The Evolution of Macroeconomic
Theory and Policy

Kamran Dadkhah

The Evolution of Macroeconomic Theory and Policy

 Springer

Kamran Dadkhah
Department of Economics
Northeastern University
Boston, MA 02115
USA
k.dadkhah@neu.edu

ISBN 978-3-540-77007-7   e-ISBN 978-3-540-77008-4
DOI 10.1007/978-3-540-77008-4
Springer Dordrecht Heidelberg London New York

Library of Congress Control Number: 2009927024

Cover design: WMXDesign GmbH

Printed on acid-free paper

Springer is part of Springer Science+Business Media (www.springer.com)

To Karen with love

Preface

If anyone had a doubt regarding the importance of macroeconomics, the financial and economic crisis of 2007–2009 should have relieved him/her of it. Furthermore, at times the unfolding drama and its historical background was an education in macroeconomics in itself. It seemed everyone was anxious to learn about the causes of the crisis, its turns and twists, and the possible remedies and their effectiveness. This is befitting since macroeconomics as we know it now was the product of another economic crisis.

On Thursday, October 24, 1929 (known as Black Thursday), the stock market crashed. Within a year, the number of jobless workers climbed to more than four million and hungry protesters took to the streets of New York. Thus began the Great Depression, which in the course of the decades to come changed the economies of industrial countries, fundamentally transformed our vision of the economy and economic policy, and brought into prominence a branch of economics that in 1933 Ragnar Frisch christened macroeconomics.

Over the next 80 years the interaction of economic events, economic theory, and economic policy resulted in a body of knowledge that is an integral part of political and economic discourse and indeed of everyday life in the United States and around the world. Economists, business leaders, policy makers, and all concerned citizens need to be familiar with macroeconomics.

Macroeconomics is best understood in a historical context. The book offers an introduction to macroeconomic theory and policy as they relate to events and developments of the past 80 years. The United States economy and its fiscal and monetary policies are the main concerns, but because the United States economy and world economies are intertwined, the stories of their interactions will also be recounted.

Let me emphasize that the book is neither an economic history of the United States nor a history of economic thought. The purpose of this book is to teach macroeconomics in the context of actual events and with emphasis on the relationships between macroeconomic theory and policy.

Students of economics, professional economists, and the interested public are the target audience. The book can be used as the main text or a supplement in advanced undergraduate and beginning graduate courses in macroeconomics. Professional economists may find it a useful reference. The book is not intended for readers with no background in economics. But anyone who is ready to expend the effort and is not put off by occasional equations could benefit from reading it.

I would like to thank Springer-Verlag editors Barbara Fess and Christiane Beisel for their help, support, and understanding during the writing of this book. I also would like to thank Anna Dittrich of Springer-Verlag and Saranya Baskar and her colleagues at Integra for their excellent work in producing the book. Colleagues, friends, and students helped with their comments and questions. In particular I would like to thank Neil Alper, Oscar Brookins, William Dickens, Tess Forsell, Amarita Natt who read all or large parts of the book and made extensive suggestions and corrections. My thanks also goes to Andrew Sum and Maria Luengo-Prado who made useful comments. Students in my graduate macroeconomics class Yuan Gao (Highfar), Emily Halle, Yelena Kuznetsov, Alicia Parillo, and Brian Sieben detected errors and made suggestions for improvement.

My great indebtedness is to Karen Challberg, who read the entire manuscript and made many corrections and helpful suggestions. Without her, the project would have never been conceived and carried out.

Contents

Chapter 1
The Great Depression and Mr. Keynes

More important, a host of unemployed citizens face the grim problem of existence, and an equally great number toil with little return. Only a foolish optimist can deny the dark realities of the moment.

From the inaugural speech of President Franklin Roosevelt, 1933

I believe myself to be writing a book on economic theory which will largely revolutionize—not, I suppose, at once but in the course of the next ten years—the way the world thinks about economic problems.

From Keynes's letter of January 1, 1935 to George Bernard Shaw

The Crash of 1929

The 24th of October, 1929, known as Black Thursday, started just like any other day. It rained in New York City, and the temperature fluctuated between a low of 44 and a high of 59 degrees Fahrenheit. The previous day, according to the *New York Times*, "firm tone" prevailed on the London Exchange, "French stocks [were] uneven," and on the German Boerse "losses due to profit-taking [were] mostly recovered." Perhaps the only indication that something was amiss was the *Times* report that in the previous day unlisted stocks had sharply declined.

But "Hell broke loose" on that Thursday. The volume was high with 12,894,650 shares traded, and prices dropped. The sharpest decline happened between 11:15 am and 12:15 pm. The high volume caused the tickers to lag more than four hours. Rumors started floating and made the situation worse. At one point the rumor was that eleven speculators had committed suicide. The decline was not confined to the New York Stock Exchange and spread to other markets. It caused panic on the Chicago Commodities Exchange.

Yet, despite the sharp drop during the day, at the close the decline was not precipitous: Dow Jones Industrials fell from 305.85 to 299.47, that is, a decline of about 2.1%. During the day the Federal Reserve Board had two extended meetings. The second meeting was presided over by Treasury Secretary, Andrew W. Mellon.

K. Dadkhah, *The Evolution of Macroeconomic Theory and Policy,*
DOI 10.1007/978-3-540-77008-4_1, © Springer-Verlag Berlin Heidelberg 2009

But the board decided that the situation was not serious enough to issue a formal declaration. Apparently the board had contemplated such an announcement but the recovery at the end of the day had resulted in putting it off. As the *Times* put it the next day: "Leaders Confer, Find Conditions Sound."

President Herbert Hoover issued a reassuring statement. In reply to a question by the press regarding the business situation, the president said:

> The fundamental business of the country, that is production and distribution of commodities, is on a sound and prosperous basis. The best evidence is that although production and consumption are at high levels, the average prices of commodities as a whole have not increased and there have been no appreciable increases in the stocks of manufactured goods. Moreover, there has been a tendency of wages to increase and the output per worker in many industries again shows an increase, all of which indicates a healthy condition.

But this optimism and confidence were misplaced. The market was on a downward trend. A crash was on the horizon although even many prominent economists, such as Irving Fisher, did not recognize it.

Although the market steadied on October 25, on the next Monday the Dow Jones Industrials fell by more than 40 points, or 13.47%. There would be further ups and downs. The market reached the low of 198.69 on November 13, that is, slightly less than 48% below the high of 381.17 reached on September 3. In other words, in 71 days the market shares, as represented by the Dow Jones Index, had lost close to half of their value and investors had lost half of their wealth.

Worse was still to come. Again the market recovered for a brief period. But the slide continued, and on July 8, 1932 the Dow Jones Index was down to 41.22. Compared to its high in September 3, 1929, the index had lost more than 89% of its value. Although the index stabilized and even showed an upward trend from 1932 to 1937, it declined in 1937. From 1942 until the end of the War the index showed a moderate upward trend, but it did not reach its high of 1929 even several years after the War. It took until November 23, 1954 for the Dow to gain its former peak (Fig. 1.1).

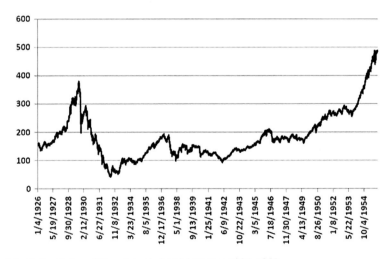

Fig. 1.1 Daily closing of Dow Jones industrial average 1926–1955

An important factor contributing to the severity of the crash was that many had bought stocks on margin. That is, they had borrowed from banks and brokers to buy stocks. An investor buys 1000 shares of stocks at $5 each. But she pays only a percentage of their value, say 10%, or $500. The remaining $4500 is her debt to the bank or broker and the stocks are collateral. If the stock price increases to $7, she can sell the stocks, pay off her debt, and pocket $2000 profit less interest on the loan and transactions costs. On the other hand, if the price falls to $3, the value of the collateral for the debt of $4500 is only $3000. So there will be a *margin call*, that is, she is asked to make up the difference. Unless she has cash lying around (in which case she probably wouldn't be buying on margin), she has to sell the same or other stocks to raise cash. But such a sell further depresses the price of stocks.

The crash of 1929 became the stuff of legends, such as investors jumping out of the windows of skyscrapers. There are many references to the era in Hollywood films. Nevertheless, what was to happen next, or perhaps had already happened and the crash was one of its symptoms, wrought far more hardship.

The Great Depression

According to the National Bureau of Economic Research (NBER), which monitors business cycles in the United States, the economy had reached its peak in August 1929. For the next 43 months, that is, all the way to March 1933, the economy would experience a decline. Recovery was slow and as late as 1936 the GDP had hardly reached its 1929 level. It was only during the World War II that the economy took off (see Fig. 1.2).

The fall in output was accompanied by massive unemployment. The number of unemployed in the United States rose from about 1.4 million in 1929 to more than 4.3 million in 1930 and reached more than 11 million in 1932 and 10.6 million in

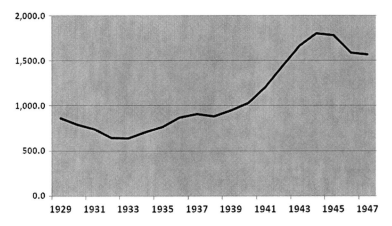

Fig. 1.2 The United States real GDP, 1929–1947 (billions of chained 2000 dollars)

Table 1.1 Unemployment in
the United States: 1929–1947

Year	Number unemployed (thousand)	Unemployment rate (%)
1929	1,383	2.9
1930	4,340	8.9
1931	7,721	15.7
1932	11,468	22.9
1933	10,635	20.9
1934	8,366	16.2
1935	7,523	14.4
1936	5,286	10.0
1937	4,937	9.2
1938	6,799	12.5
1939	6,225	11.3
1940	5,290	9.5
1941	3,351	6.0
1942	1,746	3.1
1943	985	1.8
1944	670	1.2
1945	1,040	1.9
1946	2,270	4.0
1947	2,629	4.4

1933. At the same time the unemployment rate rose from 2.9% in 1929 to 15.7% in 1933 and reached almost 23% in 1932 (see Table 1.1 and Fig. 1.3).

These numbers, horrendous as they are, do not fully reflect the human misery of those years.[1] It should be noted that in those days the social safety net that we are accustomed to now was not in place. People and families had to fend for themselves

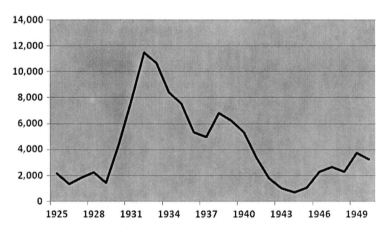

Fig. 1.3 Number of unemployed workers in the United States (in thousands)

---

[1] A good read on the conditions of the country in those years and indeed up to the early 1970s is William Manchester (1974). More recent books include David Kennedy (1999); and Adam Cohen (2009).

or at most hope for a helping hand from churches or charities. Not finding gainful employment, families would drive to other towns and cities in search of a job. Millions of all walks of life were on the road. Many would use freight trains to go from one place to another in a hopeless search for jobs. But the depression was countrywide, and the searchers would end up destitute in a different town and state. People including women slept in parks on the ground, without blankets, or protection. Hungry protestors flooded New York City. Soup kitchens sprang up to feed the hungry.

In Kentucky, coal fields turned into an armed camp and there were bloody confrontations between miners and operators, which resulted in a dozen men, including three deputy sheriffs, losing their lives. Many miners had become unemployed and their children went to school hungry. Those miners who still worked received $9–$12 per week in wages.

The depression was hardest on the youth recently out of school. Like the rest of country they were on the road in search of jobs. Among the transients who later found fame were John Steinbeck, the author of *The Grapes of Wrath* and *Of Mice and Men* and the winner of Nobel Prize for Literature in 1962, and Eric Sevareid, journalist and commentator who worked for CBS. Young girls sold their bodies for as low as ten cents just to survive. This generation suffered from malnutrition which later showed up in medical examinations when young men were drafted to fight in World War II. Many had bad teeth, and the mental health of some had been affected.

Sometimes racism compounded the tragedy. In 1931 two young white women complained that they were driven off a freight train in Chattanooga, Tennessee and raped by six black young men. Although two doctors who examined the girls did not find evidence of rape, an all white jury quickly condemned some of the young men to death. The trials received national attention, and although none of the young men were executed some spent years in jail or on the run.

Even the federal government was harsh on those who had served the country. In 1924 Congress had authorized payment of soldiers' bonuses to World War I veterans. The payment was to be made in 1945. In the desperate days of the Great Depression, veterans with their families had gathered in Washington, DC to demand the immediate payment of $500. They were called the " bonus army" and set up shanties in parks, dumps, abandoned warehouses and stores. On July 28, 1932 District of Columbia police tried to evict them. In the ensuing riot two bonus marchers were shot dead. Later, on the orders of President Hoover, federal troops commanded by General Douglas MacArthur and Major Dwight Eisenhower using machine guns and tear gas evicted the bonus army and set fire to their makeshift shanties.[2]

The depression years were also the years of prohibition and speakeasies, Al Capone and Mafia. The country witnessed a crime wave.

---

[2]General MacArthur had exceeded his authority, but Hoover assumed full responsibility for the event. See, Kennedy (1999), p. 92.

America was no more the paradise people around the world aspired to reach. In 1932, for the first time in history, emigration from the United States exceeded immigration. 103,295 people left the country while only 35,576 entered it.

It should be noted that while the suffering of the masses was going on, the rich showed the utmost callousness. They were concerned mostly with lining their pockets even during the times of tragedy.

Depression Around the World

The United States was not alone in this human tragedy; the Great Depression was a universal malaise affecting all advanced countries. England, Germany, Canada, Australia, Scandinavian countries, Belgium, the Netherlands, and France suffered, albeit to different degrees (Fig. 1.4). Among European countries France was less affected by the depression.

In 1929 the unemployment rate in England was 10.4%. Within a year it reached 16.1%, that is, almost one out of six laborers was out of work. In 1931 and 1932 the rate climbed, respectively, to 21.3% and 22.1%. In other words, almost two out of every 9 laborers were out of work. In September 1931, England abandoned the gold standard and devalued the sterling pound by 20%, closed its stock market and cut unemployment benefits. There were demonstrations by the unemployed protesting the cut in benefits. In October 1932, there were four days of riot by unemployed youth in London. Mounted police fought the crowd resulting in many injuries. In November 1931, Conservatives won the election and Ramsay MacDonald (a founder of labor Party but running without the backing of any party) won a seat and formed the cabinet.

Perhaps the worst case unfolded in Germany. Germans had suffered in World War I and its aftermath. In 1928 it seemed that recovery was underway, but in 1929 the unemployment rate climbed to 13.3%. In March 1930, there were communist demonstrations both in the United States and in Europe resulting in clashes with police. There were injuries and two persons lost their lives in Germany. Worse was still to come: unemployment rate reached 34.3% in 1931 and climbed to 43.8% in 1932. In other words, three out of every seven workers were unemployed. The situation was ripe for exploitation by a demagogue; in January 1933, Adolf Hitler became the chancellor of Germany.

Economies of less developed countries—to the extent that they were connected to the industrialized world—were also affected by the crisis.

FDR and the New Deal

Americans reacted to the dire economic situation by electing Franklin Delano Roosevelt.

The president-elect won 42 of 48 states, the exceptions being Connecticut, Maine, Vermont, New Hampshire, Delaware, and Pennsylvania. He had won 472

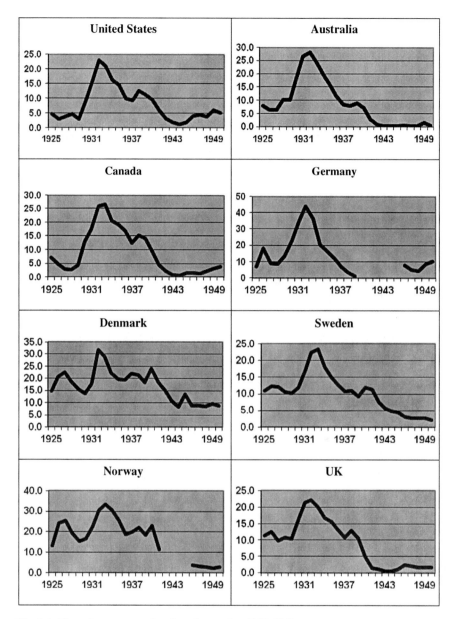

Fig. 1.4 Unemployment rates in selected countries: 1925–1950

electoral votes, while Herbert Hoover who would be called the "president-reject" by *Time* won 59. It was a landslide, the greatest since President Lincoln defeated the Democratic Party's candidate, General George McClellan in 1864.

There is little doubt that the depression was the main if not the only factor in determining the election outcome. FDR knew this and from the start set out to find a cure for the economic ills of the nation. It is not that Herbert Hoover was oblivious to the crisis. Hoover did try to alleviate the depression. He sought the advice of business and banking leaders to assist him in bolstering the economy. He wanted to expand federal construction to create new jobs and asked the governors of the 48 states (at the time Hawaii and Alaska hadn't become states) to expand public works. He asked businesses to increase production and labor to keep wages low. To "prevent hunger and cold" he named a committee to come up with a plan for reducing unemployment. He sought a joint undertaking by private and government agencies to stimulate production and accelerate public work and asked the Congress for up to $150 million for public works to create jobs. Also in January 1932 he signed a law creating the Reconstruction Finance Corporation and allocating $2 billion for loans to industries, farms, and banks in order to boost business and create jobs. Contrary to Hoover's reputation of doing nothing, a glance at the US government budget, shows that government spending were increased in absolute amount but particularly as a percentage of the GDP (Table 1.2 and Fig. 1.5). Nevertheless, Hoover did not believe in strong government action. He preferred voluntary action on the part of people. The force of the Great Depression was well beyond these well intentioned yet feeble attempts.

Table 1.2 The United States government budget: 1925–1947

Year	Receipts ($1,000,000)	Expenditures ($1,000,000)	Share of Expenditures in the GDP (%)
1925	3,641	2,924	
1926	3,795	2,930	
1927	4,013	2,857	
1928	3,900	2,961	
1929	3,862	3,127	3.02
1930	4,058	3,320	3.64
1931	3,116	3,577	4.68
1932	1,924	4,659	7.94
1933	1,997	4,598	8.15
1934	2,955	6,541	9.91
1935	3,609	6,412	8.75
1936	3,923	8,228	9.82
1937	5,387	7,580	8.25
1938	6,751	6,840	7.94
1939	6,295	9,141	9.91
1940	6,548	9,468	9.34
1941	8,712	13,653	10.78
1942	14,634	35,137	21.70
1943	24,001	78,555	39.55
1944	43,747	91,304	41.54
1945	45,159	92,712	41.56
1946	39,296	55,232	24.85
1947	38,514	34,496	14.13

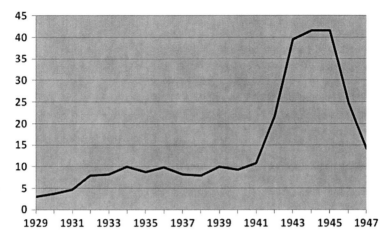

Fig. 1.5 US government expenditures as a percentage of GDP

We should note that not all actions of Hoover were beneficial to the health of the economy. In June 17, 1930 he signed into law the Smoot-Hawley Act.[3] The original intention was to help farmers by increasing tariffs on agricultural imports. But by the time the law passed Congress it imposed stiff tariffs on imports of all kind. It was a protectionist measure and became the poster child of beggar-thy-neighbor policies. Other countries retaliated and international trade declined. The Smoot-Hawley Act cannot be considered a cause of the depression but certainly it was an aggravating factor.

As the depression deepened an increasing number of Americans came to believe that strong policies could rescue the situation. Perhaps that is why FDR who pledged "a new deal for the American people" won the election.

"We Must Act and Act Quickly"

In his inaugural speech President Roosevelt described the situation in the country, named the culprits, presented his program, and described how he was going to carry it out. He noted that

> Values have shrunken to fantastic levels; taxes have risen; our ability to pay has fallen; government of all kinds is faced by serious curtailment of income; the means of exchange are frozen in the currents of trade; the withered leaves of industrial enterprise lie on every side; farmers find no markets for their produce; the savings of many years in thousands of families are gone. More important, a host of unemployed citizens face the grim problem of existence, and an equally great number toil with little return. Only a foolish optimist can deny the dark realities of the moment.

---

[3] For a background on this law, see "The battle of Smoot-Hawley," *The Economist*, December 20, 2008, pp. 125–126.

And he blamed "the unscrupulous money changers" who "stand indicted in the court of public opinion, rejected by the hearts and minds of men. The money changers have fled from their high seats in the temple of our civilization. We may now restore that temple to the ancient truths."

The president declared that "this Nation asks for action, and action now." He outlined what he intended to do. It involved direct government intervention in the economy including government employing those who could not find a job, government planning and directing the economy, and imposing regulations on the activities deemed crucial for the functioning of the economy.

> Our greatest primary task is to put people to work. This is no unsolvable problem ... It can be accomplished in part by direct recruiting by the Government itself, treating the task as we would treat the emergency of a war, but at the same time, through this employment ... stimulate and reorganize the use of our natural resources. ... we must frankly recognize the overbalance of population in our industrial centers and, by engaging on a national scale in a redistribution, endeavor to provide a better use of the land for those best fitted for the land. The task can be helped by definite efforts to raise the values of agricultural products and with this the power to purchase the output of our cities. It can be helped by preventing realistically the tragedy of the growing loss through foreclosure of our small homes and our farms. It can be helped by national planning for and supervision of all forms of transportation and of communications and other utilities which have a definitely public character. ... there must be a strict supervision of all banking and credits and investments; there must be an end to speculation with other people's money, and there must be provision for an adequate but sound currency.

In combating the economic ills of the nation his focus was domestic, and international trade was of secondary importance. "Our international trade relations, though vastly important, are in point of time and necessity secondary to the establishment of a sound national economy."

Roosevelt felt that the plan could be accomplished within the limits of the US constitution and with cooperation of the Congress. Yet he felt that he needed broad executive power to carry out the plan. Clearly, faith in the market capitalist system was shaken, and there were doubts if the problem could be solved within the strict mandates of democracy. FDR took a paternalistic view toward the economy.

The New Deal Policies

The action started from day one of the new president in office.[4] The thinking of the new administration was that the problems of the economy stemmed from overproduction. Markets and the laissez faire system had failed to bring about equilibrium. "It seemed self-evident in 1933 that America's capacity to produce had outstripped its capacity to consume." "America no longer needed its builders and promoters;

---

[4]It is not the intention of this section to present a full account of the New Deal, nor is such a feat possible in anything less than a whole book. Yet every macroeconomist needs to be quite familiar with these programs. There are a large number of books on the subject and hopefully the section whets the reader's appetite to seek and study them.

the economics of future would be less concerned with the production of more than with the administration of what there was."[5] Competition had created chaos and the antitrust laws had exacerbated the situation. There was too much production and not enough demand. There was a clear need for planning and management by the government. Therefore, government had to intervene to restore the balance between supply and demand. The government would take a number of measures to increase demand and regulate and curtail the supply.

The first order of business was to rescue farmers who were in dire conditions. Among measures taken to help farmers were the Agricultural Adjustment Act aimed at balancing supply and demand by paying subsidies to cooperating farmers, and the Emergency Farm Mortgage Act, which provided for refinancing of farm mortgages. Farmers received $100 million in loans by the end of the year.

The National Industrial Recovery Act (NIRA) of 1933 was passed to regulate the production of industry and bring about balance between consumption and production. NIRA created the National Recovery Administration (NRA) and suspended antitrust laws for two years. Each industry was to come up with codes for production and fair competition, maximum hours, and minimum wage.[6] The federal government was to oversee their enforcement.

Another purpose of NIRA was to create jobs for unemployed youth in the form of public work. For this purpose $3.3 billion was allocated. In addition, Congress allocated $500 million to be given to the unemployed through state and local governments.

NRA created a large administration and a huge amount of rules and regulation. In 1935 the Supreme Court unanimously declared NIRA unconstitutional. Worse, the whole program is judged a failure and even ardent supporters of the New Deal don't "suppose that this verdict can now be altered."[7] According to Schlesinger, the Great Depression brought a sense of urgency and engendered a sense of national solidarity. Thus, personal motivations and self interests were pushed aside. NRA, responding to the urgency, accumulated a large administrative bureaucracy and undertook huge responsibilities under the burden of which it finally crumbled. Once the sense of urgency was gone as a result of recovery, self-interest motives were back in action. The conclusion seems to have been that if self-interest could be restrained, if national solidarity could be maintained, and if organization of the enterprise could be arranged more efficiently, then everything will be all right; perhaps next time!

The fact is that huge bureaucracy is a feature of such programs. Why should we think that the head of a private corporation who is put in charge of a public administration will suddenly be transformed and guided by nothing but public interest?

---

[5] Arthur Schlesinger (1958), pp. 180–181. The reader may find the echoes of the idea of limits to growth in the 1970 s and again in the early years of the twenty-first century.

[6] These were different from the federal minimum wage laws. The first of such laws was passed in 1938 requiring a minimum wage of 25 cents per hour. Of course, each state has been free to set its own minimum wage, which could not be below the federal level.

[7] Schlesinger Jr., op. cit ., p. 175.

Such enterprises are doomed by their nature, not mismanagement, or because people lost their national solidarity. A lesson to be learned is that giving incentives to work in the best public interest is more effective.

A great achievement of the New Deal was to change the landscape of working conditions in the United States. Section 7 (a) of NIRA declared "that employees shall have the right to organize and bargain collectively through representatives of their own choosing, and shall be free from interference restraint, or coercion of employers of labor, or their agents, in the designation of such representatives or in self-organization or in other concerted activities for the purpose of collective bargaining." Further, "that employers shall comply with the maximum hours of labor, minimum wage rates of pay, and other conditions of employment, approved or prescribed by the president."

It turned out that such provisions were not strong enough and, anyway, the Supreme Court ruled NIRA unconstitutional. The National Labor Relations Act of 1935 reiterated such rights (Sec. 7), and the Fair Labor Standards Act of 1938 prohibited child labor and established minimum wage and forty-hour week.

In addition to public works, subsidies, and trying to manage supply and demand, the New Deal created a number of supervisory agencies to regulate different sectors. In 1933 an investigation of the stock market by a Senate and Banking Committee found gross abuses by banks and brokers. In 1934 the Securities and Exchange Commission was created to oversee "the key participants in the securities world, including securities exchanges, securities brokers and dealers, investment advisors, and mutual funds." "The SEC is concerned primarily with promoting the disclosure of important market-related information, maintaining fair dealing, and protecting against fraud."

The Glass-Steagall Act of 1933 created the Federal Deposit Insurance Corporation to insure each bank deposit up to $2500. To help homeowners who could not make payments, the Home Owners Loan Corporation was created. More than 20% of homeowners, including those who got the money to repair their home, used this federal assistance. The Railroad Coordination Act established a federal coordinator of transportation.

In order to stimulate the economy an inflationary policy was adopted. The President reduced the amount of the dollar's gold backing and set the price of gold at $35. Government expenditures increased drastically, from less than two billion dollars in 1933 to $8.7 billion in 1941.

The New Deal helped to create an atmosphere of hope, prevented the economy from sliding down further, and increased output and income. However, by 1936 the economy had barely reached the output level of 1929, and unemployment rate was close to three times that of pre-depression years. To make matters worse, in 1937 the country experienced a mini-recession. The real recovery and progress started in 1941 when the United States entered World War II. Thus, it is an open question whether the New Deal policies were effective in combating depression and whether they alone would have brought the prosperity that country experienced after the War.

Irving Fisher's Theory of Debt-Deflation

To be an economist at the time of the Great Depression must have felt like being a physician and seeing a person collapse in front of you or being a police officer coming upon the scene of a crime in progress. You can keep quiet or pretend that you are busy with a much deeper theoretical question, in which case you have to live the rest of your life wondering if you are for the real. Or you can jump into action and perhaps make a mistake, but then you are for the real. Among American economists who tried to explain the Great Depression was Irving Fisher.[8]

Irving Fisher definitely was the greatest American economist at least up to the mid-twentieth century, on the testimony of no less an authority than Joseph Schumpeter.

In Fisher's theory, depression occurs when there is an imbalance between aggregate demand and the aggregate output of the economy. Therefore, the shortage of demand is the culprit. Fisher rejects the classical notion that overproduction can only be in certain products (presumably being cancelled by underproduction in others). He notes that there can be general overproduction, which can take one of the two forms: very large inventories or a high rate of production. Indeed, except for brief periods, either underproduction or overproduction characterizes the economy.

Nevertheless, overproduction should not be mistaken for the cause of business cycles or depression. It is too little money that is mistaken for too much goods. The main causes are over-indebtedness and deflation. "In short, the big bad actors are debt disturbances and price level disturbances." He puts the blame squarely on the demand deficit. But he believes that this is caused by the contraction of money supply, which in turn is the result of over indebtedness. Excessive borrowing is followed by the shortage of credit and liquidity.[9]

According to this theory at any moment there is only so much debt (not necessarily an exact amount but a range) that the economy can support. In good times everyone is borrowing and banks are eager to lend. In a fractional banking system, banks keep only a fraction of deposits as reserves and could lend the rest. At the same time investors can borrow and buy stocks and other securities. Once the situation sours and a group of borrowers can't pay back their debts, there would be a chain reaction. Either a borrower has to sell her assets to pay back the debt or, worse, she could default on her debt. In other words, over-indebtedness leads to debt liquidation and through it to distress selling. As a result there will be a decline

---

[8]Irving Fisher (1867–1947) was a great economist and statistician and a pioneer in the use of mathematics and statistics in economics. He was also a campaigner for many causes including promotion of healthy living and hygiene, prohibition, eugenics, and establishing a league of nations. The ideas presented here are based on his "The Debt-Deflation Theory of Great Depressions," *Econometrica* (October 1933), pp. 337–357.

[9]The reader could see the similarities between 1929 and the credit crunch of 2007 resulting from the subprime mortgage problem and the echo of Fisher's theory in some comments made by economists and financial analysts.

in money in circulation since some bank loans are paid back and some are defaulted on. Moreover, the velocity of circulation will decline.

To make these ideas more precise, consider the equation of exchange[10]

$$PT = MV + M'V'$$

where P is price level, T volume of transactions, M currency in circulation, M' deposits in banks, and V and V' velocities of circulation respectively of M and M'.

If there is a sharp decline in the right-hand side of the above equation, we should expect a commensurate decrease in the price level. This implies a fall in the net worth of businesses, a reduction in profits, and a decline of output, trade, and employment. As a result there will be bankruptcies, pessimism and loss of confidence. Such a situation would cause hoarding of money and a further drop in the velocity of circulation.

An aggravating factor is the increase in the value of debts due to a fall in the price level. Note that an increase in the price level works in favor of debtor and against creditors, because debts are in terms of the dollar and a decline in purchasing power of the dollar means a lower real value of debt. A decline in the price level works in the opposite direction and increases the value of debts. Thus, it is conceivable that as debtors pay their debts, because of deflation the value of their debts is increased, thus setting in motion a vicious cycle.

A depression can come to an end because of universal bankruptcies, which would wipe out debts. Then there will be recovery and boom. But we need not accept this "natural" course of the economy. The government can get the economy out of depression by reflation, that is, by increasing the price level induced by an increase in the amount of money in circulation. Refusing to inflate the prices, vainly trying to balance the budget, raising taxes, and to borrow from the public, during a depression, are fatal mistakes for a democracy. The economic ills and the wrong response of the government could lead to anarchy and revolution.

In short, Fisher saw the problem as lack of demand and the solution an increase in money supply. Indeed, he claimed that President Roosevelt did this and in March 1933 brought an end to the depression.

Fisher corresponded with President Roosevelt and even met him. He gave advice but had little or no impact on the actual policy of the government. Fisher was against government meddling in the economy and opposed Roosevelt's policies including the National Industrial Recovery Act and the Agricultural Adjustment Act. He was for the devaluation of the dollar and increase in money supply. One reason for Fisher's lack of influence on policy may have been that in 1929 when the stock market had started its downward spiral, he confidently predicted a stable and upward trending market. He put his money where his mouth was and lost a considerable amount of money. The wrong prognostication also cost him reputation and credibility.

---

[10]We shall discuss in more details this equation and the theory behind it in Chap. 9.

Money and the Great Depression

Fisher believed that recession was a monetary phenomena and monetary expansion could prevent or remedy the situation. A number of studies have tried to substantiate the proposition that the Great Depression was caused by the Federal Reserve policy. Indeed, the monetary explanation of the Great Depression has many adherents and in recent decades has informed the policy choices of the Federal Reserve.

On the other hand, a number of studies have tried to refute such a vision. Since the depression started in 1929, a glance at the monetary data (see Fig. 1.6) shows that money could not have been the cause; at most it can be assigned the role of an aggravating factor. Some have disputed even that. Money could have been the effect and not the cause, and contracted as a result of depression. In other words, money may have been endogenous and reacting rather than exogenous and causative.

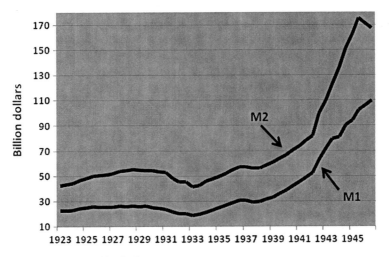

Fig. 1.6 Money supply 1923–1946

The fact is that we still do not know what caused the Great Depression and we may never know for sure. On the other hand, at times of panic and market turmoil it is prudent for the Federal Reserve to calm down the markets and investors through expansionary monetary policy. This is exactly what the Fed did in 1987 and then in 2007 when the subprime problem had reduced the liquidity in international markets and threatened a recession.

The Keynesian Vision of the Economy

"I believe myself to be writing a book on economic theory which will largely revolutionize—not, I suppose, at once but in the course of the next ten years—the

way the world thinks about economic problems."[11] In a way John Maynard Keynes
was right. The tone of reviews of his work changed from 1936 to 1946, and within
the span of two decades of the publication of the *General Theory* most economists
were of Keynesian persuasion and within three decades policy makers around the
world were following his advice. Even today after many ups and downs, in truth we
are all Keynesians.

Keynes's vision of the capitalist economy can be summarized in the ex-ante
inequality of investment and savings. Consider an economy which produces a certain amount of goods and services. Those involved in production receive a total
amount of income equal to the value of output or Gross Domestic Product (GDP).
The income takes the form of wages and salaries, rental income, profit, and interest
income. A portion of this income is paid to the government in the form of taxes.
What remains is disposable personal income, which recipients spend a portion, but
not all, of on consumption. The ratio of consumption to disposable personal income
and even to the GDP is more or less stable; for instance, in the present day United
States, it is about two thirds of the GDP. The expenditures on consumer goods con-
stitute demand for products. The rest of income is saved.

On the other hand, entrepreneurs decide on the amount of investment. Note that
this is physical investment in the form of factories, equipment, buildings and so
on and not in the form of buying stocks or bonds. The amount of investment, at
least partially, is dependent on the outlook of the economy and the expectations of
the investors. Thus, aggregate investment could be quite volatile. When investors
are optimistic about the future and sense high returns on their capital, investment
increases, and when pessimism is the order of the day investors refrain from taking
any risk. Such behavior is not unreasonable. Investment requires time to bear fruit
and requires investors to take risks of forecasting errors, changing conditions, and
competition. Only if they are confident about the future of the economy and believe
in the viability of projects would they invest. One or two percentage points reduction
in the cost of borrowing would not make a lot of difference. Thus, Keynes emphasized the marginal efficiency of capital[12] and downplayed the role of interest rate.

The sum of consumption, investment, and government expenditures determines,
ex post, the amount of income. For the time being, let us assume that government
balances its budget and its total expenditures is equal to the tax revenues. If investment is less than savings then income declines. A lower income causes consumption
to decrease, which in turn causes income to decrease further. The process continues
until something stops this downward process. On the other hand, if investment is
greater than savings, income will increase leading to higher consumption and even
higher income. Now the multiplier effect works in the other direction.

---

[11] From Keynes's letter of January 1, 1935 to George Bernard Shaw, The General Theory and After,
Part I Preparation, Vol. XIII of the *Collected Writings of John Maynard Keynes*, Donald Moggridge
(ed.), MacMillan, 1973, p. 492.

[12] Keynes's marginal efficiency of capital is the same as the internal rate of return. It is the discount
rate which makes the present value of the future stream of revenues generated by an investment
project equal to the replacement cost of capital required by that investment.

The level of income thus determined may or may not be commensurate with the full employment of the productive capacity of the economy, particularly the full employment of the labor force. In the Keynes theory there is no guarantee that full employment will be reached. Prior to Keynes it was thought that full employment was the rule and unemployment was caused by temporary fluctuations around the normal state of the economy. In Keynes's theory full employment is the exception; unemployment and, at times, shortage of labor force are the rule.

But then how are the level of employment, output, and aggregate supply determined? In the classical system, employment is determined in the labor market. Labor employed plus the existing physical capital and the technology in the economy determine the level of output through production function. Output determines income and demand. Anyone who is willing to work at the going wage rate will find employment. Therefore, whoever is unemployed is *voluntarily* unemployed; hence the moral stigma attached to unemployment prior to WWII. In contrast, in the Keynesian model aggregate demand determines the level of output, which in turn gives rise to the actual level of employment. The actual employment may, therefore, be above or below full employment. The difference between actual and full employment level of output gives rise to *involuntary unemployment.* Hence no stigma is attached to at least certain types of unemployment, and it is the duty of the government as the representative of society to help those who cannot find gainful employment.

It may be argued that if there are unemployed workers willing to work, the wage rate would drop and more will be employed reducing unemployment. The process will continue until all who are willing to work at the going wage rate find employment. We postpone a full discussion of such issues to Chap. 3. Here we note that if wages are downwardly rigid, the adjustment may be slow. In the meantime because of the shortage of demand, prices may be decreasing and despite a decline in nominal wages, real wages may be stable or even on the rise.

We can make the above argument more precise by starting with the consumption function, which determines the amount of demand for consumption goods C, resulting from any amount of disposable personal income $Y - T$ that is,

$$C = \alpha + \beta(Y - T)$$

where Y denotes the GDP, T the amount of taxes, and β is the marginal propensity to consume

$$\beta = \frac{\Delta C}{\Delta(Y - T)}$$

that is, the amount of additional consumption resulting from one dollar increase in income.[13] In addition, we can talk of average propensity to consume, that is

$$APC = \frac{C}{Y - T}$$

---

[13]More generally, since consumption is a function of income, β is the derivative of consumption with respect to disposable personal income $\beta = dC/d(Y - T)$.

Investment which is the demand for capital goods is independent of income and has a large random component.

$$I = \bar{I} + U$$

Where $\bar{I}$ is determined by such factors as interest rate and U is dependent on such factors as expectations of profit (what Keynes referred to as the marginal efficiency of capital) and as a result is quite volatile.

Total demand is determined as (see Fig. 1.7):

$$Y = C + I + G$$

Now there is no reason that the sum of consumption, investment, and government expenditures equals the amount of income that coincides with aggregate demand necessary for the full employment of productive resources. This is especially so because of the random component of investment. If the aggregate demand is greater than the full employment income, then we experience inflation; if it is less then we have recession; only if the two coincide do we have the classical case. In this sense, the classical economic theory is a special case of Keynes's theory; hence the title of the book, *The General Theory*.

There are two more elements that have to be added to this story. First, under-investment is the prevalent mode of the capitalist economy. The reason is that investors are risk averse and, therefore, act cautiously toward good news and drastically cut their commitments when facing bad news. Thus, an economy left to its own devices would drift toward recession more often than toward full employment and inflation.

The second point, due to Keynes's favorite student, Richard Khan, is the multiplier effect of investment. Since the sum of consumption, investment, and government expenditures, ex-post, is equal to income, we can write:

$$Y = C + I + G = \alpha + \beta(Y - T) + I + G$$

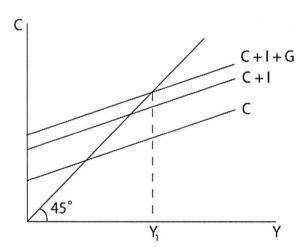

Fig. 1.7 Keynesian theory of aggregate demand

Solving for Y we have

$$Y = \frac{1}{1-\beta}[\alpha + I + G - \beta T] = \bar{\alpha} + k(I + G) - \beta k T$$

where $\bar{\alpha} = \alpha/(1-\beta)$ and $k = 1/(1-\beta)$. Thus, every dollar addition to investment would add k units to income. The multiplier k, is greater than one because marginal propensity to consume is a positive fraction. For example, if $\beta = 0.75$ the multiplier will be 4. The implication is that once there is a shortage of investment, the economy will fall into a downward spiral.

The shortfall in aggregate demand due to the inadequacy of investment can be made up by an increase in government expenditures (Fig. 1.8). As the formula above shows the multiplier for both investment and government expenditures is the same, and one dollar increase in investment or government expenditures would increase income by k dollars ($4 in our example). Thus, the Keynesian remedy is government expenditures; hence his advocacy of public works and his admiration for President Roosevelt's New Deal, but not for all the reforms that involved an expansion of government bureaucracy.

The economic rationale for this conclusion is that an increase in government expenditures, say, building a new road or buying a new squadron of fighter jets will increase the income of those who build these items for the government. But the recipients of the additional income will spend part of it on consumption, which in turn would enhance the income of the producers of consumer goods. The process continues, and income of the nation is increased several folds depending on the marginal propensity to consume.

Shorn of all its trimmings, we can see how Keynes transformed our view of the workings of the economy. Keynes changed the question from "should the government intervene in the economy?" to "When to intervene in the economy?" This is the insight that has survived to the present day.

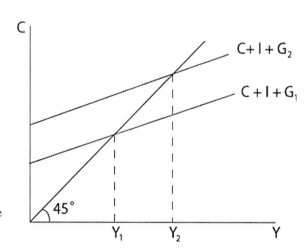

Fig. 1.8 Effect of an increase in government expenditures on aggregate income

John Hicks and the IS-LM Model

Keynes had provided a vision of the economy. But this was not enough. For one thing the book was difficult to read, contained inconsistencies, and parts of it were open to different interpretations. Economists and policy makers required a common language (a code book), even a limited one, to be able to communicate. They needed a tool, something like the apparatus of supply and demand, to find common ground and delineate their differences. John Hicks, a brilliant economist and Nobel Laureate (1974) obliged by devising the IS-LM model. IS stands for investment-savings and LM for liquidity and money.

Hicks allowed investment to be a function of interest rate although this dependence may be weak (low elasticity of investment with respect to interest rate). Thus, we can write

$$Y = \bar{\alpha} + kI(r) + kG - \beta kT$$

where r stands for the real interest rate, that is, nominal rate of interest less the expected rate of inflation. The equation shows an equilibrium relationship between the real income and the real rate of interest. The higher the rate of interest, the lower is investment and consequently income. Thus, the equation—which is referred to as the IS curve—can be represented as a downward sloping line in (Y,r) plane (Fig. 1.9).

Next he considered the demand for and supply of liquidity or money,[14] which depends on income and the nominal rate of interest. An increase in income results in a higher demand for money and an increase in the interest rate will decrease the

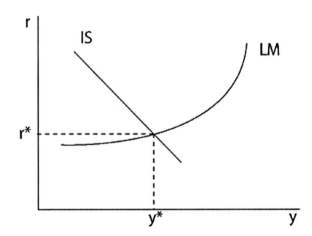

Fig. 1.9 IS-LM representation of the Keynesian model

---

[14]Money is an asset with low and even negative (considering inflation) rates of return. So it may be asked why anyone would hold money balances. Three motives have been forwarded for why individuals, firms, and governments hold money. They need money to pay for purchasing goods, services, and assets (transactions demand), for a rainy day (precautionary demand), and for taking advantage of the opportunities to buy high yield assets (speculative demand).

demand. The reason is that the more income a nation has the more transactions will be made; hence the more money needed. But the interest rate is the price of money, and an increase in the price will cut the demand.

Of course the demand is for the purchasing power of money (real balances). The supply of money M is determined by the Federal Reserve (the central bank), and its purchasing power is M/P where P is the price level.[15] We can write the equilibrium in the money market as

$$L(Y,r) = \frac{M}{P}$$

where we have assumed the expected rate of inflation to be zero and therefore nominal and real rate of interests are identical. The LM curve is upward sloping because, given a certain amount of real balances, an increase in income requires an increase in the interest rate to keep the equilibrium (Fig. 1.9).

An increase in government spending will have the same effect in the IS-LM model as in the Keynesian cross. It shifts the IS curve to the right resulting in higher income and interest rate (Fig. 1.10). The economic explanation is that the additional expenditures creates income for those who supply goods and services to the government. Again the multiplier effect works to increase the aggregate income beyond the initial increase in government expenditures. But there is a difference here. The increase in income increases demand for money, which given the supply of money would increase the interest rate. Thus, there will be drop in investment, which to some extent will negate the initial effect of the expansionary fiscal policy. Nevertheless, because investment is not too sensitive to interest rate, this secondary effect would be small.

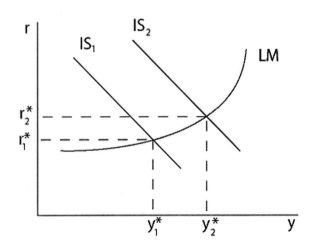

Fig. 1.10 Effects of an expansionary fiscal policy

---

[15] Here it is assumed that the central bank has full control of the nominal money supply. This is not a precise statement. For a fuller discussion of this point see Chap. 9.

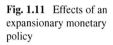

Fig. 1.11 Effects of an expansionary monetary policy

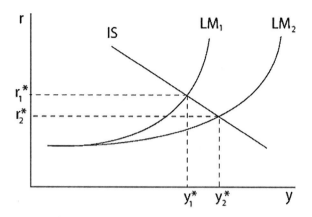

A tax cut will also shift the IS curve to the right and will have an expansionary effect.

An increase in money supply would shift the LM curve to the right causing a reduction in the rate of interest and an increase in income (Fig. 1.11). The economic rationale is that an increase in money supply would reduce the price of money, the interest rate. This in turn increases investment, which would increase the level of income. The increase in income leads to a higher demand for money putting pressure on interest rate. The rise in interest rate, to some extent, modifies the increase in investment and income.

It should be evident that a decrease in money supply will have the reverse effects. The interest rate will increase causing investment and income to decrease. Again, the reduction in income, to some extent, will modify the effects of the drop in money supply. The reason is that the lower income will reduce the demand for money. Also note that we can analyze the effects of an increase in price level, *mutatis mutandis*, in the same way as a change in money supply.

Monetary policy would be ineffective if the economy is operating at the horizontal segment of the LM curve (Fig. 1.12). This is the case of the *liquidity trap*, where the interest rate is at the lowest possible level and the additional liquidity would not have any effect on the interest rate and on investment. The same could happen if the perception of risk or other factors cause a freeze on credit, in which case the expansion of money supply by the Fed would be ineffective.

On the other hand, if we assume investment to be interest rate inelastic (IS curve being almost vertical), then fiscal policy would be quite potent (Fig. 1.12).

The IS-LM model despite its simplicity proved quite useful and was the basis of macroeconomic theory as well as the main vehicle of policy analysis in governments around the world. David Laidler believes that it provided a common language for economists to communicate.[16] But it is more than that. The IS-LM captures several main features of macroeconomic reality that other more "sophisticated" models have failed to do. In the 1970s, the model came under heavy criticism from the

---

[16]David Laidler (1999).

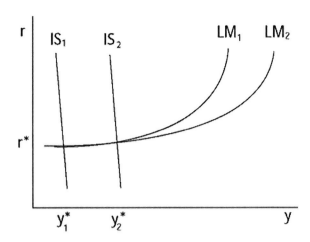

Fig. 1.12 The liquidity trap

New Classical economists and later from the adherents of real business cycle models (see Chaps. 7 and 8). It fell out of favor in some classrooms where some real business cycle theorists avoided it as if it were religiously sinful to mention it. Yet, even today in policy circles and discussions among economists on macroeconomic issues, it is not difficult to discern the shadow of the IS-LM.

Keynes and FDR

We may ask at this point, "to what extent Keynes's analysis influenced and informed the New Deal policies?" FDR and Keynes were contemporaries, the message of the *General Theory* and policies of the New Deal have strong affinity, and some younger admirers of FDR later became enthusiastic Keynesians. Yet it is hard to make a direct connection between FDR's policies and Keynes's analysis. The New Deal policies were formulated in 1933 while the *General Theory* was published in 1936. Keynes has changed our outlook on the working of the economy and the role of government and he has influenced macroeconomic policies. But his influence manifested itself after the War in setting up the international economic order (see Chap. 2) and later in formulating domestic economic policies of the United States (see Chap. 4) and other countries.

The Fundamental Question

The fundamental issue raised by the Great Depression was and is whether a decentralized capitalist system operating on its own would attain a stable equilibrium characterized by full employment. If it does not have such equilibrium, or has multiple equilibria, or the full employment equilibrium is not stable, then the system cannot be left to itself. Prior to the Great Depression we had two visions of the capitalist system. First, the mainstream economists believed that the system has a stable equilibrium, albeit attained in the long run. Second, the Marxists who believed that the system is doomed; it may have ups and downs but in the long run it will collapse and will be replaced by the socialist system. Keynes believed in the capitalist system but was concerned that we may not live long enough to see the long run. If millions were unemployed and hungry, it would be little consolation to tell them to wait because everything will be fine in 10, 20, or 30 years from now.

Keynes's vision was that the system on its own may linger on less than full employment for many years. Therefore, it was necessary for the government to step in and rescue it. The alternative would be to risk social unrest and the demise of the system as a whole through a socialist revolution or Fascist putsch. Such a fear was not unwarranted. Already Russia had fallen into Communists' hands and Germany, Italy, and Spain were moving toward Fascist states.

In the classical economic vision, prices and wages are determined in the market as the result of the interaction of supply and demand. Supply and demand of commodities and services including labor are determined by the decisions of the multitude of individuals and firms. Those decisions, in turn, are based on market signals in the form of prices and wages. Every individual is sovereign and master of his/her own destiny. Every individual strives to maximize his/her pleasure, or more precisely, utility. Every firm is after maximizing its profit. Everyone has the incentive to do the utmost. The beauty of the system is that while each individual and firm is after self-interest, the overall result is the best outcome for the economy and society. Since wages are flexible and the system is competitive, supply of and demand for labor are equalized at full employment level. If there were unemployed workers, real wages would go down until all of them find employment. And if there were unfulfilled vacancies, real wages would increase to attract more workers to offer their labor.

The Marxian vision is based on the following analysis. The aggregate profit in the economy—but not individual firms' profits—depends on the surplus value in the economy. The surplus value is the amount of value created by workers but not paid for by capitalists who "exploit" the workers. But each firm's profit depends on its cost and price. The price is determined in the market while each firm's costs depend on its stock of capital and the technology utilized. Thus, each capitalist has an incentive to innovate and to introduce new machinery and technology. This cuts into the amount of labor employed causing a reduction in surplus value. Thus, while the particular firm's profit is raised, overall profit, which depends on aggregate surplus value, declines. This causes ups and downs in the economy, brings unemployment and misery to workers. Furthermore, each crisis is deeper than the previous one, finally resulting in a revolution in which the ancien régime is overthrown and replaced by socialism.

In this scheme of things, workers as well as capitalists are pawns. Workers are victims and are unable to control their destiny except in the final stage when they band together and overthrow their yokes. But capitalists too are pawns in this game. They are bad not because they have no heart or are bad people. Indeed, they may be god-fearing people. It is their destiny to play the role of the bad guy. Should they decide to give away all their wealth, they just cease to be capitalists and in a way slow down the progress of history.

Whereas the Marxian vision resembles a Biblical story with redemption at the end, the classical economics vision believes that free enterprise and free market can create a feasible heaven on earth. In the Marxian vision workers, and perhaps even capitalists, are victims. If a worker is unemployed, it is the fault of "the system." In the classical economics vision everyone is sovereign, and if a worker is unemployed it is because he or she has chosen not to work. It is always possible to find a job at some wage.

The Keynesian vision falls somewhere in between. Definitely, there are individuals who decide not to work. But there are those who are the victims of the shortage of demand: they are involuntarily unemployed. But there is more to the story. The Marxian vision does not allow for any intervention in the market because it is useless and at best will hinder the progress toward socialism. In classical economics, the intervention is neither needed nor desirable. Any government meddling in the economy would detract from the optimal outcome produced by the market. In contrast, the Keynesian vision claims that intervention is possible and desirable. Not only can government improve the lot of people and create jobs for involuntarily unemployed, but it is its duty to do so.

It is the Keynesian vision that has triumphed and has been the outlook of people and governments around the world since World War II. It is important to keep the distinction between the three visions—particularly Keynesian and classical—in mind. Because, as the coming chapters will show, they will appear in several reincarnations and the arguments for and against them will influence policymakers.

Paternalistic Economic Policy

Keynes was a great economist and he changed the way we think. Indeed, whether we like it or not, to a great extent, we are all Keynesians. But there is a strand of paternalism in his analysis and policy prescriptions. Keynes came from the privileged class of the British society and his attitude may be understandable. It is not difficult for such a person to believe that he/she has to take care of the less fortunate or guide the society to the right path. "Keynes was a 'do-gooder' in the best sense of the term. Given his background, it is not surprising that he was somewhat paternalistic and thought of the United Kingdom as being governed by an intellectual élite who would guide and persuade the general public."[17] An instance of such paternalistic attitude is when he assured Hayek that should his (Keynes's) theories produce dangerous effects (such as inflation) he would swing the public opinion in the right direction.[18] Indeed it is not unusual for the guiding light, in some instances, to consider himself or herself above the convention and code of conduct or even the law and constitution.

---

[17] J. C. Gilbert (1982), p. 13.
[18] F. A. Hayek (1983), June 11, p. 39.

FDR was also a patrician and had a paternalistic approach to policy. In his inauguration speech he noted

If I read the temper of our people correctly, we now realize as we have never realized before our interdependence on each other; that we can not merely take but we must give as well; that if we are to go forward, we must move as a trained and loyal army willing to sacrifice for the good of a common discipline, because without such discipline no progress is made, no leadership becomes effective. We are, I know, ready and willing to submit our lives and property to such discipline, because it makes possible a leadership which aims at a larger good. This I propose to offer, pledging that the larger purposes will bind upon us all as a sacred obligation with a unity of duty hitherto evoked only in time of armed strife.

With this pledge taken, I assume unhesitatingly the leadership of this great army of our people dedicated to a disciplined attack upon our common problems.

Action in this image and to this end is feasible under the form of government which we have inherited from our ancestors. Our Constitution is so simple and practical that it is possible always to meet extraordinary needs by changes in emphasis and arrangement without loss of essential form.

It is to be hoped that the normal balance of executive and legislative authority may be wholly adequate to meet the unprecedented task before us. But it may be that an unprecedented demand and need for undelayed action may call for temporary departure from that normal balance of public procedure.

I am prepared under my constitutional duty to recommend the measures that a stricken nation in the midst of a stricken world may require. These measures, or such other measures as the Congress may build out of its experience and wisdom, I shall seek, within my constitutional authority, to bring to speedy adoption.

But in the event that the Congress shall fail to take one of these two courses, and in the event that the national emergency is still critical, I shall not evade the clear course of duty that will then confront me. I shall ask the Congress for the one remaining instrument to meet the crisis–broad Executive power to wage a war against the emergency, as great as the power that would be given to me if we were in fact invaded by a foreign foe.

For the trust reposed in me I will return the courage and the devotion that befit the time. I can do no less.

We encounter the same paternalistic streak in the 1960 s and the administration of President John Kennedy (see Chap. 4 for a discussion of economic policy of that period). Milton Friedman noted that the paternalistic attitude in the inaugural speech of the President is not "worthy of the ideals of free men in a free society."

The paternalistic "what your country can do for you" implies that government is the patron, the citizen the ward, a view at odds with the free man's belief in his own responsibility for his own destiny. The organismic, "what you can do for your country" implies that government is the master or the deity, the citizen, the servant or votary. To the free man, the country is the collection of individuals who compose it, not something over and above them.[19]

The above discussion is not against social programs, but a particular attitude toward society and economy and certain types of programs. Paternalistic policies and programs may bring some benefits but they are usually accompanied by one or more detrimental side effects. These include huge bureaucracy and suffocating regulations, corruption and abuse of public funds, and long term harm to those who

---

[19]Milton Friedman (1962), pp. 1–2.

allegedly are to be helped by the policy. Perhaps an example of paternalistic programs outside the realm of economics but with important economic consequences could help illustrate the last consequence. Consider a government mandate to teach children of immigrants in their native language. Ostensibly the program is instituted to help such kids. But if children of immigrants are to live a successful life in the adopted country of their parents, they need to learn the language even better than the natives. Failure to be fluent in the language will doom them to failure ever after.

Goals of economic and social policies and the way to achieve them are essential to economic analysis and to the subject of the present book. In the next chapter we shall talk about the welfare state.

Chapter 2
The Post-War Economic Order

I believe that we should make available to peace-loving peoples
the benefits of our store of technical knowledge in order to help
them realize their aspirations for a better life.
Inaugural speech of President Truman, 1949

Idleness is not the same as Want, but a separate evil, which men
do not escape by having an income. They must also have the
chance of rendering useful service and feeling that they are
doing so. This means that employment is not wanted for the sake
of employment, irrespective of what it produces.
William Henry Beveridge, *Full Employment in a Free Society*

By mid 1943 the tide of war had turned against the Germans. The Russians had started their counterattack and soon were near Kiev in Ukraine. By the fall of that year Mussolini was deposed and American troops landed in Italy. Perhaps a sane person would have surrendered. The Allies now could look forward to the end of the war and the kind of world that would emerge although planning for the post-war economic environment had started as early as 1942 in the United States and England. In both countries the planners—Harry Dexter White in the United States and John Maynard Keynes in England—were at work to come up with arrangements and innovations that would prevent a repeat of the 1930s. Their efforts culminated in the Bretton Woods Conference of 1944, and both can be considered as architects of the post-War international economic order.

No doubt the Great Depression and the War had scarred the world and had changed both the economic landscape and the outlook of nations and governments on world affairs. Post War realities as well as people's expectations demanded new economic arrangements and policies both domestically and in international relations.

Domestically, the time of minimal government and hands off business and the economy was over. Governments were held responsible for the smooth functioning of the economy and the economic well being of their citizens. Furthermore, at the time of war everyone had made sacrifices; the rich did not sacrifice more because they had more. Thus, during peacetime everyone was entitled to share more equally. One group should not monopolize the resources and enjoyment during the peace and ask everyone to sacrifice during war. The welfare state was born.

K. Dadkhah, *The Evolution of Macroeconomic Theory and Policy*,
DOI 10.1007/978-3-540-77008-4_2, © Springer-Verlag Berlin Heidelberg 2009

Internationally the old monetary system had failed and there was no reason to revive it. Yet, the world economic powers did not have the courage to design a completely new system and decided on a more flexible version of the gold standard. But the follies of the beggar-thy-neighbor policies were obvious, and efforts were made to liberalize international trade.

What completed the international scene was the confrontation between the United States and Western Europe—the free world of capitalism and democracy—and the Soviet Union and its satellites representing socialism or, more aptly, state capitalism and dictatorship. The old enemies had been vanquished, but new enemies had emerged.

The United States had emerged as the dominant power, and the old world of European powers had crumbled. Worse, Europe was economically devastated and needed help to get back on its feet. On the other hand, while during the War the Soviet Union had been an ally and Joseph Stalin had been nicknamed "Uncle Joe," few in positions of power in the West had any illusions about the nature of the Soviet system. A confrontation between the free world and the Soviet Union was expected once the war was over. If anyone had any doubts, Stalin's behavior after the War disabused them of any hope for a change in the nature of the oppressive regime in the Soviet Union.

The age of colonialism was over and many countries were struggling for independence and would soon achieve it. The confrontation with the Soviet Union could be fought in any region in the world. In particular, the poor countries, some of them newly independent, were susceptible to communist propaganda and agitation. The United States as the leader of the free world felt an obligation to help the poor countries both as a moral obligation and as a strategic instrument in the confrontation of the free world against the Soviet Union.

A new age had started, and both the domestic scene in the United States and the international economic order would undergo drastic change.

The G.I. Bill

On June 22, 1944 President Roosevelt signed into law the Servicemen's Readjustment Act of 1944, which became known as the G.I. Bill.[1] It provided, authorized, and funded benefits for returning veterans (specifically those who had served from September 16, 1940 to the end of the War) in four areas: health, education, housing, and employment.

It provided for the health care of veterans and allocated $500 million for the construction of additional hospitals.

---

[1] It was "An Act to provide Federal Government aid for the readjustment in civilian life of returning World War II veterans." Thus, it is called The Servicemen's Readjustment Act of 1944. A good read on the subject is *Over Here: How the G.I. Bill Transformed the American Dream* by Edward Humes, 2006.

But perhaps the most important aspect of the bill and the provision for which it is best known was in the area of education. The federal government would pay university tuition, fees, and costs of books of veterans up to $500 per year and pay for their living expenses of $50 per month for those without dependents and $75 for those with dependents.

The Bill also authorized the Administrator of Veterans Affairs to guarantee 50% of loans for the purchase or construction of homes, farms, and businesses up to $2000. This may seem like a small amount compared with present day housing prices but indeed enabled many veterans to buy homes.[2]

Finally, it provided for job counseling and unemployment benefits for returning veterans.

The impetus for the bill may have been the prevention of the sorry experience of World War I veterans (see Chap. 1). It also reflected the changed attitude toward the role of government in a democratic society. Whatever the motive, the G.I. Bill had a great impact on American society. Up to World War II, higher education was generally, although not exclusively, available to upper class youth. The G.I. Bill changed that and opened the door of universities and colleges to sons and daughters of all strata of the society. In this respect it is noteworthy that the Bill did not confine its provisions to men or whites; it was for all veterans including women and blacks. One consequence of the bill was to foster the expansion of universities; another was to open homeownership to many more families.

The importance of the G.I. Bill is that it made a big difference in the lives of several million veterans and transformed American society. But it also showed how the government could improve the lots of many and improve the distribution of resources without imposing undue regulations on the economy or interfering with the working of the free market.

In 1984 the G.I. Bill was updated so that later generations of veterans could receive home loan guarantees and help with their education. The new bill is known as Montgomery G.I. Bill after its sponsor congressman Gillespie Montgomery of Mississippi.

The Employment Act of 1946

The Great Depression was an enormous shock to Americans. Many could not forget it many decades later and their behavior and psyche were affected by it. Immediately after the War, there was fear of the repeat of the Great Depression. The end of the War meant that government expenditures and purchases would be scaled back, while at the same time a large number of veterans would be discharged and return to civilian life. Thus, a huge additional labor supply would coincide with a decline in aggregate demand. The memory of recessions following World War I was still alive.

---

[2]Based on data from the US Census Bureau, I estimated the median price of a house in the United States to be about $2500 in 1940 and $6250 in 1950.

Some economists, including Alvin Hansen, forwarded the *stagnation theory* based on which, in the long run, a capitalist system would tend toward stagnation. Some also forwarded *underconsumptionist* theories.

Many believed that the experience of the Great Depression should not be repeated. The loss of output and the loss of livelihood and dignity of the unemployed were too much to bear more than once. John Maynard Keynes had shown the way for avoiding another depression. The cause of depression was a lack of effective demand compared to the amount of aggregate supply that would be available with the full employment. The government could and should step in and by managing the aggregate demand prevent wild fluctuations in output and employment.

Proponents of government action used employment data contained in a book by former Vice President Henry Wallace[3] to document the depth of the problem during the Great Depression. Wallace had projected the labor force in the United States from 1900 to 1944. After subtracting the number of frictionally unemployed—that is, those moving between jobs whose unemployment is a condition for the smooth working of the labor market—he arrived at the number of jobs needed for full employment. A comparison of the estimated employment data with the projected number needed for full employment showed that a large number of Americans were unemployed during that period.[4]

That depression had to be avoided and the government had a duty to do so was not in dispute anymore. The question was how and to what extent the government should be involved in the economy. Is each individual entitled to have a job? How would that entitlement be achieved? At one extreme were those who considered

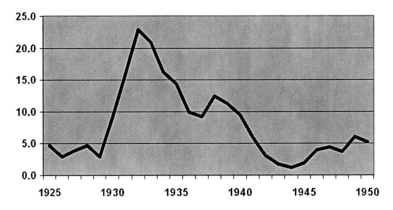

Fig. 2.1 Annual unemployment rate in the United States: 1925–1950

---

[3]Henry A. Wallace (1888–1965) was the Vice President during FDR's third term (1941–1945). He also served as FDR's Secretary of Agriculture and Secretary of Commerce. In 1948 Wallace ran as the presidential candidate of Progressive Party and lost to President Harry S. Truman.

[4]Henry Wallace, *Sixty Million Jobs* (1945). The general pattern of unemployment in Wallace's data resembles that shown in Fig. 2.1. The last year in Wallace's data was 1944.

employment a basic *right* and those who advocated some kind of planning. At the other were those who thought that government intervention in the economy ran opposite to American values. There had to be a compromise and the result was the Employment Act of 1946.

The sponsors of the Employment Act wanted the government to declare that all Americans were "entitled to an opportunity for useful, remunerative, regular, and full-time employment." It was the duty of the government to provide continuous full employment in the economy and the tool would be government expenditures. Such a goal would have been unrealistic, unattainable and detrimental to the economy. Instead Sect. 2 of the act declared the federal government has the responsibility "to use all practical means ... to promote maximum employment, production, and purchasing power."[5]

The President was to transmit an Economic Report to Congress. It was to contain data on the condition of the economy, forecast of future trends, a review of the federal government's economic program, and a program for carrying out the policy of maximum employment, production, and purchasing power.

Thus, in the post war era the government was to be held responsible for the employment and well being of its people. The era of minimal government, responsible only for internal and external security, had come to an end. This was not confined to America; indeed, the transformation of the role of government in the US was less drastic compared to European nations. The mid 1940s ushered in the welfare state in many European countries (see below).

In 1976 Senator Hubert Humphrey and Representative Augustus Hawkins sponsored a bill to revive the intents of the original Employment Act by recognizing the rights of all Americans to gainful employment. The end result was the Full Employment and Balanced Growth Act of 1978, which again did not recognize such a right.

The Council of Economic Advisers

Section 4 of the Employment Act of 1946 created the Council of Economic Advisers (CEA) in order to "appraise programs and activities of the Government ... and to formulate and recommend national economic policy to promote employment, production, and purchasing power under free competitive enterprise." The Council would be composed of three individuals whose "training, experience, and attainments" made them "exceptionally qualified" for the job.

During the years many luminaries of the economics profession have served on the Council. They include two Nobel laureates (James Tobin and Joseph Stiglitz), three future Chairmen of the Board of Governors of the Federal Reserve (Arthur Burns, Alan Greenspan, and Ben Bernanke), and top economists (including among others Arthur Okun, Martin Feldstein, John Taylor, Alan Blinder, and Gregory Mankiw).

---

[5]For a short history of the Employment Act and opposing views see G. J. Santoni (1986).

The CEA is charged with advising the President on economic matters and preparing an *Economic Report of the President*. This annual publication includes an assessment of the economic conditions of the country, economic policies of the government and their intended results, and a compendium of macroeconomic data tables.

As a part of the executive branch, the influence of the CEA and its economists depends on the views and attitudes of the President and their closeness to that of the CEA chairman and its staff. The Administration hasn't always heeded the advice of economists. Faced with policies they could not support, some have decided to keep quiet, some have returned to academia, and some like Martin Feldstein, the CEA chairman under President Reagan, have been outspoken.

It seems that the profile of the CEA rose during the early years of its operation. Its influence peaked in the early 1960s during the administrations of Presidents Kennedy and Johnson. After the 1970s and particularly in the past two decades its influence, with ebbs and flows, has waned. One reason may be the demise of the fixed exchange rates system in 1971 and the current system of flexible rates (see Chap. 6). In a fixed exchange regime monetary policy is ineffective as a counter-cyclical measure and fiscal policy is effective (see Chap. 5). In a system of flexible exchange rates, the situation is reversed and monetary policy is effective in avoiding recessions or at least ameliorating their effects while fiscal policy is less effective. Hence the prominence of monetary policy and the Federal Reserve System as the center of economic policy and the rising profile of the Fed's chairman.

The Birth of the Welfare State

The New Deal ushered in many elements of the welfare state including the establishment of social security and unemployment insurance. Yet as a comprehensive state policy we may date, with no pretence of being precise, the birth of the modern welfare state[6] as 1942 and the submission of the Beveridge Report[7] in England. It called for a "comprehensive policy of social progress," and "An attack upon Want," "Disease, Ignorance, Squalor, and Idleness." The report called for a revolutionary approach to the problem of social security and a comprehensive program, not a piecemeal approach. Furthermore,

---

[6]Here we speak of the modern welfare state. Welfare of citizens has been the concern of governments for many centuries. It is not difficult to find precedence for welfare measures in ancient China or other parts of the world. Here we are talking of a deliberate, comprehensive, and sustained policy of modern governments.

[7]The report is entitled *Social Insurance and Allied Services* and was prepared by a committee under the chairmanship of Sir William H. Beveridge. The members of the committee were drawn from different departments concerned with the well being of citizens including Home Office, Ministry of Labour and National Service, Ministry of Health, and Treasury. The report was submitted to the British Parliament in November 1942.

social security must be achieved by co-operation between the State and the individual. The State should offer security for services and contribution. The State in organizing security should not stifle incentive, opportunity, responsibility; in establishing a national minimum, it should leave room and encouragement for voluntary action by each individual to provide more than that minimum for himself and his family.

All modern governments are welfare states; the difference is the degree with which they interfere in the market to deliver services. Providing education, health care, unemployment compensation, insurance against catastrophic outcome, and taking care of citizens who could not take care of themselves have become normal duties of all governments. There is no reason to believe that one scheme of income distribution is better than the other. Nevertheless, we can argue that at least the starting point of life should be reasonably equal for all members of society regardless of their families' positions.

Over time the welfare state has had both its defenders and detractors. At times the phrase has been made into a code word for derision against government meddling in the economy. But the rationale for it remains persuasive. A glance at any society shows that there are those who have more than they even can keep account of and those who can hardly make ends meet. If we take some developing nations we even encounter people whose survival is at risk or barely survive with a dollar or two per day. Why is there such dispersion in income and wealth?

One can consider human society engaged in a vast economic game, which has its own rules and regulations. There will always be losers and winners because people are different. Human beings are not born equal; some are stronger, some more intelligent, and some more beautiful. Some work harder and some are lucky. Of course the starting points of players are not equal either. Some are born into rich families and some in dirt-poor environments. In the jargon of economics, the initial endowments are vastly different.

In nature the rule is the survival of the fittest; why shouldn't that apply to human society? Let the market determine the outcome and let us accept it as the best. Indeed, the fundamental theorem of welfare economics shows that once equilibrium is reached under the free market no one can be made better off unless someone else is made worse off (Pareto optimality). In other words, improving on market equilibrium requires interpersonal comparisons and value judgments. And it may be asked that "who are we to make value judgments?"

But there is more than one problem with the above argument. First, the rules of the game are human-made and there could be a different set of rules that would result in a less unequal distribution of income. Why is it that property rights should be enforced by the government? Let the market or the survival-of-the-fittest take care of that. Think of armed shareholders who may pay a visit to a bandit CEO's house who has helped himself to a great reward when the company shares have gone down.

The fact that initial endowments are not equal is also a consequence of human-made rules. Furthermore, Pareto optimality does not depend on initial distribution of wealth. For every distribution of initial wealth there is a different outcome, and every one of them is Pareto optimal. It is not true that there exists a value free initial

distribution of wealth. Acceptance of any initial distribution of wealth or rules of
inheritance involves moral and value judgment.

But even if we accept the rules of the game still there are circumstances in which
markets fail and the outcome is not optimal. These situations clearly call for intervention. These cases are extensively discussed in microeconomics and public economics and we need not elaborate here. Yet a great contribution of Keynes and
Keynesian economics was to show that the free enterprise system might fail in the
macro sense. It could fail to bring equilibrium at a level of employment that everyone willing and able to work can find gainful employment at market wages; hence,
involuntary unemployment would occur.

The opponents of welfare state point to three problems. Welfare programs create vast bureaucracies, are fraught with waste, corruption, and fraud, interfere with
efficient functioning of markets, and create an underclass of loafers who live out of
handouts. The challenge of any government or any party advocating welfare for all
is to come up with a mechanism to provide services without adverse effects. Thus,
the question is not whether we should take care of our fellow citizens, but how.

Figures 2.2 and 2.3 show public and private social expenditures in the United
States, Sweden, and the OECD.[8] Social expenditures include pension, unemployment benefits, health, education, and other benefits.

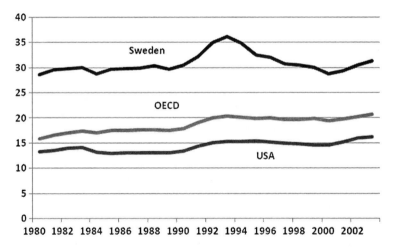

Fig. 2.2 Public social expenditures as a % of the GDP

---

[8]The Organization for Economic Co-Operation and Development was established in 1961 and
presently has 30 members. They include Canada, the United States, Mexico, many European
countries, Australia, Japan, and Korea. Member countries are committed to market economy and
democracy.

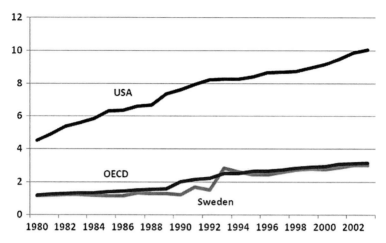

Fig. 2.3 Private social expenditures as a % of the GDP

The Bretton Woods Agreement

On the international front, the most urgent issue was the restoration of a credible monetary system. Such a system was a prerequisite for the expansion of trade. The restrictive inter-war policies of beggar-thy-neighbor had brought losses to everyone and had to be avoided. It was also hoped that the system would help eliminate exchange controls. In July 1944, representatives of 44 countries gathered in the Mount Washington Hotel in Bretton Woods, New Hampshire, USA to forge the post-war international monetary order and exchange rates regime. The preparatory work had started long ago, and the United Kingdom and the United States had each brought a plan to the meetings.

The British plan, referred to as Keynes Plan after its principal author, called for an international clearing union with an international currency that could be used to settle the accounts between members. Members with surplus in their international balance would commit funds to the union and members with deficit in their international balance would use credit extended to them by the union. Such an overdraft facility would be in an international currency and in the books of the union. Needless to say, the plan favored the United Kingdom and other countries in similar position while putting the burden of footing the bills on the United States.

The American plan, referred to as the White Plan after its principal author Harry Dexter White,[9] called for the establishment of a fund. Members would subscribe

---

[9]Harry Dexter White (1892–1948) was a Harvard educated economist and a high ranking official in the US Department of Treasury. He was the principal architect of the Bretton Woods Agreement, the IMF, and the World Bank. White has been accused by several sources of being a Soviet spy. He died of a heart attack three days after testifying before the House Committee on Un-American Activities (he had had several heart attacks before that testimony).

gold and currency from which the fund would extend credit to members experiencing temporary deficit. The final Bretton Woods Agreement was principally based on the White Plan.

An international monetary system can be characterized by four main features: an international currency, how exchange rates are determined, a central authority to manage the system and if necessary back the currency, and a mechanism for correcting disequilibrium, i.e., eliminating chronic deficits or surpluses. For example, during the Gold Standard regime, gold was the international currency. By defining the gold content of their currencies each and every country determined its exchange rates with all other currencies. Thus, the ratio of the gold contents of every two currencies was equal to their exchange rate and, as long as the gold contents remained constant, the exchange rates were fixed. During the 19th and early years of 20th centuries Britain played the role of the central authority and through the Bank of England supervised the system. Small deficits and surpluses resulted in changes in the book entries in the Bank of England. The account of deficit countries would be debited and that of the surplus countries credited. Large imbalances would trigger shipments of gold between countries resulting in expansion or contraction of money supply in that country.

The Bretton Woods Agreement chose the gold-backed-dollar as its international currency. The value of the dollar was fixed in terms of gold at $35 per ounce. Thus, while nominally gold was still the international currency, members had to express the par value of their currency in terms of gold or the dollar. Hence the international monetary system hammered out at the Bretton Woods conference was called the gold exchange standard.

The ratio of par values determined the exchange rates between currencies. For example, if the par value of the Swedish kronor was 5.2 per dollar and that of the Egyptian pound 0.44 per dollar, then the exchange rate between the kronor and the Egyptian pound would be 11.818 kronor per Egyptian pound or 0.085 Egyptian pounds per kronor. Thus, the exchange rates were fixed.

Furthermore, the members had to contain the fluctuations in the rate within 1% of the parity, which meant that in the most extreme case (one country being 1% above and the other 1% below parity) the exchange rates would be 2% above or below the fixed rates. Central banks were obligated to maintain dollar reserves and to maintain parity by intervening in the market, i.e., by buying or selling the dollar at the official rate.

Thus, the dollar became the international currency and the United States the financial center. The coordination mechanism was to work through the IMF (see below).

The International Monetary Fund (IMF)

The IMF was officially established on December 27, 1945 and began operation on March 1, 1947. The membership was initially open to countries participating in the Bretton Woods conference.[10] The par value of each nation's currency would be determined in gold or the US dollar. The par values would determine the exchange rates between currencies. After such determination all trading between member states would be carried out on that basis (except for a prescribed trading margin). The working assets of the fund were contributed by the members. Each country had a quota, part of which was paid in gold and the rest in that country's currency. The United States had the largest quota and the total working capital of the fund was expected to reach $8.8 billion.

The members were entitled to borrow from the fund to cover temporary imbalances in their international transactions. But if a fundamental disequilibrium developed, the country, with the agreement of the IMF, could devalue its currency. Such arrangements were meant to avoid any devaluation "war" between countries.

As will be discussed in Chap. 6, in 1971 the United States severed the tie between the dollar and gold and effectively ended the Bretton Woods system. With the collapse of the Bretton Woods system in 1971, the IMF lost its raison d'êtres and became another useless bureaucracy providing jobs for educated middle class individuals of different countries. Today it continues its existence and is still in search of a mission.

The Bank for Reconstruction and Development (the World Bank)

The Bretton Woods Agreement also envisioned the establishment of a bank for Reconstruction and Development. The genesis of the bank was a proposal by Harry Dexter White in 1942. At the beginning the bank was meant as a vehicle for financing the reconstruction of war-ravaged Europe. The idea of development was added later on—particularly at the insistence of developing countries with the acquiescence of White—while Keynes and the British were against it.

Data on World Bank loans (Table 2.1) confirms that in the early years the bank's loans were extended to Europe and to a lesser extent Latin America, while Africa, Asia, and the Middle East received none. It is after 1950 that the bank paid attention to developing countries.

Table 2.1 Distribution of world bank lending (%)

Region	1946–49	1950–59	1960–69	1970–79	1980–89	1990–95
Africa	0	15	12	14	15	15
Asia	0	38	40	38	43	37
Europe	81	20	12	12	9	16
Latin America	19	22	28	24	26	25
Middle East/North Africa	0	5	7	11	7	7

Source: *The World Bank, Its First Half Century*, by Kapur et al. (1997).

---

[10]The Soviet Union was one of the 44 countries participating in the conference, but it decided not to join the fund. Later on, nations other than the original 44 joined the fund.

The bank's capital would be raised from members' subscription. Part of each member's quota was to be paid within a year and the rest as needed. The bank would make loans from its own capital or by borrowing in the international financial markets. In addition the bank could guarantee a loan by a third party to a member country, thus reducing the risk and therefore the cost of the loan.

The World Bank's loans were made for specific projects and would only cover the foreign exchange portion of such projects. Each loan had to be guaranteed by the government of the receiving country. Over the years the bank's objectives have evolved. Nevertheless, in a world with disparity among countries and with problems of poverty, corruption, and AIDS, it has played an important role. Surely, it can play a more significant role in alleviating such problems as AIDS in Africa.

It was unfortunate that in recent years the Bank was embroiled in needless controversy. In 2005, President Bush nominated Paul Wolfowitz, deputy secretary of Defense to be the president of the World Bank. His appointment was controversial, and later he was embroiled in a controversy involving his relationship with a bank senior officer. It was alleged that he had granted her excessive salary raise. Fortunately that undignified episode is over. Wolfowitz resigned in 2007 and was succeeded by Robert Zoellick, who has brought calm and stability to the bank.

General Agreement on Tariffs and Trade (GATT)

In 1947 a group of countries[11] signed an agreement to promote free trade by cutting tariffs and removing barriers to international trade. The pact which came to be known as the General Agreement on Tariffs and Trade (GATT) went into effect on January 1, 1948. The idea of free trade and its effects on growth and well being of nations have been debated for centuries among economists and politicians. There have been many who have thought that by closing the doors and avoiding imports or by following mercantilist policies a country could gain income and employment for their people. Such policies were tried after World War I in many countries including the United States as embodied in the Smoot-Hawley Act. The upshot was that everyone lost. If everyone follows a beggar-thy-neighbor policy, you end up with a neighborhood populated by beggars. The idea behind the GATT was to avoid the same mistakes.

The echo of the Great Depression and the influence of the Keynesian ideas is quite apparent in the preamble to GATT:

> Recognizing that their relations in the field of trade and economic endeavour should be conducted with a view to raising standards of living, *ensuring full employment* and a large and steadily growing volume of real income and *effective demand*, developing the full use of the resources of the world and *expanding the production and exchange of goods.*

---

[11] They included Australia, Belgium, Brazil, Burma, Canada, Ceylon, Chile, China, Cuba, Czechoslovakia, France, India, Lebanon, Luxemburg, the Netherlands, New Zealand, Norway, Pakistan, Rhodesia, Syria, South Africa, United Kingdom, and the United States.

> Being desirous of contributing to these objectives by entering into reciprocal and mutu-
> ally advantageous arrangements *directed to the substantial reduction of tariffs and other
> barriers to trade and to the elimination of discriminatory treatment in international com-
> merce* [emphasis added].

While GATT has been less glamorous and talked about than either the IMF or the
World Bank, it has been more enduring and more effective in promoting trade and
growth in the world. The original agreement was followed by further talks[12] that
resulted in further tariff reductions and the expansion of the agreement into other
areas including services and patents.

In 1995 the World Trade Organization (WTO) was born, which currently has
153 members. WTO is the main organization for promoting international trade and
resolving trade dispute between member countries.

The Marshall Plan

World War II was over but Europe was devastated. Factories and roads had been
destroyed, international commerce and trade had been disrupted, and industrial production was recovering at a very slow pace. To add to the misery there had been crop
failures and bad harvest. There were shortages and hunger everywhere. It was not
surprising that Europeans were discouraged, desperate, and angry. Perhaps nothing
can illustrate the hopelessness of Europe better than neo-realist films made by the
brilliant Italian directors Vittorio de Sica, Roberto Rossellini, and others.

On the horizon loomed the specter of a communist takeover of European countries. Some like Albania, Poland, Czechoslovakia, and others were already written
off. But others such as Italy, Greece, France, and Austria were not safe. People in
these countries were desperate and easy prey to communist propaganda. Up to the
spring of 1947, the United States had provided credit and aid to Europe. Although
substantial in sum, these had the nature of relief funds, and credits and loan had
strings attached to them. The fact was that Europe needed long term growth and
a hope for the future. The United States had the means to rescue Europe, and the
Truman administration rose to the challenge.

Secretary of State George Marshall[13] announced the plan for the European recovery in his commencement speech at Harvard University on June 5, 1947. According
to Marshall, Europe was in a critical situation because

---

[12] Among the more famous ones are the Kennedy round (1962–1967), Tokyo round (1973–1979),
Uruguay round (1986–1994), and the Doha round (2001–2008). The Doha round ended in failure. Negotiators from different countries gathered in Geneva Switzerland in July 2008. Despite
extended discussion they could not reach an agreement. The sticky point was developing nations'
demand to be able to impose temporary tariff barriers to control prices or block a surge in imports.
On one side stood the United States and on the other China and India.

[13] General George C. Marshall (1880–1959) as the Chief of Staff of the United States Army (1939–
1945) was instrumental in the Allies' victory in World War II. He served as Secretary of State
(1947–1949) and Secretary of Defense (1950–1951) during the Truman administration. He was
awarded the Nobel Peace Prize in 1953 to honor his "great work for the establishment of peace."
During the ceremony in the University of Oslo, communists protested by shouting and throwing
leaflets.

Long-standing commercial ties, private institutions, banks, insurance companies and ship-
ping companies disappeared, through loss of capital, absorption through nationalization or
by simple destruction. In many countries, confidence in local currency has been severely
shaken. The breakdown of the business structure of Europe during the war was complete.
... Raw materials and fuel are in short supply. Machinery is lacking or worn out. ... Thus
a very serious situation is rapidly developing which bodes no good for the world.

He added:

Europe's requirements for the next three or four years of foreign food and other essential
products—principally from America—are so much greater than her present ability to pay
that she must have substantial additional help, or face economic, social and political deterioration of a grave character.

The remedy lies in breaking the vicious circle and restoring the confidence of the
European people in the economic future of their own countries and of Europe as a whole.

The consequences [of the crisis] to the economy of the United States should be apparent
to all. It is logical that the United States should do whatever it is able to do to assist in
the return of normal economic health in the world, without which there can be no political
stability and no assured peace.

[G]overnments, political parties or groups which seek to perpetuate human misery in
order to profit therefrom politically or otherwise will encounter the opposition of the United
States.

It would be neither fitting nor efficacious for this Government to undertake to draw
up unilaterally a program designed to place Europe on its feet economically. This is the
business of the Europeans. The initiative, I think, must come from Europe. The role of this
country should consist of friendly aid in the drafting of a European program and of later
support of such a program so far as it may be practical for us to do so. The program should
be a joint one, agreed to by a number, if not all European nations.

From its inception to 1952 when the Marshall Plan was ended, the United States
spent about $13 billion. Using the GDP deflator as a measure of price change and
comparing 2006 to 1950 (the mid year of the Marshall Plan), the amount spent by
the US is equivalent to $92 billion in 2006 prices. Alternatively, $13 billion was
about 4.4% of the United States GDP in 1950. In 2006 4.4% of the US GDP was
more than $580 billion. Thus, the sum was substantial and required a real sacrifice
by the US taxpayers.

The effect of the Marshall Plan on the recovery of Europe has been the subject of
many inquiries. Some have argued that except for the first two years of the plan, the
annual amount of the aid was small compared to the amount of domestic capital formation of the recipient countries. It is also said that European economies had already
started on the path to growth when the Marshall Plan went into effect. Finally, some
have emphasized the role of economic reforms in Europe, for instance, the German
economic and monetary reform of 1948.

There can be no doubt, however, that the Marshall Plan played a crucial role in
reviving the economies of Europe. Table 2.2 shows the amount of American aid as
a percentage of domestic capital formation in four European countries.

It can be seen that the amount, particularly in the first years, was substantial.
The $13 billion dollars of aid helped to relax the foreign exchange constraint of the
recipient countries and "thus solved the catch-22 of having to export in order to pay
for imports but being unable to produce for export without first importing materials

Table 2.2 American aid as a percentage of gross domestic capital formation

	1948	1949	1950	1951
United Kingdom	9	11	10	2
France	14	12	10	7
West Germany	31	22	11	7
Italy*	27	34	10	9

*As a % of net domestic capital formation.
Source: Lucrezia Reichlin (1995)

and machinery."[14] It also gave European governments the resources to fund social and welfare programs and at the same time continue with economic liberalization. Further, the aid was both an economic and political boost that brought confidence to Europe and jump-started the growth. Finally, it fostered American style management in Europe. None of these, of course, detracts from the importance of economic reforms of these countries. Indeed, the main lesson of the Marshall Plan for international intervention is that only foreign aid combined with domestic reforms could succeed. There has to be a close partnership between donor and recipient country with the latter having resolved to succeed.

The Point Four

In his inaugural address of Thursday, January 20, 1949, President Truman outlined four major courses of action for peace and freedom. The first point noted the continued support for the United Nations and related agencies; the second referred to the Marshall Plan for the European recovery and the removal of barriers to world trade; the third point was about the North Atlantic security plan (NATO).

> Fourth, we must embark on a bold new program for making the benefits of our scientific advances and industrial progress available for the improvement and growth of underdeveloped areas. More than half the people of the world are living in conditions approaching misery. Their food is inadequate. They are victims of disease. Their economic life is primitive and stagnant. Their poverty is a handicap and a threat both to them and to more prosperous areas. . . . I believe that we should make available to peace-loving peoples the benefits of our store of technical knowledge in order to help them realize their aspirations for a better life. And, in cooperation with other nations, we should foster capital investment in areas needing development.

The idea of the Point Four was that a vast area of the world and a large part of humanity were in the grip of poverty. Whatever the reason, poverty would create a fertile ground for the communists to sow the seeds of discontent, revolution, and takeover by a puppet of the Soviet Union. The United States had the resources and

---

[14] Barry Eichengreen (2007), p. 65.

technology to help the people of poor nations out of their poverty and thus deprive the Soviet Union of an easy prey.

In October 1950, the United States signed the first Point Four agreement with Iran. Technical assistance was provided in the fields of agriculture, public health, and education. In later years the Point Four program was merged with other international aid programs of the United States.

Many Point Four programs were small and diffused projects which could not compete with spectacular projects (Aswan Dam, for instance) in grabbing headlines. Yet their usefulness could not be denied. Some have wondered why despite American aid to some countries, the population developed a hostile attitude toward the United States and in some countries the communist parties gained ground. Indeed, why did in some countries, leftist revolutions or coup d'états occur? A possible answer to these questions rests on the following observations.

First, anti-Americanism is more a reflection of the insecurity of a nation that needs to find a culprit for its own failings. The alternative to blaming the United States for all ills in the world is to accept responsibility for some of them. Second, the lure of communism has been due to income inequality rather than poverty. The selling point of Marxism and communism is the promise of security and equality for everyone; "from each according to his/her ability, to each according to his/her need." It promises to take the wealth of the wealthy and share its fruits with everyone. Many members of communist parties and definitely most of the party leaders in developing countries have been members of the middle class and, in many cases, upper class. Finally, the spirit of rebellion and revolution is directly correlated with economic well-being. It is hard to find a revolution that occurred during a time of famine or misery. Most revolutions are preceded by a period of economic prosperity.

The discussion above points to one conclusion. There is a connection between economics and politics but the relationship is neither simple nor mechanical. The emphasis should be on incentives, partnership, and respect for the dignity of the aid recipient.

The Brave New Post War World

In many respects the post World War II world was a different world. On the domestic front national governments assumed an increasing role in the economy. This was true in the United States and around the world. Internationally, countries became more intertwined than before. The idea of a free market for exchange rates was set aside in favor of fixed and managed rates. This was not surprising given that the memory of the Great Depression was still fresh. Nevertheless, countries were expected to open their markets to each other, promote trade, and to help each other. The march toward globalization had started and more was to come.

Chapter 3
Laying the Foundations of Keynesian Economics

I give you the toast of the Royal Economic Society, of economics
and economists, who are the trustees, not of civilization, but of
the possibility of civilization.
John Maynard Keynes, at the end of his speech on the occasion
of his retirement from the editorship of the *Economic Journal*
in 1945

Keynes had propounded a new vision of the economy, and Hicks had turned this vision into a tractable model and a way for economists to analyze economic problems. Indeed Keynes's vision resonated well with many younger economists and some decision makers. But now the real work had started. A few decades were needed to flesh out the theory, fill the gaping holes in it, and show that indeed it was a good approximation to economic reality. But if the new vision and set of policies associated with it had to have any chance, its approval had to be more widespread than in the academic circles. Decision makers and the general public had to be convinced that the Keynesian prescription was worth trying and once adopted it would bear the promised fruits. In this chapter we shall concentrate on the theoretical and empirical development of Keynesian theory and in the next chapter discuss its policy effectiveness.

To begin with, Keynesian theory relied on aggregate variables such as national income, consumption, investment, government expenditures, and unemployment rate. It posited relationships between these variables which were not based on microeconomic theory that started with optimizing consumers and firms;[1] rather they were claimed to be empirically observed and verifiable. Thus, the theory required compilation of national income account data and an apparatus to substantiate assumed economic relationships. At the same time if the government was to "manage" the economy, it required detailed information regarding the direction of important economic variables. Further, it needed reliable forecasts of the same variables and a model to evaluate policy options. The shared requirements of theory and policy led to the development of national income accounting and econometrics.

---

[1] This lack of microfoundations was one of the main points of controversy among economists. We shall discuss it in Chap. 7.

K. Dadkhah, *The Evolution of Macroeconomic Theory and Policy*,
DOI 10.1007/978-3-540-77008-4_3, © Springer-Verlag Berlin Heidelberg 2009

The foundations of such activities were laid before the War but they continued with renewed vigor after it.

In many ways the Keynesian model was incomplete, but nowhere as significantly as in the case of price level. Keynes had assumed price level to be constant. Further, concentrating on the Great Depression, he had analyzed the situation where the labor supply and, therefore, output are infinitely elastic. Hence, his model concentrated on aggregate demand and lacked a supply equation. Early on Lawrence Klein (Nobel Laureate 1980) extended the model to include labor market, aggregate supply, and price level.

Another line of inquiry involved fleshing out the components of theory. Keynes had simply referred to consumption or investment functions and demand for money. But what were the shapes of these functions and would they account for all or most of observed facts about consumption, investment, and demand for money. In addition, there was the nagging question of microfoundations. The aggregate relationships posited by Keynes, such as consumption, investment, and demand for money function, should be the sum of individual behaviors. Could we, for example, start from the optimizing behavior of individual consumers and derive the demand for consumption goods and show that its aggregate over all consumers corresponds to the Keynesian consumption function? If this is not possible, what micro behavior is the basis of the aggregate consumption function?

Finally, a group of economists modified the Keynesian model to explain long-run economic growth. Keynes's theory pertains to short-run fluctuations in advanced economies. But once these economies were out of the depression and the expected post war stagnation did not materialize, the issue of economic growth gained attention. More important, in the post-war era many former colonies gained independence, and people and policy makers of developing countries became more enthusiastic about growth and development. The issue of long-run economic growth, therefore, gained urgency and international recognition. Why were some countries poor and some rich? What was needed to start and sustain economic growth? Roy Harrod, Evsey Domar, and Robert Solow (Nobel Laureate 1987) and others tried to answer such questions.

Aggregate Supply and Aggregate Demand

The Keynesian model concentrated on the demand side of the economy and even then it assumed that the price level was constant. The price level appeared in the LM curve to transform the money supply into "real balances" and make it compatible with all other variables in the model which were in constant prices. As long as the economy was in throes of depression, the question of price level could be set aside. But when the economy started on the path to recovery the questions of price level and inflation became significant. Particularly as the economy got closer and closer to full employment, the issues of prices, wages, and inflation gained urgency. It is important to note that before WWII, the main concern of economists was deflation. After the war the government played a larger role in the economy and, compared to pre-war peacetime, its expenditures increased drastically. Thus, inflation and not deflation became a major concern. The Keynesian model had to be expanded to include the determination of price level. Otherwise, as many critics of Keynes had charged, the model was a special case of the classical model and applicable to the case of a depression only when wages are inflexible.

A less than satisfactory solution for introducing price level is to add a vertical supply line at the point of full employment to the IS-LM model. As long as the intersection of IS and LM curves lie to the left of full employment, the price level would decrease, shifting the LM curve to the right, increasing the income level and bringing it closer to the full employment. If the point of intersection is to the right of full employment, the price level would increase, the LM curve shifts to the left, income decreases and gets closer to the full employment. At the point of full employment the price level stays constant. Figures 3.1 and 3.2 depict these situations

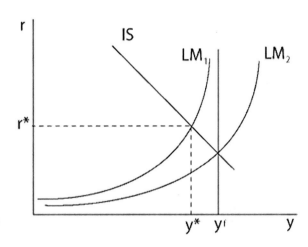

Fig. 3.1 Less than full employment and falling price level

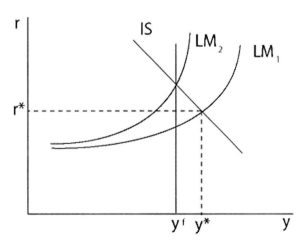

Fig. 3.2 Overheated economy and inflation

where Y^f denotes the full employment output and Y^* and r^* are, respectively, the short run equilibrium levels of income and interest rate.

A more satisfying solution is to explicitly derive aggregate demand and supply functions.

To obtain the aggregate demand curve, consider again the IS-LM equations:

$$Y = C(Y - T) + I(r) + G$$

$$L(Y,r) = \frac{M}{P}$$

Note that for every level of prices P, there is a point of intersection of IS and LM which determines the corresponding level of income. A decrease in price level, P, acts the same as an increase in money supply; the LM curve shifts to the right, interest rate decreases and income increases. Given the amount of government expenditures and taxes, each price level is associated with a given amount of aggregate income. Connecting these points in the Y-P plane we have the aggregate demand curve, which is downward sloping because the lower the price level the higher is income. We can depict the loci of such pairs of P and Y in the P-Y plane and designate it as aggregate demand curve (Fig. 3.3).

To obtain the aggregate supply function, consider the following equations:

$$Y = f(N)$$

$$\frac{W}{P} = f'(N)$$

$$N = \varphi \left(\frac{W}{P} \right)$$

The first equation is the production function stating that output is a function of the amount of labor employed N. The reason is that we are still dealing with the

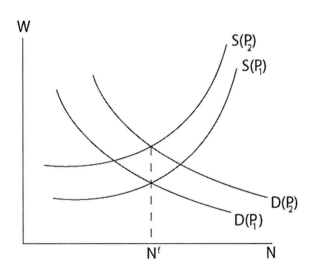

Fig. 3.3 Supply and demand for labor: the classical case

short-run, and capital stock is assumed to be constant or its change is negligible compared to the stock of capital.

The second equation is a demand for labor function, stating that firms hire workers to the point that the marginal product of labor is equal to the real wage rate. This directly comes from microeconomics of optimizing firms. Finally, based on microeconomics, the supply of labor depends on real wages. The worker maximizes her utility by deciding on the amount of time to work—which brings income—and the amount of time to allocate to leisure. The higher the real wage rate the more willing she would be to sacrifice leisure and earn income. Thus, the amount of labor supply increases with the increase in the real wage rate. The last two equations determine the equilibrium value of employment (Fig. 3.3).

Since both supply and demand for labor depend on real wages, in equilibrium, total employment remains constant. All those who are willing to work at going market wages find employment; there is no involuntary unemployment. Since output and income depend on employment, the amount of supply is constant at Y^f (that is, the amount of income produced with the full employment of the labor force) and the aggregate supply curve is a vertical line (Fig. 3.4). There is only one point of equilibrium at full employment. Increasing demand through fiscal or monetary policy would only increase the price level with no effect on income or employment.

Figure 3.4 depicts the classical case. If the economy is not at full employment, prices will decline until the equilibrium is reached. Historical evidence showed that this may not occur or it may take a very long time to happen. Hence Keynes's famous saying that "in the long run we are all dead."

Alternatively, we can consider the pure Keynesian case, where price level is fixed and aggregate supply is infinitely elastic (Fig. 3.5). Here an increase in aggregate demand would only increase aggregate output and employment. The price level is not affected because there is so much unused productive capacity in the economy that the increase in demand would not result in bidding up prices.

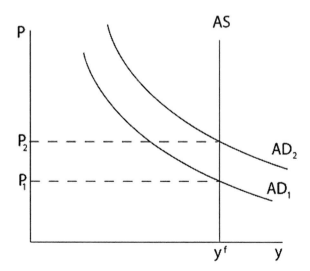

Fig. 3.4 Aggregate supply and demand: the classical case

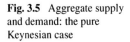

Fig. 3.5 Aggregate supply
and demand: the pure
Keynesian case

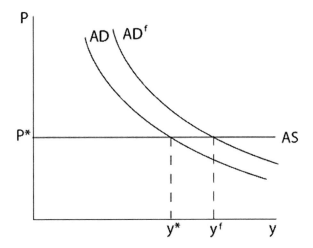

An alternative to these extreme cases is to separate wage rate from the price index in one of the equations. One could assume that workers respond to nominal wages and the price level differently. For instance, they would be happier to receive 10% wage increase even if prices rise by 10%—leaving real wage constant—than to have no wage increase and prices remain constant. Such a situation, however, is called money illusion and goes against the postulate of rationality in economics because in the two cases the real wage rate—that is, the purchasing power of the laborer—remains constant but the laborer reacts differently. Yet such a situation may not be unreasonable. An increase in wage or salary is direct money in the worker's pocket. The price index is the average of prices across country and for a typical consumer. Not everyone is affected equally.

A modern way to address such a situation is to assume that workers' estimate of the price index P^e differs from the actual price level affecting demand for labor by firms. Thus,

$$\frac{W}{P} = f'(N)$$

$$N = \varphi\left(\frac{W}{Pe}\right)$$

Now while demand for labor may change as a result of change in prices, supply of labor may be differentially affected or not at all (Fig. 3.6). In other words, the change in aggregate price from P_1 to P_2 increases demand for labor but workers perceive the equilibrium level of prices differently; they hang on to what they thought to be the equilibrium price before it went up.

Again, since output and income depend on employment, for each level of price, we have a different level of income. The loci of combination of Y and P will be designated as aggregate supply, which together with aggregate demand would determine both income and price level (Fig. 3.7).

We can analyze the effects of monetary and fiscal policies on output, employment, and price level. An increase in money supply or government expenditures

Fig. 3.6 Supply and demand for labor

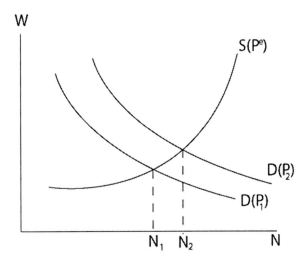

Fig. 3.7 Aggregate demand and supply

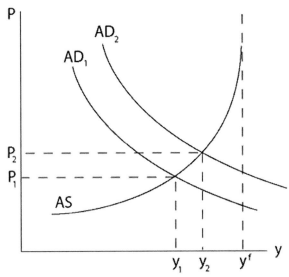

would shift aggregate demand to the right causing an increase in both income and price level. On the other hand, an increase in taxes or reduction in government expenditures or money supply would reduce income and the price level.

National Income Accounting

National income accounts are the fact sheets of the economy. They show how much has been produced (gross domestic product GDP, national income), how it is distributed (wages and salaries, corporate profits, rental income, interest, and others), and how it is used (consumption, investment, government expenditures, exports, imports, and changes in inventory). The accounts give a picture of material wealth production and its circulation in the economy. They are indispensable for understanding the economy and form the basic facts upon which academics and other researcher test their macroeconomic theories. They play a crucial role in formulating fiscal, monetary, tax, and other economic policies. They form the background for many business and government decisions. And the importance of national accounts to the general public is evidenced by the extensive coverage of their releases and revisions in popular media.

The history of the quest for a factual picture of aggregate economy dates back to 1664 England and William Petty, who put together a crude picture of income and expenses in that country.[2]

In the United States, policy response to the Great Depression necessitated an understanding of the overall state of the economy, which was prevented by a lack of data. Simon Kuznets (Nobel laureate 1971) of the National Bureau of Economic Research (NBER) was commissioned by the Department of Commerce to develop estimates of national income. Kuznets coordinated the work at NBER and the Department of Commerce, and in 1934 the report *National Income, 1929–1932* was presented to the US Senate.

Requirements of wartime planning during World War II increased the demand for national income data. In 1942 estimates of more detailed annual data became available. The supplement to the July 1947 issue of the *Survey of Current Business* presented the US national income and product statistics within a complete and consistent accounts system.

Since then the national account system has undergone many revisions to improve its precision and coverage. The last comprehensive revision to improve National Income and Product Accounts (NIPA) was implemented in 1999. The Bureau of Economic Analysis (BEA) at the US Department of Commerce is in charge of compiling national account data. Experts and scholars inside and outside the Bureau have contributed to the improvements of the accounts.

After the war many advanced countries started the compilation of national accounts. In the late 1940s and in 1950s many developing countries opted for planning to develop their countries and pull their nations out of poverty. National planning required data at both the macro and micro level. Most developing countries inaugurated a system of national accounting. Today almost all countries compile national account data on a regular basis.

This brings up the question of comparability of the data across countries. Efforts have been made to make national accounts of different countries comparable. The United Nations, the Commission of the European Communities, the International Monetary Fund, the Organization for Economic Co-operation

---

[2]For a brief pre-modern history of national income accounting the reader is referred to "The Accounts of Society" by Nobel laureate (1984) Richard Stone, who received his prize "for having made fundamental contributions to the development of systems of national accounts and hence greatly improved the basis for empirical economic analysis."

and Development, and the World Bank have published a conceptual framework for national income accounting known as the *1993 System of National Accounts* (SNA 1993). A description of the system can be found on the web at http://unstats.un.org/unsd/sna1993/toctop.asp.

The Bureau of Economic Analysis (BEA) has participated in preparing SNA 1993 and has designed the major improvements to the US national accounts system, to incorporate, to the extent possible, the SNA's concepts.

The Rise of Econometrics

Econometrics and macroeconomic theory and policy are intertwined and there is no way to tell the story of one without elaborating the role of the other. As a science, economics needs to validate its propositions with reference to facts. Econometrics is a way to organize our facts and relate them to theory. The idea of using data and statistical methods to substantiate economic propositions and connect economic theory with the real world was not new. It can be traced back to the 19th century and before.[3] Before WWII Jan Tinbergen (Nobel laureate 1969) developed a comprehensive macroeconomic model for the Netherlands. There was active research in other countries as well. But the rise of econometrics after WWII was to a great extent due to the post War interventionist policies of governments in the United States and Western Europe, the amenability of the Keynesian economics to empirical verification, and the availability of national income data.

After the War many countries adopted interventionist policies. Advanced Western countries intended to attain maximum possible employment and to stabilize their economies by shortening the duration and ameliorating the effects of recessions. Developing countries aimed for growth and development through indicative planning. Thus, there was a need to know more about the economy and to be able to forecast its future course. More important, governments needed to assess the effects of their policies and their decisions in a tangible and quantitative manner. They needed data on the economy, which were provided by newly established government agencies to compile national account data. They required techniques to distill the information; hence the rising importance of econometrics.

The rise of econometrics was further helped because the Keynesian model was presented as a set of explicit equations relating measurable variables to each other. At the same time there was the revolution in computing technology. Large computers capable of processing large amounts of data and carrying out complex computations became available.

In using econometrics, economists and policy makers pursue three goals: structural analysis (verifying or falsifying economic propositions), forecasting, and policy evaluation.

---

[3] There are a number of books on the history of econometrics including *The History of Econometric Ideas* (1990) by Mary Morgan and *A History of Econometrics* (1987) by Roy Epstein.

Consider the well known economic proposition that an increase in price would lower demand. How do we know this is true? It seems reasonable to collect data on both quantity and price and see if they are negatively correlated. This is what Danish economist E. P. Mackeprang did in his 1906 dissertation. Using annual data on price and demand for sugar in England from 1824 to 1852, he first detrended the data by computing

$$D_t = \log\left(100\frac{d_t}{\bar{d}_t}\right), \qquad P_t = \log\left(100\frac{p_t}{\bar{p}_t}\right)$$

where $\bar{d}$ and $\bar{p}$ are, respectively, the five-year moving averages of demand and price. His estimated regression equation was

$$D_t = 2.835 - 0.418P_t$$

The estimated coefficient of the price variable confirmed the hypothesis that an increase in price reduces demand. Although quite simple, the above example illustrates what econometricians have been doing since then to test economic hypotheses.

There are two reasons for forecasting. First, it is the ultimate test of an economic proposition. It is always possible to come up with a story or theory that fits the known facts. Similarly, it is possible to find an equation that fits the data. Therefore, the ultimate test of a theory is to predict facts that were not known when the forecast was done. Second, any decision hinges on the forecast of the future. To carry an umbrella or not depends on whether we forecast rain or not. Similarly, any decision by governments, businesses, and individuals, explicitly or implicitly is based on a set of forecasts. In particular, government budget decisions and monetary policy of the central bank are made on the basis of forecasts. The Fed would decide to lower interest rates if it forecasts a downturn in the economy. On the other hand, it would increase the rate if the forecast shows a tendency for inflation to accelerate.

The third goal of econometrics is to quantify the consequences of one or several proposed policies. Suppose the government decides to lower taxes across the board by either 15% or 25%. One consequence of such policy is a shortfall in government revenues in the first or the first two years of its implementation. But how much would be the reduction in total tax collection under each alternative? Further, the proponents of the policy argue that the tax cut would boost income and employment. Again, the question is, by how much? In order to make a sensible decision, policy makers, the legislature, and citizens need to have a clear idea of the magnitude of both cost and benefits of a policy.

In order to estimate economic models for the above purposes, we need data. Economic data comes in three varieties: cross section, time series, and panel data. Cross section data pertains to the characteristics of a sample or population at a given point in time. For example, we may collect data on income, consumer expenditures, wealth, and size of the family for a random sample of families in Boston, in several major cities, or across country. Time series refer to data on a particular variable over time. For example, the GDP, the Federal Funds Rate, or money supply in the US from 1950 to 2008. The frequency of data may be annual or quarterly (the GDP), monthly (money supply), daily (exchange rates), or even minute by minute (in case of financial data).

If we collect the same set of data from the same sample at fixed intervals, then we have a panel data. For instance, the labor department may choose a sample of workers and collect data on their age, education, wage, race, sex, and employment every year or every five years. Such a data will form a panel data. Alternatively, we may form a panel data of time series like consumption, income, interest rate, investment, money supply and other aggregate variables for a number of countries in the OECD.

Each type of data requires its own estimation methods and inference theory. These issues are beyond the scope of the present book, and the reader is referred to econometrics books. One question, however, needs to be answered here. If econometrics is the application of statistical theory to economic data and models, why do we need a different subject? Statistical theory is based on carefully designed experiments and random samples. In economics, experiments are exceptions and their results questionable. Economics is an observational science and data is collected as a process unfolds and without investigators being able to control any of the variables. Thus, the main task of econometrics is to build methods of estimation that mimic the process which created the data and to account for deviations from the ideal settings of statistical theory. Below, we shall discuss two such complications in econometrics estimation: simultaneity and errors in variables. The reason for the choice of these topics is their particular importance in the development of economic theory.

Simultaneity and Identification

The issues of simultaneity and identification play a crucial role not only in empirical macroeconomics but also in theoretical macroeconomic controversies. Most economic processes involve several relationships. For instance, modeling a market behavior involves a supply and a demand schedule. In macroeconomics the IS and LM equations each consists of a number of equations that are collapsed into one equilibrium condition. Such models are referred to as systems of simultaneous equations because several variables are simultaneously determined by the model. In the demand and supply system, quantities supplied and demanded as well as the price are determined under the equilibrium condition. Similarly, the IS-LM model simultaneously determines the level of output and the real interest rate. In the context of the larger model, once we have these two variables, we can determine consumption and investment.

Consider a model of demand and supply of a product, say, oranges.

$$
\begin{aligned}
Q^d &= \alpha_0 + \alpha_1 P + \alpha_2 Y + u \qquad & \alpha_0, \alpha_2 > 0, \ \alpha_1 < 0 \\
Q^s &= \beta_0 + \beta_1 P + v \qquad & \beta_0 < 0, \beta_1 > 0 \\
Q^d &= Q^s
\end{aligned}
$$

where Q^d, Q^s, P, and Y are, respectively, quantity demanded, quantity supplied, price, and income, u and v are random variables representing variations in quantity demanded and supplied that are not explained by the model, and α's a β's are coefficients of the model. Since there are three equations, three variables can be determined by this model. They are called endogenous variables as opposed to exogenous variables, which are given or determined outside of the model. In the above system, Q^d, Q^s, P are endogenous and Y is exogenous. It should be noted that the classification of variables into endogenous and exogenous is based on economic, not mathematical, considerations. There is no mathematical argument behind saying Y is exogenous; it is no different from any other variable in the equation. Rather, economic logic tells us that the aggregate income of consumers is not determined in the market for oranges.

The system of equations above is called the *structural model* because it describes the structure of the system. If we want to test a hypothesis then we need to estimate the coefficients of the structural model. The problem is that by estimating the equations using ordinary least squares we end up with biased and inconsistent estimates. To see this, let us solve the equations for the endogenous variables to obtain the *reduced form* of the model. That is,

$$P = \frac{\alpha_0 - \beta_0}{\beta_1 - \alpha_1} + \frac{\alpha_2}{\beta_1 - \alpha_1} Y + \frac{u - v}{\beta_1 - \alpha_1}$$

$$Q = \frac{\beta_1 \alpha_0 - \beta_0 \alpha_1}{\beta_1 - \alpha_1} + \frac{\beta_1 \alpha_2}{\beta_1 - \alpha_1} Y + \frac{\beta_1 u - \alpha_1 v}{\beta_1 - \alpha_1}$$

where $Q = Q^d = Q^s$. As can be seen P depends on v which is the error term of the supply equation. Therefore,

$$E(u \mid P) \neq 0$$

Estimating the supply equation by regressing Q on P would result in biased and inconsistent estimates. This is because the dependency of P on u violates the basic assumptions needed to establish the unbiasedness and consistency of the OLS estimator. The same is, of course, true if we estimate the demand equation using OLS. This is the problem of *simultaneity bias*.

Norwegian economist Trygve Magnus Haavelmo (1911–1999) discovered the problem of simultaneity in econometrics. He made many contributions to economics and econometrics and won the Nobel Prize in economics in 1989. Henri Theil (1924–2000) devised the method of two stage least squares (2SLS) to consistently estimate systems of simultaneous equations. Later, he and Arnold Zellner devised a more efficient technique called the three stage least squares (3SLS). There are also limited information maximum likelihood (which is equivalent to 2SLS) and full information maximum likelihood (equivalent to 3SLS) for the estimation of simultaneous equations.

Let us rewrite the reduced form in a more compact form

Fig. 3.8 Identified supply curve and unidentified demand curve

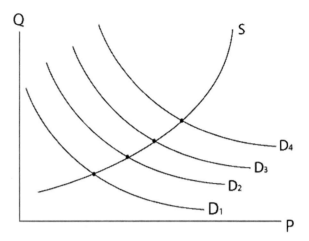

$$P = \pi_{01} + \pi_{11}Y + \varepsilon_1$$
$$Q = \pi_{02} + \pi_{12}Y + \varepsilon_2$$

Observe that we can estimate the reduce form model consistently.[4] Thus, if our goal is to forecast P and Q, we will have no problem. But if our objective is structural analysis or policy evaluation, we need to estimate the structural model. If we are to test a hypothesis regarding the effect of price on the quantity supplied we need to have an estimate of β_1, and if we want to analyze the effect of an income tax on the demand for this commodity we need an estimate of α_2. It turns out that we can obtain a consistent estimate of β_1. Note that by dividing π_{12} by π_{11} we get β_1. We say that β_1 is identified. But the parameters of the demand function are not identified. This can be seen graphically in Fig. 3.8. We have several demand curves each corresponding to a different level of income. What we observe are the intersection points of demand and supply, which can be seen to trace the supply curve. Thus, if we regress Q on P we get the supply curve; the demand curve is unidentified.

Errors in Variables

An important assumption in econometric analysis is that the error term and the explanatory variables are independent of each other or at least uncorrelated.

$$E(u|x) = 0$$

As we saw, this assumption breaks down in the case of a simultaneous equations system. The same is true when a lagged dependent variable is among explanatory

---

[4]A consistent estimator converges to the true parameter with high probability as the number of observations increases.

variables and when explanatory variables are measured with error. This case is of particular importance because Friedman used it to operationalize his consumption function. Furthermore, in many recent studies the instrumental variable estimator has been used to overcome the question of endogeneity. Consider the regression model

$$y_i = \alpha + \beta x_i^* + u_i$$

where u_i is white noise. Let us assume that variable x^* is measured with error:

$$x_i = x_i^* + \varepsilon_i$$

Estimating β by regressing y on x and using OLS will result in biased and inconsistent estimate. We cannot do much about the bias, but to obtain a consistent estimate we use instrumental variable estimator. Suppose that we can find a variable z which is correlated with x^* but uncorrelated with u. Then we can obtain an instrumental variable estimate of β which is consistent. Thus,

$$\hat{\beta} = \frac{\sum\limits_{i=1}^{n} (y_i - \bar{y})(x_i - \bar{x})}{\sum\limits_{i=1}^{n} (x_i - \bar{x})^2}$$

is biased and inconsistent, but

$$\hat{\beta}_{inst} = \frac{\sum\limits_{i=1}^{n} (y_i - \bar{y})(z_i - \bar{z})}{\sum\limits_{i=1}^{n} (x_i - \bar{x})(z_i - \bar{z})}$$

is biased but consistent.

Adaptive Expectations Model

Invariably all economic decisions depend on the expectations of the future. Firms' decisions to invest in any project depend on the expectations of future profits and their outlook on the economy. Consumers may increase or curtail their demands depending on their expectations of inflation and the outlook of the job market. Similarly, central bankers decisions to raise or lower nominal interest rate hinges on their forecast of growth and inflation rates. Since decisions of economic agents—consumers, investors, firms, governments, and others—determine or affect economic outcomes, expectations are among the most important explanatory variables in economic analysis. Therefore, it is not surprising that expectations play an important role in economics.

There are surveys of consumers, manufacturers, economists, and others, which form the bases of consumers' confidence, expectations of inflation, and other indices. The data, subject to all qualifications of survey data, are useful sources of information for decision makers. There have been studies of the efficacy of such indices and definitely they deserve more thorough and systematic investigations.

From the point of economic theory, however, expectations pose several important and difficult questions. First, if we allow a theory to base its explanation of economic phenomena on an exogenously determined expectations variable, we have provided the theorist with the ultimate *deus ex machina*. If there is a lot of investment in plants and equipment and the economy is on the upswing, it is because of optimistic expectations of the population, and if people refrain from spending and the economy is tanked, then it is due to those pessimistic expectations. The same is true about theories whose validity depends on assuming the trend line to change without any warning.

Second, even if we allow for the expectations to be the main determinants of all economic events, the question remains as to what determines the expectations. Still a third question pertains to testing economic hypotheses. Data on the expectations of many economic variables do not exist. In cases where such data is collected on a regular basis, many economists question their validity in reflecting the state of expectations in the economy.

For these reasons economists have proposed two models of expectations formation: adaptive expectations, which we shall present here, and rational expectations, which is discussed in the next chapter.

Consider the behavior of nominal wage rate in a market where labor has collective bargaining power. Suppose that the rate of growth of wage rate is determined by the expected rate of inflation plus a fixed percentage. The relationship, however, is not exact and we have

$$W_{t+1}^{\cdot} = \frac{W_{t+1} - W_t}{W_t} = \pi_{t+1}^e + \alpha + u_{t+1}$$

where W is money wage rate and π the inflation rate, the superscript e denotes expectation, and u is a random variable reflecting all other factors influencing the growth rate of the wage rate. But inflation rate expectation is not an observable variable. Then how could we estimate the equation? We need to model the process of expectations formation. One way would be the adaptive expectations scheme proposed by Paul Cagan. It posits that people learn from the error of their forecast and correct their future expectations. But they do so only partially. Suppose workers expected the inflation rate this year to be 3% and it turned out to be 5%. It is not unreasonable to estimate the inflation rate to be 4.5% next year. If that happens then expectations are formed by a model of the form:

$$\pi_{t+1}^e - \pi_t^e = \gamma(\pi_t - \pi_t^e)$$

where in our example, $\gamma = 0.75$. The above equation is equivalent to

$$\pi_{t+1}^e = \gamma \pi_t + (1 - \gamma) \pi_t^e$$

Note that we also have

$$\pi_t^e = \gamma \pi_{t-1} + (1 - \gamma) \pi_{t-1}^e$$

Making the substitution, we get

$$\pi_{t+1}^e = \gamma \pi_t + (1 - \gamma) \gamma \pi_{t-1} + (1 - \gamma)^2 \pi_{t-2}^e$$

Continuing in this way

$$\pi_{t+1}^e = \gamma \sum_{i=0}^{\infty} (1 - \gamma)^i \pi_{t-i}$$

Now the wage equation becomes

$$\dot{W}_{t+1} = \gamma \sum_{i=0}^{\infty} (1 - \gamma)^i \pi_{t-i} + \alpha + u_{t+1}$$

Of course, we need not extend the lags to infinity. We can agree on a cutoff point beyond which the past inflation rates are insignificant in forming our expectations of the future. In the above equation the rate of growth of money wage depends on a distributed lag of inflation rates. It is also called the moving average form of the equation. Since the right hand side variables are observable, in principle, we can estimate the parameters of the model.

While the above equation is practical, we could do better. Note that we also have

$$\dot{W}_t = \gamma \sum_{i=0}^{\infty} (1 - \gamma)^i \pi_{t-i-1} + \alpha + u_t$$

Multiplying the above equation by $1 - \gamma$ and subtracting from our wage equation we get

$$\dot{W}_{t+1} = \alpha \gamma + (1 - \gamma) \dot{W}_t + \gamma \pi_t + u_{t+1} + (1 - \gamma) u_t$$

The new equation is called the autoregressive form. Note that there are only a few variables on the RHS of the autoregressive equation and its estimation is easier than the moving average form. Nevertheless, the estimation of the autoregressive model poses its own econometric problems. The topic, however, is well beyond the scope of our discussion here.

There are many other examples where the adaptive expectations model could prove useful. We shall discuss one such example in the section on consumption function.

Partial Adjustment Model

Based on microeconomic theory, once the optimal level of a variable is determined, economic agents should immediately move to that position. For example, once the optimal level of output is determined each firm has to immediately acquire the necessary capital stock to produce it. Yet we observe inertia in many economic variables. The consideration of costs of adjustment and uncertainty as to the optimality of the new position may delay complete adjustment. One model that captures such a feature of economic variables is the partial adjustment model. Such a model has particular relevance to modeling aggregate investment behavior, which we shall discuss in a later section.

Let us denote the optimal value of a variable y, say productive capacity or capital stock of firm, by y^*. Further suppose that y^* depends linearly on the volume of sale x:

$$y_t^* = \alpha + \beta x_t + u_t$$

where u_t is white noise. The firm would like to immediately increase its productive capacity to its optimal level. Cost considerations, however, compel the firm to move partially toward the optimal level:

$$y_t - y_{t-1} = \gamma(y_t^* - y_{t-1}) \qquad 0 < \gamma < 1$$

Therefore,

$$y_t^* = \frac{1}{\gamma}y_t - \frac{1-\gamma}{\gamma}y_{t-1}$$

Substituting for y^* in the first equation, we get

$$y_t = \gamma\alpha + (1-\gamma)y_{t-1} + \gamma\beta x_t + \gamma u_t$$

The main purpose of this model is to start with optimization but end up with an operational equation that could be estimated using the available data. Note that whereas y^* is unobservable, y is.

Discounting and Present Value

In modeling consumption and investment we make frequent reference to the present value of a stream of income. Indeed the concept of present value and discounting are central to many economic arguments. Here we briefly discuss these concepts.

If you lend $100 today at the annual rate 5% then in a year you will have $105=$100(1+0.05)$. It follows that $105 next year is equal to $100=$105/(1+0.05)$ today. In other words, a promissory note worth $105 payable next year is worth $100 today. This is called discounting.

Now consider an asset that will pay D_t for the next six years, that is $t = 1, \ldots, 6$. Further assume that the nominal rate of interest is expected to be i_t, then the present value of such an asset would be:

$$PV = \frac{D_1}{1 + i_1} + \frac{D_2}{(1 + i_1)^2} + \frac{D_3}{(1 + i_1)^3} + \frac{D_4}{(1 + i_1)^4} + \frac{D_5}{(1 + i_1)^5} + \frac{D_6}{(1 + i_1)^6}$$

$$= \sum_{t=1}^{6} \frac{D_t}{(1 + i_t)^t}$$

If instead of 6 years we assume that the asset pays dividends or interest for n years, and all D_t's are equal to D and we expect the interest rate to stay constant at i, then the present value of that asset would be:

$$PV = D \frac{1 - \frac{1}{(1+i)^n}}{i}$$

If $D = 1$ and the payment continues forever, then we have:

$$PV = \frac{1}{i}$$

hence the conclusion that the price of bonds and interest rates are inversely related.

The inverse relationship between price and the yield of bonds is easily observed on daily data of financial websites. When the price of a bond—government, corporate, or municipal—increases its yield declines. The opposite happens when the price decreases. The economic rationale behind this relationship should be clear. If there is a significant increase in the supply of bonds, the price of bonds should go down. Looking at it differently, it means that there are many more borrowers who should compete for the existing resources. Therefore, they have to be willing to pay higher rates to attract lenders to lend them money. The opposite happens when there are more lenders, who would settle for lower rates. At the same time the higher demand for bonds leads to an increase in their price.

The relationship has significance for policy. As we shall see in Chap. 13, the US government decided to spend a few trillion dollars to rescue the economy during the 2007–2009 recession. This necessitated the issuance of new bonds. An increase in government borrowing would increase the interest rate but reduce the price of existing bonds. A large amount of the US government debt is held by China, which stands to lose a considerable amount should bond prices decline. The US government needs to take this fact in mind since a reaction to offload bonds by the Chinese government may have adverse effects on the bond market and the US economy.

The Consumption Function

Consumption is the largest component of the GDP. In the United States, consumption comprises two thirds of the GDP and more than 95% of the disposable personal income (see Figs. 3.9 and 3.10). In recent years one main reason for growth in the

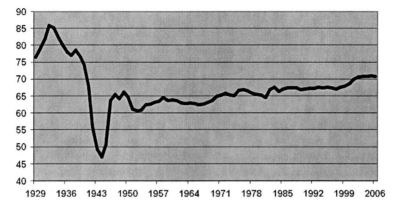

Fig. 3.9 The ratio of consumer expenditures to GDP in the United States: 1929–2006

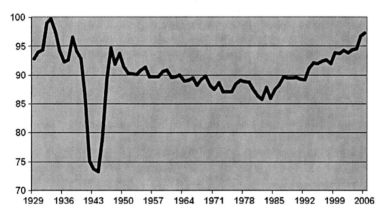

Fig. 3.10 The ratio of consumer expenditures to disposable personal income in The United States: 1929–2006

United States has been the growth of domestic consumption. Many emerging countries such as China and India also would need to boost their domestic consumption if they want to have sustained growth in the long run. It is not surprising, therefore, that modeling consumption has been a preoccupation of macroeconomists. But there is more to the story of consumption function: it is the cornerstone of Keynesian theory. Keynes had noted that aggregate consumption, that is the total value of goods and services that the populace uses for sustenance and pleasure, depends on aggregate income. This proposition seemed non-controversial and intuitively appealing. People and nations with less income had to devote all or most of it to consumption. As a person or nation gets richer, there will be more savings. Thus, as income increases the proportion of income devoted to consumption decreases and that of saving increases. Furthermore, both personal observation and statistical analysis seemed to corroborate Keynes's thesis. On the other hand, the Keynesian theory crucially depended on the multiplier effect because an increase in government expenditure would be magnified by the multiplier and added to the national income. For instance, if the multiplier was 10, then an increase of $100 billion in government expenditures would increase the GDP by $1000 billion, while a multiplier of 5 would result in only $500 billion increase in the GDP.

The multiplier, in turn, depended on the proportion of additional consumption resulting from additional income. Suppose as a result of an increase of $50 billion in national income, consumption is increased by $45 billion. The ratio $0.9 = 45/50$ is called *marginal propensity to consume*. Since income less consumption is called saving, *marginal propensity to save* is $0.1 = 5/50$. The multiplier is the inverse of the marginal propensity to save, that is, $10 = 1/0.1$. But, if marginal propensity to consume is 0.8, then the multiplier is 5.

Keynes had also introduced the notion of *average propensity to consume*, defined as the ratio of total consumption to total income. For instance in 1956 total consumer expenditures in chained 2000 dollars was 1425.4 billion dollars or 63.19% of the GDP and 89.66% of the disposable personal income for the same year. In 2006 the total consumer expenditures reached 11415.3 billion dollars or 70.88% of the GDP and 97.27% of the disposable personal income for the same year.

Keynes believed that marginal propensity to consume was lower than the average propensity. If true, then over time average propensity to consume would decline. Consider the consumption function of Chap. 1 and divide through by disposable personal income. Then

$$\frac{C}{Y - T} = \frac{\alpha}{Y - T} + \beta$$

The left hand side is the average propensity to consume. Since α is positive, the marginal propensity to consume β is lower than average.

This observation led some economists to predict that after the War, because of a rise in income, average propensity to consume will decline and the amount of savings will be greater than is absorbable by investment. If there is a reduction in government expenditures then the aggregate demand would be short of what is needed for full employment. Indeed, some advanced the stagnation thesis that in the long run a capitalist system would be stagnant.

For a theory to survive, it has to look in the face of the facts and come out intact; else it has to be adjusted and if adjustments are too drastic then the theory has to be abandoned. Keynes's consumption theory at first seemed to be doing all right as some found short run consumption functions to conform to its postulates. But the function faced three drastic setbacks. First, Simon Kuznets published estimates of consumption and income for the United States dating back to 1869. The data showed that the ratio of consumption to income had remained reasonably stable. In other words, while in the short run consumption function had an intercept α, in the long-run consumption was proportional to income and the intercept was equal to zero. How could we reconcile a flatter short run consumption function with a steeper long-run function passing through the origin?

Second, the predicted postwar stagnation did not occur. Figures 3.9 and 3.10 show the average propensity to consume for the United States from 1929 to present. During the Great Depression the propensity to save soared because income fell drastically. During the War we witness a sharp decline of consumption relative to income because resources of the country were mobilized for the war and because there were restrictions on consumption. But during the post War period we have a stable and slightly rising propensity to consume. Thus, there was not, and neither is there today, any danger of stagnation due to the lack of consumption. Anyone who doubts that should visit a shopping mall to notice the difficulty of finding a decent parking space. Consumer expenditures have been a major factor in the prosperity of the US economy in the past 60 years.

A third failure of the function is the lack of correspondence between increased (decreased) income and consumption in some years. In other words, there are periods during which income has increased (decreased) while consumption has decreased (increased).

Several economists tried to reconcile the Keynesian consumption function with the above mentioned facts. Among them were two future Nobel laureates, Milton Friedman, who forwarded the permanent income hypothesis, and Franco Modigliani, who together with Albert Ando suggested the life cycle hypothesis.[5]

Permanent Income Hypothesis

Consider a consumer who would live for T periods and whose lifetime utility depends on his consumption. At time $\theta = t$, his lifetime utility can be written as

$$\overline{U} = \sum_{\theta=t}^{T} \frac{U(C_\theta)}{(1+\delta)^{\theta-t}}$$

where δ is the rate of time preference. The consumer maximizes her utility subject to the constraint:

$$\sum_{\theta=t}^{T} \frac{C_\theta}{(1+r)^{\theta-t}} = \sum_{\theta=t}^{T} \frac{Y_\theta}{(1+r)^{\theta-t}}$$

where r is the interest rate and we have assumed that the consumer's initial endowment as well as her bequest are zero. Maximizing the utility subject to constraint results in the following set of equations:

$$U'(C_{\theta+1}) = \tfrac{1+\delta}{1+r} U'(C_\theta), \quad \theta = t,\dots,T-1$$
$$\sum_{\theta=t}^{T} \frac{C_\theta}{(1+r)^{\theta-t}} = \sum_{\theta=t}^{T} \frac{Y_\theta}{(1+r)^{\theta-t}}$$

---

[5] James Duesenberry forwarded the relative income hypothesis, but it has fallen out of favor in economics.

Fig. 3.11 Intertemporal
optimization of consumption

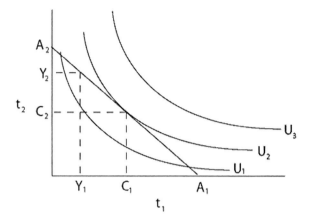

Figure 3.11 depicts this situation for the case of $T = 2$, that is, a consumer who is concerned with the maximization of her utility over a two-period horizon. She earns Y_1 in the first and Y_2 in the second period. The budget constraint is the line A_1A_2. By borrowing at the rate r she can have

$$A_1 = Y_1 + \frac{1}{1+r}Y_2$$

in the first period. Or by saving all her income in the first period and lending it out, she could have

$$A_2 = Y_2 + (1+r)Y_1$$

in the second period. Any point on the line A_1A_2 is open to the consumer and she chooses the combination of consumption C_1 in the first period and C_2 in the second to maximize her utility.

Going back to the general case, note that the right hand side of the second equation is the present value of the consumer's stream of income. In other words, had there been a perfect loan and credit market, the consumer could have borrowed this much today to be paid in the future (with interest) from her earnings. Thus, it signifies the individual's present value of both human and nonhuman capital. If indeed our imaginary consumer could assemble this present value then from now till eternity she could earn

$$Y_t^* = r \sum_{\theta=t}^{T} \frac{Y_\theta}{(1+r)^{\theta-t}}$$

We shall call Y^* the permanent income. Actual or observed income, Y may deviate from permanent income by the amount of transitory income y. Thus, we have

$$Y_t = Y_t^* + y_t$$

Friedman postulated that consumption consists of permanent consumption, C^*, that depends on permanent income

$$C_t^* = \beta Y_t^*$$

and a random variation called transitory consumption, c. Thus, for the total consumption, C we can write

$$C_t = \beta Y_t^* + c_t$$

Since permanent income is unobservable, we may assume that the consumer has an estimate (expectation) of her permanent income and in each period updates the expectation using the adaptive expectations formula

$$Y_t^* - Y_{t-1}^* = \gamma(Y_t - Y_{t-1}^*)$$

or

$$Y_t^* = \gamma \sum_{i=0}^{\infty} (1 - \gamma)^i Y_{t-i}$$

Substituting in the consumption function,

$$C_t = \beta \gamma \sum_{i=0}^{\infty} (1 - \gamma)^i Y_{t-i} + c_t$$

Lagging the above equation one period and multiplying it by $1 - \gamma$, we have

$$(1 - \gamma)C_{t-1} = \beta \gamma \sum_{i=1}^{\infty} (1 - \gamma)^i Y_{t-i} + (1 - \gamma)c_{t-1}$$

Subtracting it both side from the previous equation, we shall get the consumption function.

$$C_t = (1 - \gamma)C_{t-1} + \beta \gamma Y_t + c_t - (1 - \gamma)c_{t-1}$$

which is empirically more appropriate. Estimating the equation using annual US data, we get the following results:
For the period 1929–2006[6]

$$\Delta C_t = 1.883 + 0.425\,\Delta C_{t-1} + 0.558\,\Delta Y_t$$
$$(7.033)\ (0.069) \qquad\qquad (0.068)$$
$$R^2 = 0.806 \quad DW = 1.92$$

---

[6]Note that since the estimated equations involve first difference and its lagged value, in each case we lose two observations. Thus, our estimation periods are 1931–2006 and 1948–2006.

For the period 1946–2006

$$\Delta C_t = -3.008 + 0.395\,\Delta C_{t-1} + 0.628\,\Delta Y_t$$
$$(9.460)\ (0.076)\qquad (0.077)$$
$$R^2 = 0.803\ \ DW = 2.16$$

In both periods the constant term is not significantly different from zero as the theory predicts. The short run marginal propensity to consume is 0.558 for the longer period, 1929–2006, and 0.628 for the period after the War. The long rum MPC for the long period is 0.97 but for the post War period is estimated as 1.04, which is either an anomaly explainable by the margin of error or it is a reflection of foreign trade deficit of the recent years.

Cross Section Estimate of Propensity to Consume

In order to account for the lower marginal propensity to consume in cross section data, Friedman wrote the actual or observed income and consumption of individual i as the sum their permanent and transitory components

$$C_i = C_i^* + c_i \qquad and \qquad Y_i = Y_i^* + y_i$$

In other words, permanent income and consumption are measured with random errors, which are respectively, y_i and c_i. Furthermore, he assumed that these errors are not correlated with each other or the permanent components. Thus,

$$E(c_i) = E(y_i) = 0, \quad \forall i$$

and

$$E(C_i^* c_i) = E(Y_i^* y_i) = E(c_i y_i) = 0, \quad \forall i$$

Now suppose we estimate the long run consumption function

$$C_i^* = \beta Y_i^* + u_i$$

by replacing permanent consumption and income by observed consumption and income in the regression model, the estimated marginal propensity to consume

$$\hat{\beta} = \frac{\sum_{i=1}^{n} C_i Y_i}{\sum_{i=1}^{n} Y_i^2} = \frac{\beta \sum_{i=1}^{n} Y_i^{*2} + \beta \sum_{i=1}^{n} Y_i^* y_i + \sum_{i=1}^{n} Y_i^* c_i + \sum_{i=1}^{n} c_i y_i}{\sum_{i=1}^{n} Y_i^{*2} + \sum_{i=1}^{n} y_i^2 + 2\sum_{i=1}^{n} Y_i^* y_i}$$

would be biased because both the numerator and denominator have random components. Moreover, the estimate is inconsistent because asymptotically we have

$$\text{plim } \hat{\beta} = \beta \frac{\sigma_{\tilde{Y}*}^2}{\sigma_{\tilde{Y}*}^2 + \sigma_{\tilde{y}}^2}$$

The solution is to use instrumental variable estimator. But in this case the instrument is rather simple and consists of a vector of ones. Instead of estimating MPC using OLS one can simply take the ratio of the average of observed consumption to observed income:

$$\hat{\beta}_{inst} = \frac{\sum\limits_{i=1}^{n} C_i}{\sum\limits_{i=1}^{n} Y_i}$$

But now

$$\text{plim } \hat{\beta} = \frac{\beta E(Y_i^*) + E(c_i)}{E(Y_i^*) + E(y_i)} = \beta$$

In other words, the simple ratio of average observed consumption to average observed income provides us with an asymptotically unbiased estimate of marginal propensity to consume consistent with long run estimates from time series data.

Life Cycle Hypothesis

The life cycle hypothesis is another attempt to reconcile the Keynesian consumption function with the observed facts about consumption. It was proposed by Albert Ando and Franco Modigliani in 1963.[7] They observe that people in the early years of their life consume more than their income and have negative savings. In the middle years of life individuals and families earn more than they consume and have positive savings. Finally, in the later years (during retirement) they consume more than their income and, therefore, draw down their savings (Fig. 3.12).

Thus, looking at a cross section of families we observe that people with lower income—those at the beginning or end of their lives—consume proportionately more than their income, whereas those with higher income—those in their productive years—consume a smaller portion of their income. On the other hand, if the age distribution of the population is relatively stable, when we look at time series of individual or family consumption over a long period of time we would observe a constant ratio of consumption to income. That is the same pattern that we observe in the national aggregate data. Thus, in cross section data and in the short time series

---

[7]We should also mention the contributions of Richard Brumberg, who was a student of both Modigliani and Friedman and whose death in 1954 cut short a promising career. His dissertation was entitled, "Utility Analysis and Aggregate Consumption Functions: An Empirical Test and its meaning" (Johns Hopkins University, 1953); and he published three papers, two of them with Modigliani, on the subject of consumption of function.

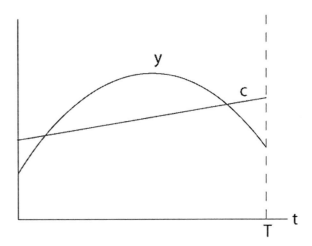

Fig. 3.12 The life cycle of income and consumption

data during a particular business cycle we observe MPC < APC, and in the time series data over the long run we notice MPC = APC.

In order to test their hypothesis, Ando and Modigliani observed that life cycle data could come from two sources: labor and assets. They made the following simplifying assumptions to make the hypothesis operational and amenable to econometric testing. First, lifetime labor income is proportional to current income, and second, lifetime income from assets is equal to the current value of assets. The second assumption is justified on the ground that the value of an asset is equal to the discounted value of its future stream of income. Thus, the consumption function could be written as

$$C_t = \beta_0 + \beta_1 Y_t + \beta_2 A_{t-1} + u_t$$

where A_{t-1} denotes the value of assets at the beginning of the period. Ando and Modigliani estimated many versions of their consumption function. An example is

$$C_t = 8.1 + 0.75 Y_t + 0.042 A_{t-1}$$
$$(1.0) \ (0.05) \quad (0.009)$$
$$R^2 = 0.998 \quad DW = 1.26$$

and in first difference form as

$$\Delta C_t = 0.52 Y_t + 0.072 \Delta A_{t-1}$$
$$(0.11) \quad (0.018)$$
$$R^2 = 0.929 \quad DW = 1.85$$

If we reestimate the equation today with annual data from 1929 to 2006 we get

$$C_t = 96.6 + 0.82 Y_t + 0.032 A_{t-1}$$
$$(45.7) \ (0.02) \quad (0.004)$$
$$R^2 = 0.999 \quad DW = 1.78 \quad \rho = 0.786$$

and in difference form:

$$\Delta C_t = 0.73 Y_t + 0.072 \Delta A_{t-1}$$
$$(0.05) \quad (0.007)$$
$$R^2 = 0.784 \quad DW = 1.74$$

If we confine the estimation period to the post World War II era (1946–2006), then the comparable results are:

$$C_t = 145.9 + 0.81 Y_t + 0.036 A_{t-1}$$
$$(42.4) \quad (0.02) \quad (0.003)$$
$$R^2 = 0.999 \quad DW = 1.99 \quad \rho = 0.636$$

and

$$\Delta C_t = 0.78 Y_t + 0.037 \Delta A_{t-1}$$
$$(0.05) \quad (0.007)$$
$$R^2 = 0.794 \quad DW = 2.23$$

Several differences between our estimates and those of Ando and Modigliani should be mentioned. Ando and Modigliani used as their dependent variable an estimate of consumption calculated as consumer expenditures excluding the purchase of durable goods but including their depreciation; we have used consumer expenditures. Moreover, they used labor income; here we have used disposable personal income which includes rental, interest, and dividends income.[8] All variables in our regression are in chained 2000 prices. This is the reason for the difference in the constants of regressions between our estimates and those of Ando-Modigliani. Data on assets are available in current prices only; we used the price index for disposable personal income to convert assets into constant 2000 prices. Finally, the new equation is estimated using Cochrane-Orcutt and Hildreth-Lu methods to correct for serial correlation (the two methods resulted in identical parameter estimates).

Despite differences in the definition of variables, the lapse of four decades, and different estimation methods, the above results are remarkably similar to those of Ando and Modigliani, which is a testimony to the robustness of the life cycle hypothesis.

The Investment Function

Investment plays two important roles in the economy. In the long run, it is the addition to capital stock and therefore addition to the productive capacity of the economy. An economy without investment or lower than optimal level of investment

---

[8] The use of labor income—estimated as personal income less proprietor, rental, interest, and dividend income proportionately adjusted for taxes—in most models resulted in marginal propensity to consume exceeding one or very close to one and constant terms that were out of line.

would stagnate or even decline. In the short run, investment is an important component of aggregate demand. Its volatility is the main cause of fluctuations in the economy. Thus, understanding investment and its determinants is a basic task of macroeconomics. But investment is a complex issue and even today we do not have a firm understanding of the subject. In particular, investment involves risk and forecasts of the future, an aspect that has not been dealt with in macroeconomic models.

A naïve approach to evaluating investment is to consider it as a stream of expenditures and revenues. Suppose a project would cost I_0 and I_1 dollars in the first two years (the present year is denoted by 0) and starting with the year two will generate R_t, $t = 2, \ldots 10$ dollars net revenues over the next nine years. The present value of this project would be:

$$PV = I_0 + \frac{I_1}{1+i} + \sum_{t=2}^{10} \frac{R_t}{(1+i)^t}$$

where i is the expected rate of interest. One can argue that, aside for the risk, if the present value is positive then the project is worth undertaking. An alternative measure would be the internal rate of return, that is, the rate that would make the present value equal to zero.

$$I_0 + \frac{I_1}{1+ir} + \sum_{t=2}^{10} \frac{R_t}{(1+ir)^t} = 0$$

Solving for ir we can compare it to actual interest rate. If ir is greater than i, then the project is viable.

We may formulate and test a more appropriate model of investment by first determining the optimal value of the stock of capital and then considering a gradual move toward such a target. If the optimal capital stock is K_t* then we need to fill the gap $K_t^* - K_{t-1}$. The move toward optimal stock of capital may take time for several reasons: uncertainty about the optimal level of capital and adjustment cost for expanding facilities and training the new staff. Partial adjustment model, discussed above, is one way that empirical models have operationalized the move toward the optimal capital stock. Partial adjustment models differ in their lag structure whose determination is an empirical matter.

Consider an optimizing firm that makes investment decisions to maximize its profit. The objective function can be written as

$$\sum_{t=0}^{T} \frac{1}{(1+i)^t} [P_t f(K_t, L_t) - w_t L_t - P_t^i I_t]$$

subject to

$$I_t = K_t - K_{t-1} + \delta K_{t-1}$$

where i is the rate of interest, P price of output, K capital stock, L labor force, w

wage rate, P^i price of investment goods, and δ depreciation rate. Denoting profit by $\Pi = \Pi(K)$, signifying that it depends on the stock of capital, we have

$$\Pi(K_t) = P_t f(K_t, L_t) - w_t L_t$$

The Lagrangian is

$$l = \sum_{t=0}^{\infty} \frac{1}{(1+i)^t} [\Pi(K_t) - P_t^i I_t] + \sum_{t=0}^{T} \lambda_t [I_t + (1-\delta)K_{t-1} - K_t]$$

$$= \sum_{t=0}^{\infty} \frac{1}{(1+i)^t} [\Pi(K_t) - P_t^i I_t] + \sum_{t=0}^{T} \frac{q_t}{(1+i)^t} [I_t + (1-\delta)K_{t-1} - K_t]$$

where $q_t = (1+i)^t \lambda_t$. Solving the maximization problem we will have

$$q_t = P_t^i$$

and

$$\frac{\partial \Pi(K_t)}{\partial K_t} = \Pi'(K_t) = \frac{1}{1+i} [\delta q_{t+1} + i q_t - \Delta q_{t+1}]$$

In other words the capital stock should be expanded to the point where its marginal profit equals the user cost of capital, which equals the sum of depreciation rate and interest rate times the price of capital goods less the change in the price of capital goods. The condition gives us K^* the optimal level of capital stock. Denoting the user cost of capital by c_t we can write

$$K_t^* = \alpha + \beta c_t + u_t$$

Using partial adjustment model we can write

$$K_t - K_{t-1} = \gamma \alpha + \gamma \beta c_t - \gamma K_{t-1} + \gamma u_t$$

or

$$I_t = K_t - K_{t-1} + \delta K_{t-1} = \gamma \alpha + \gamma \beta c_t + (\delta - \gamma) K_{t-1} + \gamma u_t$$

And if we assume the output (income) to be proportional to capital stock, that is,

$$Y_t = \frac{K_t}{\mu}$$

then we can write

$$I_t = \alpha \gamma + \gamma \beta c_t + (\delta - \gamma) \mu Y_{t-1} + \gamma u_t$$

Note that when estimating the above model we may have to drop the user cost variable as this is unobservable or replace it with lagged value of investment. With

more elaborate partial adjustment models we can get investment functions of the
form[9]

$$I_t = \beta_0 + \beta_1 \Delta Y_t + \beta_2 \Delta Y_{t-1} + \beta_3 I_{t-1} + \beta_4 K_{t-1} + \beta_5 K_{t-2} + \varepsilon_t$$

Tobin's q

Let us rewrite the optimality condition relating marginal profit to user cost of capital
as

$$\Pi' + \frac{1-\delta}{1+i} q_{t+1} = q_t$$

or

$$\frac{\Pi' + [(1-\delta)/(1+i)]q_{t+1}}{q_t} = 1$$

This is Tobin's marginal q: the denominator is the price of one unit of capital
goods today while the numerator is the profit from that unit this period plus the value
of that unit next period less depreciation and discounted to present. It is reasonable
to say that if the firm is in equilibrium, the ratio is equal to one. If, however, the
ratio is greater than one, it would be profitable to add to the capital stock whereas if
the ratio is less than one capital stock should be reduced. Note that marginal q is not
observable and has to be estimated with perhaps unrealistic assumptions.

Under the assumption of constant return to scale, marginal q would be equal to
average Q defined as the total value of the firm divided by the cost of replacing its
capital stock. If a company's shares are traded in the market, one can get a market
valuation of the firm. Given some estimate of the cost of replacing the firm's capital
stock, we can arrive at a good estimate of the average Q:

$$Q = \frac{MV_t}{P_t^i K_t}$$

where MV is the market value of the firm or the present value of its future stream of
income and $P^i K$ is the replacement cost of the existing capital.

Demand for Money

One half of the IS-LM model deals with equilibrium between demand for and
supply of money. The model assumes that money supply is exogenously determined,[10] while demand depends on income and the rate of interest. Formulation

---

[9]See Jorgenson and Siebert (1968), pp. 681–712.

[10]In Chap. 9 we take up the question of the determinants of money supply. Here we assume that
the central bank can fix the amount of money supply.

and estimation of demand for money posed three fundamental questions. The first was the question of definition of money and whether it should be defined narrowly as the sum of currency plus demand deposits (M1) or broadly as M1 plus saving and time deposits (M2). The important issue here was which definition would result in a more stable demand for money function over time. Needless to say, we may find that under different political and economic conditions and different institutional arrangements, different definitions of money result in a more stable demand function. For instance, in a developing country where financial institutions are primitive, currency in circulation may be the appropriate measure of money. On the other hand, in an advanced country M2 may be the appropriate measure. In the United States, prior to 1981, the velocity of circulation for M1, while not constant, shows a smooth trend. But after 1981 the velocity is quite erratic. Hence the use of M2 would result in a more stable demand for money function.

Second, does demand for money depend on interest rate? As we may recall this question goes to the heart of the controversy between Keynesians and monetarists. Monetarists concede that only in the short-run is demand for money affected by the rate of interest. Finally, is demand for money related to income or wealth? This question gains more importance as more and more people own stocks and other financial assets. How would an increase in money supply affect not only prices of goods and services but also prices of financial assets? Should the central bank pay attention to the activities in the capital market? And should it try to deflate a bubble? Answers to the above questions would determine the nature of theories of demand for money.

We can look at the question of the definition of money in a broader context. Money performs three functions: unit of account, means of payment, and store of value. As such any asset with intrinsic or legal value (fiat money) can perform these tasks. The difference between different definitions of money revolve around the degree of their liquidity. Thus, we can imagine that at different times and different places varying measures of money may be appropriate. For instance, in a country where banking system is undeveloped, the useful definition of money may be currency in circulation because many merchants and businesses may not easily accept checks. On the other hand, in developed countries means of payments have expanded and include credit cards.

In the United States M2 has a more stable velocity of circulation, while over time, velocity of M1 has shown increasing volatility (see Fig. 3.13), and as we shall see M2 has a more stable demand (Table 3.1). It seems, therefore, that M2 is a better measure for the United States.

A few theories of demand for money have been proposed. One by Tobin attributes the holding of money to a preference for reducing risk. Another by Baumol resorts to the cost of visiting banks to withdraw money as an incentive to hold money. On closer examination one finds them rather outlandish. Here we discuss Friedman's simple yet theoretically acceptable explanation. Money is an asset with a price—the rate of interest—which provides a number of services and which easily and with low transaction costs can be exchanged for other assets.

It follows that a simple constrained utility maximization model would tell us that demand for money is positively related to the amount of wealth and negatively to

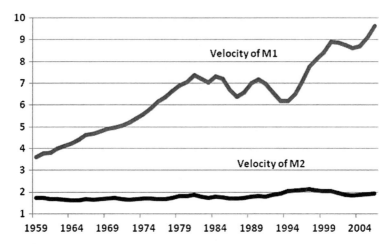

Fig. 3.13 Velocity of circulation

its price, the rate of interest. Note that we are talking about demand for a certain amount of purchasing power or real balances. Hence money is divided by the price level to make it into money at constant prices: *M/P*. This necessitates us to consider real as opposed to nominal wealth in the economy.

From an econometric point of view, there are three problems to be resolved before proceeding with estimation. First, what should be the appropriate rate of interest? As interest rates are connected (see Chap. 9), we need not dwell too much on the subject. The rate on short term commercial papers, Treasury bills, or the rate on saving deposits could be considered.

Second, should we include human capital into total wealth? Such a measure does not exist and different researchers have used a variety of assumptions to get around it. We may argue that total income is proportional to total assets and it is more accurately estimated. Note that even the value of physical assets is not as easily estimated as the GDP.

Third, we should be cognizant of inertia in many economic processes. Therefore, it is advisable to include the lagged dependent variable among explanatory variables.

$$\ln\left(\frac{M_t}{P_t}\right) = \beta_0 + \beta_1 \ln\left(\frac{M_{t-1}}{P_{t-1}}\right) + \beta_2 \ln Y_t + \beta_3 \ln(1 + r_t)$$

The Growth Model of Harrod and Domar

In Chap. 1 we noted that Keynes's analysis as well as Hicks's IS-LM model pertained to the short run, which excluded the issue of growth. The main concern of the short run analysis was the fluctuations in the economy resulting from inadequacy of

Table 3.1 Estimated results for the demand for money function

Explanatory Variables	$\ln(M1/P)$			$\ln(M2/P)$		
	1960–2006	1960–1979	1980–2006	1960–2006	1960–1979	1980–2006
Constant	1.106	0.080	2.506	0.954	-0.706	1.204
	(0.426)	(0.681)	(0.383)	(0.356)	(0.141)	(0.773)
$\ln(M/P)_{-1}$	0.703	0.923	0.817	0.389	0.577	0.610
	(0.090)	(0.124)	(0.073)	(0.100)	(0.128)	(0.146)
$\ln(Y)$	0.133	0.071	-0.097	0.486	0.521	0.247
	(0.062)	(0.036)	(0.059)	(0.092)	(0.124)	(0.156)
$\ln(1+r)$	-0.107	-0.074	-0.157	-0.091	-0.146	-0.062
	(0.018)	(0.026)	(0.024)	(0.013)	(0.017)	(0.022)
R^2	0.991	0.919	0.989	0.998	0.998	0.995
ρ	0.823		0.497	0.862		0.854

Figures in parentheses are standard deviations of estimated coefficients.

demand. But in the long run the concern would be growth of the economy. We need growth not only because we would like to live better but also because an increase in population generates more demand for goods and services and requires employment opportunities for an expanding labor force. It was Keynes himself who had called economists "the trustees of the possibility of civilization."

The challenge of modeling growth was taken up by Roy Harrod (1939), a student of Keynes, and after the war by Evsey Domar (1946). Harrod's model differs from Domar's in that the former involves expectations of variables. But over time the two models have been merged and Domar's version which is simpler (and perhaps more mechanical) has gained currency. Here we introduce this more famous version.

Keynes's model was designed for the short run and in reference to the Great Depression. Therefore, it rested on three crucial assumptions:

1. Supply is infinitely elastic because there is a large pool of unemployed workers and unutilized production capacity. Thus, once we generate demand, output expands to meet it.
2. Investment is autonomous and independent of savings. It depends on the mood of the investors and their expectations of future profits.
3. The capital stock in the economy is constant because it takes time for investment to turn into working capital and the model is concerned with the short run. In other words, the time span of the model is shorter than the gestation period of investment projects.

By relaxing these assumptions, Domar devised the following system of equations. The first makes output dependent on capital stock where β is the output/capital ratio; the second makes investment equal to savings and, therefore, no more independent of the state of the economy; the third is the saving counterpart of the consumption function stating that savings depend on income with s being the marginal propensity to save. Finally, the last equation states that the change in capital stock, K, is equal to investment minus depreciation, where δ is the average rate of depreciation.

$$Y = \beta K$$
$$I = S$$
$$S = sY$$
$$\frac{dK}{dt} = I - \delta K$$

If we ignore the second equation, that is, the restriction that investment should be financed by saving, we arrive at the *actual rate of growth*. In the short run a country can invest more or less than its savings. It is in the long-run that excepting unusual circumstances—such as the case of the United States since WWII when other countries happily kept dollar balances—savings govern investment.

For the actual rate of growth we have

$$\frac{dY}{dt} = \beta \frac{dK}{dt} = \beta I - \beta \delta K$$

Substituting for K from the production function and dividing through by Y, we have

$$\frac{1}{Y}\frac{dY}{dt} = \beta\frac{I}{Y} - \delta$$

Thus, the actual rate of growth is equal to the ratio of investment to output times output/capital ratio less the depreciation rate. This explains the emphasis on investment in developing countries after WWII.

If we take the equality of investment and saving into account, we have

$$\frac{1}{Y}\frac{dY}{dt} = \beta s - \delta$$

In other words, in the long run, the growth rate of the economy is equal to the product of output/capital ratio and marginal propensity to save minus the rate of depreciation. This growth rate is called the *warranted rate of growth*. The actual rate of growth may deviate from this rate in the short run. But, since over a period of time investment should equal to savings, in the long run the actual rate would be equal to the warranted rate of growth.

Thus, the Harrod-Domar model posited that the main constraint to growth is capital stock. This was true in many developing countries. Furthermore the rate of growth depended on marginal propensity to save and output capital ratio. A country that wanted to grow needed to save or somehow obtain the financial resources (foreign aid or investment, for example). Furthermore it should use a technology that maximized output from a given amount of capital. This latter conclusion pointed to the importance of using advanced technologies and reinforced the desirability of foreign investment as a source of modern technology.

But what about employment of a growing labor force? Let the labor supply in the economy grow at the rate n:

$$\frac{1}{L}\frac{dL}{dt} = n$$

and let the output labor ratio be α

$$Y = \alpha L$$

Then starting with a position of full employment, in order to maintain it, that is, to find jobs for all the new laborers, the output should grow at the rate:

$$\frac{1}{Y}\frac{dY}{dt} = \frac{1}{\alpha L}\alpha\frac{dL}{dt} = n$$

But there is no guarantee that in any economy we have

$$\beta s - \delta = n$$

If $\beta s - \delta < n$, then we will have chronic, indeed worsening, unemployment problem. If $\beta s - \delta > n$, then we face continuous shortage of labor and possibly inflation. In other words, the economy will face no problem if it happens that the labor force grows at a rate equal to the warranted rate of growth. On either side of this razor edge of the steady state, the economy is in trouble.

From the above analysis a country could draw a particular growth policy, although such a conclusion does not necessarily follow from the model. A country facing rapid growth of population and, therefore, increase in labor force could choose one of several policies or a combination of them. First, the country may try to limit its population growth. In addition to jobs, a rapidly growing population needs more investment in education, health, and housing. Such expenditures may, at least in the short run, reduce the economic growth rate. Hence, government may have a stronger incentive to control the population. Second, the country may encourage investment in advanced technologies, thus increasing β and consequently the warranted rate of growth to bring it in line with the increase in labor force. India, under the influence of socialist ideas, decided to choose technologies that by reducing α would require more workers for the same amount of output. Such policies would harm economic growth and the well being of people in the long run.

As a positive theory with testable implications, the Harrod-Domar growth theory is not a great success. If the theory was correct almost all economies in the world should face either chronic inflation or high unemployment as a matter of structure. But the theory is simple and it requires a reasonably small set of data to work with it. Thus, it proved a useful tool for macroeconomic scenario analysis and planning in developing countries.

Solow's Model

The Harrod-Domar model is based on the Leontief production function of the form

$$Y = \min(\alpha L, \beta K)$$

which does not allow for the substitution of labor for capital or vice versa. It is exactly this lack of substitutability that leads to the conclusion that the warranted rate of growth must be equal to the growth rate of labor force or else the economy is in trouble.

Solow posited a more general production function of the form

$$Y = F(K, L)$$

But he assumed that the function was homogeneous of degree one, that is, it exhibits constant returns to scale. Thus, letting $k = K/L$, we can write:

$$F(K,L) = LF\left(\frac{K}{L},1\right) = Lf(k)$$

Change in capital stock is equal to investment, which in turn, depends on savings. Thus,

$$\frac{dK}{dt} = I = sLf(k)$$

On the other hand

$$\frac{dk}{dt} = \frac{d}{dt}\left(\frac{K}{L}\right) = \frac{L\frac{dK}{dt} - K\frac{dL}{dt}}{L^2}$$
$$= \frac{1}{L}\frac{dK}{dt} - k\frac{1}{L}\frac{dL}{dt}$$

or

$$\frac{dk}{dt} = sf(k) - nk$$

This is the famous differential equation of Solow's growth model. It cannot be solved without specifying the production function. For instance if we assume the production function to be Cobb-Douglas of the form

$$Y = AK^\alpha L^{1-\alpha}$$

then the differential equation becomes:

$$\frac{dk}{dt} = sAk^\alpha - nk$$

This is the Bernoulli equation. To solve it divide the equation through by k^α and let $z = k^{1-\alpha}$. Further, let $z(0)$ denote the value of z at time $t = 0$; then

$$z = \left(z(0) - \frac{sA}{n}\right)\exp\left(-n(1-\alpha)t\right) + \frac{sA}{n}$$

and

$$k^{1-\alpha} = \left(k(0)^{1-\alpha} - \frac{sA}{n}\right)\exp\left(-n(1-\alpha)t\right) + \frac{sA}{n}$$

Needless to say, the solution is involved; hence, the recent emphasis on computational methods for discerning the behavior of economic models (see Chaps. 8 and 11 for a discussion of computational methods).

Solow Residual

Under the assumptions of the Solow model, increases in capital and labor should account for the growth rate of the US economy. Under reasonable assumptions, however, these factors fall short of explaining the historical growth rate of the economy. The part of growth rate that cannot be explained by these factors is referred to as *Solowresidual*. It is generally agreed that technological progress and improved know-how is the source of the residual.

To be more specific, consider the production function of Solow's model, and let us calculate the growth rate of output:

$$\frac{dY}{dt} = \frac{\partial F}{\partial K}\frac{dK}{dt} + \frac{\partial F}{\partial L}\frac{dL}{dt}$$

Dividing both sides by Y, and multiplying the first term on the right hand side by K/K and the second by L/L, we have

$$\frac{1}{Y}\frac{dY}{dt} = \frac{\partial F}{\partial K}\frac{K}{Y}\frac{1}{K}\frac{dK}{dt} + \frac{\partial F}{\partial L}\frac{L}{Y}\frac{1}{L}\frac{dL}{dt}$$

In a competitive economy each factor is paid the value of its marginal product. Thus, $\partial F/\partial K$ is equal to the compensation of the services of capital and when multiplied by K/Y, we get the share of capital in output. Similarly, $\partial F/\partial L$ multiplied by L/Y is the share of labor in output. In sum, we have

Rate of growth of output = Share of capital in output times rate of growth of capital

+ Share of labor in output times rate of growth of labor

The formula provides a simple way of accounting for growth. Now a back-of-envelope calculation shows that, in the long run, employment has grown by about 2% average annually and the share of labor in output has been around 2/3. Since we have assumed the production function to be homogeneous of degree one, based on the Euler Theorem,[11] the share of capital equals 1/3. Capital as measured by private fixed assets shows a growth rate of 2.5%. Thus, we have:

$$\frac{1}{3}2.5\% + \frac{2}{3}2\% \approx 2.17\%$$

But the US economy has grown at the rate of 3.3% average annually. Note that even if we change the shares of capital and labor, it does not solve the problem, because there are no weights between zero and one and adding up to one that would make the above sum equal to 3.3%.

Thus, in our calculations, the Solow residual is about 1.13%(=3.3%–2.17%) average annually. There has been a vast literature to substantiate, measure, and

---

[11] For a proof see Kamran Dadkhah (2007), pp. 271–274.

explain the Solow residual. In Chap. 11 we discuss recent theories of growth that try to explain the Solow residual.

The Golden Age of Macroeconomics

After the publication of the *General Theory* and particularly after the War, macroeconomics made great progress. In fact this period all the way to late 1960s could be called the golden age of macroeconomics. It was an extraordinary period both in terms of progress in understanding and modeling the economy and in terms of confidence economists showed in their ability to understand and direct the economy (see the next chapter). Economic theory left behind the era of discovering and validating economic propositions on the basis of "introspection" and pronouncing general musings on the way the economy worked. Economic relationships were derived on the basis of either factual observation or utility and profit optimization and then tested econometrically using time series data. The microeconomic as the foundation had been codified by Paul Samuelson and John Hicks and econometrics was on the rise due to the work of Jan Tinbergen, Lawrence Klein (Nobel laureate 1980), Trygve Haavelmo, and those working in Cowles Commission.[12] No more generalities and philosophical musings would do. Milton Friedman expounded the methodology of positive economics, which would judge the validity of a theory based on its ability to explain facts and to forecast as yet unknown future developments. Large macroeconomic models were built to explain and forecast every facet of the national economy.

There was a tacit agreement that microeconomics based on individual and firm optimization behavior would explain the behavior of markets and industries. Keynesian economics, while loosely basing itself on microeconomics would explain aggregate behavior. The combination was called the *neoclassical synthesis*. It was an uneasy partnership as macro behavior did not necessarily follow from microeconomic premises. As long as Keynesian policies kept the economy at near full employment with price stability, there was little to complain about. When stagflation—rising unemployment and inflation—resulted in the breakdown of the international financial order (Chap. 6), the consensus came under attack and unraveled in the 1970s. Still the achievements of economists of that period and particularly their emphasis on empirical work enriched economics.

---

[12]For an account of Cowles Commission's role in the development of econometrics see Carl Christ (1994), pp. 30–59.

Chapter 4
Keynesian Economics in Action

The unfinished business of economic policy includes (1) the achievement of full employment and sustained prosperity without inflation, (2) the acceleration of economic growth, (3) the extension of equality of opportunity, and (4) the restoration of balance of payment equilibrium.
Economic Report of the President, 1962

Our tools of economic policy are much better tools than existed a generation ago. We are able to proceed with much greater confidence and flexibility in seeking effective answers to the changing problems of our changing economy.
Economic Report of the President, 1965

I am more than half-convinced that he had, in truth, an abnormal gift, and a sense, something—I know not what—that in the guise of wall and door offered him an outlet, a secret passage of escape into another and altogether more beautiful world. At any rate, you will say, it betrayed him in the end. But did it betray him? There you touch the inmost mystery of these dreamers, these men of vision and the imagination. We see our world fair and common, the hoarding and the pit. By our daylight standard he walked out of security into darkness, danger, and death. But did he see it like that?
H. G. Wells, "The Door in the Wall"

With the election of President John F. Kennedy, a group of young, idealistic and talented intellectuals and technocrats were assembled in Washington, DC. Among them were young economists who had come of age after the war and had been schooled in Keynesian economics. The first edition of Paul Samuelson's (Nobel Laureate 1970) *Economics: An Introductory Analysis* was published in 1948. This book was responsible for spreading the Keynesian gospel not only in the United States but around the world. Their outstanding beliefs were that a better world was possible and that they had the know-how to build it. Their views on economic matters are reflected in the Economic Reports of the President for those years. The economy was considered machinery that could be fine-tuned to deliver a desirable combination of inflation and unemployment rates. The Keynesian influence was quite apparent.

K. Dadkhah, *The Evolution of Macroeconomic Theory and Policy*,
DOI 10.1007/978-3-540-77008-4_4, © Springer-Verlag Berlin Heidelberg 2009

The goal of the Employment Act is "maximum employment," or—to put it the other way round—minimum unemployment. Ideally, all persons able, willing, and seeking to work should be continuously employed. Involuntary unemployment is an individual and social evil. ... But zero unemployment is unattainable.

Given the existing structure of the economy and the nature of the processes by which prices and wages are determined, a serious attempt to push unemployment close to zero would produce a high rate of price inflation. ... Happily, however, the conflict between the goals served by price stability and the goal of minimum unemployment is only partial. Stabilization policy—policy to influence the level of aggregate demand—can strike a balance between them which largely avoids the consequences of a failure in either direction. Furthermore, the degree of conflict can be diminished by private and public policies which improve the functioning of labor and product markets [*Economic Report of the President 1962*].

The tool of the stabilization goals was government's fiscal policy. In particular, the government would reduce taxes and increase its expenditures. President Kennedy argued for a tax cut and asked the Congress to reduce tax rates. In an address to the Economic Club of New York, the President said

But the most direct and significant kind of federal action aiding economic growth is to make possible an increase in private consumption and investment demand—to cut the fetters which hold back private spending.

The final and best means of strengthening demand among consumers and business is to reduce the burden on private income and the deterrents to private initiative which are imposed by our present tax system—and this administration pledged itself last summer to an across-the-board, top-to-bottom cut in personal and corporate income taxes to be enacted and become effective in 1963.

I'm not talking about a "quickie" or a temporary tax cut, which would be more appropriate if a recession were imminent. Nor am I talking about giving the economy a mere shot in the arm, to ease some temporary complaint. I am talking about the accumulated evidence of the last five years that our present tax system, developed as it was, in good part, during World War II to restrain growth, exerts too heavy a drag on growth in peace time; that it siphons out of the private economy too large a share of personal and business purchasing power; that it reduces the financial incentives for personal effort, investment, and risk-taking. In short, to increase demand and lift the economy, the federal government's most useful role is not to rush into a program of excessive increases in public expenditures, but to expand the incentives and opportunities for private expenditures.

In that and other speeches, President Kennedy argued that the budget deficit resulting from the proposed tax cut would and could not be eliminated by reducing government expenditures. Rather the tax cut would stimulate output, and once the goal of full employment is reached enough revenue is produced to balance the budget.

Our true choice is not between tax reduction, on the one hand, and the avoidance of large federal deficits on the other. It is increasingly clear that no matter what party is in power, so long as our national security needs keep rising, an economy hampered by restrictive tax rates will never produce enough revenues to balance our budget—just as it will never produce enough jobs or enough profits. Surely the lesson of the last decade is that budget deficits are not caused by wild-eyed spenders but by slow economic growth and periodic recessions, and any new recession would break all deficit records.

In short, it is a paradoxical truth that tax rates are too high today and tax revenues are too low and the soundest way to raise the revenues in the long run is to cut the rates now. The experience of a number of European countries and Japan have borne this out. This country's own experience with tax reduction in 1954 has borne this out. And the reason is that only full employment can balance the budget, and tax reduction can pave the way to that employment. The purpose of cutting taxes now is not to incur a budget deficit, but to achieve the more prosperous, expanding economy which can bring a budget surplus.

The tax cut was enacted in 1964. Figure 4.1 shows the receipts and expenditures of the federal government during the period 1946–1972. The graph indeed bears out the President's contention that a reduction of tax rates would have a beneficial effect on government revenues and consequently on the budget deficit. Figure 4.2 shows that after a decrease in the share of government receipts in the GDP, it started an upward trend in 1966. Of course in the same year the share of

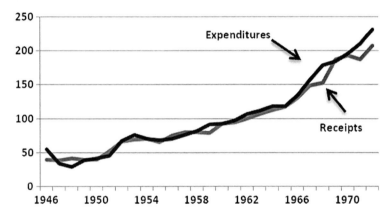

Fig. 4.1 Receipts and expenditures of the United States government (billions of current dollars)

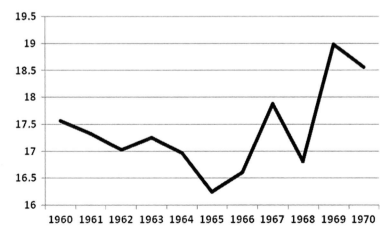

Fig. 4.2 Government revenues as a percentage of the GDP

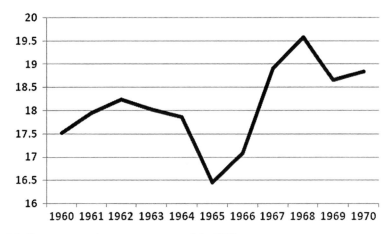

Fig. 4.3 Government outlays as a percentage of the GDP

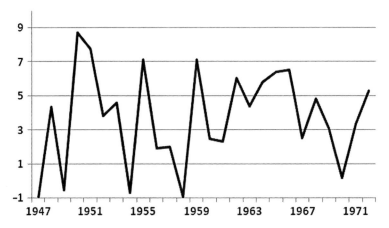

Fig. 4.4 The growth rate of the US economy (percentage change in the GDP)

government expenditures in the GDP also increased (Fig. 4.3). Thus, the impetus came from both the tax cut and increased spending; in other words, a combination of lower taxes and higher expenditures fueled a long period of boom. The government resorted to deficit spending to fuel economic prosperity and growth and succeeded for a few years. Figure 4.4 shows the growth rate of the US economy as measured by the percentage change in the GDP. Between 1962 and 1968 we observe higher than average growth rate with less volatility in growth rate.

During the same period the country made great strides in bringing disenfranchised groups, such as African Americans, into the mainstream of political and economic activities. The government also inaugurated an ambitious program called The Great Society, which would move the country toward a welfare state. The government would provide a safety net for individuals, would extend help to everyone to realize his/her potential, and the fruits of progress would be more equally distributed.

What in particular distinguish this period are general optimism and the confidence in economic policy to achieve social and economic objectives.

> No longer will we tolerate widespread involuntary idleness, unnecessary human hardship and misery, the impoverishment of whole areas, the spoiling of our natural heritage, the human and physical ugliness of our cities, the ravages of the business cycle, or the arbitrary redistribution of purchasing power.
>
> Our tools of economic policy are much better tools than existed a generation ago. We are able to proceed with much greater confidence and flexibility in seeking effective answers to the changing problems of our changing economy.
>
> The accomplishments of the past four years are a measure of the constructive response that can be expected from workers, consumers, investors, managers, farmers, and merchants to effective public policies that strive to define and achieve the national interest in
>
> - full employment with stable prices;
> - rapid economic growth;
> - balance in our external relationships;
> - maximum efficiency in our public and private economies.
>
> These perennial challenges to economic policy are not fully mastered; but we are well on our way to their solution.
>
> As increasingly we master them, economic policy can more than ever become the servant of our quest to make American society not only prosperous but progressive, not only affluent but humane, offering not only higher incomes but wider opportunities, its people enjoying not only full employment but fuller lives.[1]

The Achilles' heel of the whole enterprise was the Philips curve—or more appropriately its mechanical version—which did not hold up. Recall that the Economic Report of the President (1962) had spoken of striking a balance between unemployment and inflation. Such a balance turned out to be elusive. Combined with an unpopular war (fought with heavy reliance on technology and know-how), the era of high expectations came to an end. The overheating of the economy unraveled the Keynesian vision of the economy.

Okun's Law

The idea of full employment or maximum employment was central to the Employment Act of 1946. Unemployment on the one hand causes hardship for the unemployed and, therefore, is a social problem. On the other hand, the society loses output that could have been if everyone were gainfully employed. The amount of loss to the society equals the difference between actual GDP and what it could be under the condition of full employment.

---

[1] *Economic Report of the President*, 1965, pp. 20–21.

The problem is that if we take full employment literally and insist that everyone should be employed, the economy would be under heavy inflationary pressure. At every moment a percentage of workers are between jobs (frictional unemployment). How could we balance the goal of maximum possible output with price stability? Arthur Okun suggested that 4% unemployment would best achieve both goals. It should be noted that price stability was vaguely defined.

Okun defined the level of GDP[2] consistent with 4% unemployment rate as the *potential GDP*, and the difference between actual and potential GDP as unrealized potential or gap. He found an inverse relationship between unemployment rate and the growth rate of output, which is known as Okun's law. Below we shall discuss two versions of this law. Such relationships are considered short term because they rest on the assumption that either other factors remain constant or their combined effects is constant.

The first version relates the change in unemployment rate to the growth rate of GDP. Recall that unemployment rate is equal to one minus rate of employment:

$$u = 1 - \frac{L}{H}$$

Where u is the unemployment rate,[3] L employment, and H the labor force. Note that the labor force is equal to the civilian noninstitutional working age population times the labor force participation rate. Therefore, the rate of growth of the labor force is equal to the sum of the growth rate of population and growth rate of participation rate. On the other hand, the rate of growth of employment depends positively on the growth rate of output, and negatively on the growth rate of capital and productivity. It follows that, in addition to the growth rate of GDP, growth rates of productivity, capital stock, population, and labor force participation affect unemployment rate. Okun's law implicitly assumes that, in the short run, the combined effects of all these factors (other than the growth rate of GDP) amount to a constant term. Thus, we can write:

$$u_t - u_{t-1} = \alpha_0 + \alpha_1 \dot{Y}_t + \varepsilon_t$$

where $\dot{Y}$ denotes the growth rate of GDP and ε is a stochastic term. If we estimate this equation using annual US data from 1948 to 2006, we get

$$u_t - u_{t-1} = 1.35 - 0.39\dot{Y}_t$$
$$(11.15)\,(0.03)$$
$$R^2 = 0.76,\ DW = 1.70$$

---

[2]Today we generally talk about gross domestic product (GDP); in the 1960s economists were concerned with gross national product (GNP) and Okun defined potential GNP.

[3] Usually unemployment rate is expressed as percentage of the labor force, which requires u to be multiplied by 100.

where figures in parentheses are standard deviations. Thus, every 1% increase in the growth rate of GDP reduces the unemployment rate by about 0.4 percentage point from the previous year. Alternatively, if we want to reduce the unemployment rate by a full percentage point, we need 2.5% growth in the GDP.

An alternative formulation relates unemployment rate to the ratio of potential gap. If we let $\bar{Y}$ denote potential GDP, then Okun's law can be written as

$$u_t = \alpha_0 + \alpha_1 \left(\frac{\bar{Y}_t - Y_t}{\bar{Y}_t} \right) + \varepsilon_t$$

The problem with this formulation is the computation of potential GDP. Each method of computation of potential GDP could result in a different level of unemployment rate. Of course we may choose a method based on its goodness of fit.

The Phillips Curve

In 1958 Alban William Phillips published a truly influential paper.[4] He noted that the change in price of a commodity is inversely related to its excess supply. If we apply the same to the labor market, we should find changes in money wage rate to be inversely related to unemployment rate, which is a measure of excess supply in the labor market. In addition, he noted that the level of unemployment and increase in import prices should also have a bearing on this relationship. He found empirical support for this hypothesis in the United Kingdom economy. Analyzing separately the data for the periods 1861–1913, 1913–1948, and 1948–1957 he found evidence of an inverse relationship between unemployment rate and the rate of change in money wages in the United Kingdom. Anticipating future developments he also noted the connection to the inflation rate. Under the assumption of 2% productivity increase per year stable level of product prices would be associated with an unemployment rate slightly less that 2.5%. On the other hand, stable money wage rates would require an unemployment rate of 5.5%.

Two years later Paul Samuelson and Robert Solow (1960) presented similar results for the United States.[5] They connected the rate of inflation to unemployment rate and named the inverse relationship the *Phillips curve* (Fig. 4.5). Samuelson and Solow were careful to emphasize the short run nature of the relationship. Moreover, they pointed out that the curve could shift for a variety of reasons. Yet the policy implication they inferred from the relationship was quite clear. Under the graph labeled "Modified Phillips Curve for U.S.," it read "This shows the menu of choice between different degrees of unemployment and price stability, as roughly estimated from last twenty-five years of American data."[6] Samuelson and Solow

---

[4] A. W. Phillips (1958), pp. 283–299.
[5] Paul Samuelson and Robert Solow (1960), pp. 177–194.
[6] Op. cit., p. 192.

Fig. 4.5 The tradeoff
between inflation and
unemployment rates: the
Phillips curve

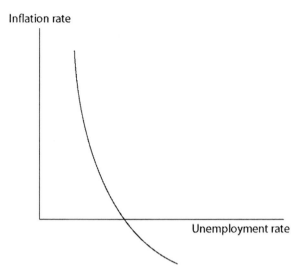

speculated that the United States could achieve price stability at the cost of 5–6%
unemployment. On the other hand, to achieve 3% unemployment rate the nation had
to accept 4–5% inflation.

Simply put, there existed an inverse relationship between unemployment and
inflation rate, and policy makers could choose among different combinations of the
two. Indeed, there were rhetorical discussions asking if a nation could not tolerate
a bit of inflation to allow more people to work. Some added that after all inflation
hurts the rich and unemployment the poor. To keep social peace, the rich should be
ready to pay a small price.

Figure 4.6 depicts such a relationship for the US economy for the years
1948–1968. The inverse relationship is quite discernible. If we confine ourselves

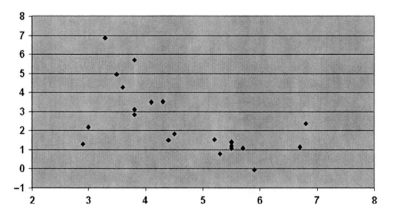

Fig. 4.6 Inflation rate (GDP deflator) vs. unemployment rate 1948–1968

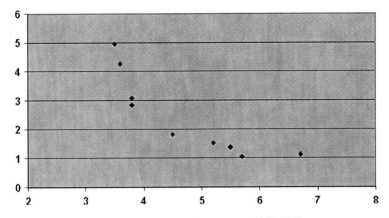

Fig. 4.7 Inflation rate (GDP deflator) vs. unemployment rate 1960–1969

to the shorter period of 1960–1969 (Fig. 4.7), the Phillips curve is even more pronounced. Thus, it is not surprising that economists and policy makers bought into the idea and based their theories and policies on the relationship.

Note that the Phillips curve is a tradeoff between the unemployment rate and inflation rate. Therefore, as long as the unemployment rate is constant, the inflation rate should remain almost constant. Moreover, if the unemployment rate is increasing then the inflation rate should decrease or at the least does not increase. The proponents of the theory were in for a rude awakening at the end of the 1960s and early 1970s when the US economy experienced the so called stagflation, that is, an increasing unemployment rate accompanied by an increasing rate of inflation.

Stagflation

If the Phillips curve held up as advertised then we could see either rising unemployment and lowering inflation, or rising inflation and lowering unemployment. But we could not see both unemployment and inflation rates increasing. Yet this is what happened after 1968 (Figs. 4.8 and 4.9). For some months both inflation and unemployment rates were on the rise. The phenomenon was dubbed stagflation to signify a stagnating economy which experiences inflation. The experience put an end to the idea of tradeoff between unemployment and inflation. Indeed, a closer examination of data on inflation and unemployment over a longer period of time showed that either the Phillips curve did not exist or that it shifted over time (Fig. 4.10).

The breakdown of the original Phillips curve prompted economists to come up with the reason for and the mechanism by which the Phillips curve shifted. It seemed obvious that after a certain point an increase in inflation could not possibly lower the unemployment rate. Hence Milton Friedman and Edmund Phelps came up with the idea of the natural rate of unemployment. Once the economy reaches this level of unemployment, an increase in inflation would not do any good. But then why

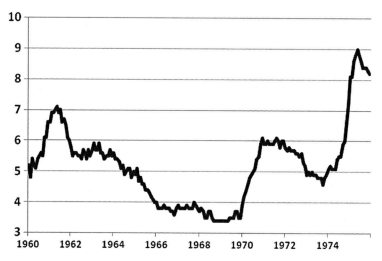

Fig. 4.8 Monthly unemployment rate

Fig. 4.9 Monthly inflation rate

does the curve shift. The answer seems to be an adjustment in the expectation of inflation. Once people expect inflation, they would adjust their wage demands, and therefore it takes a higher rate of inflation to effect the same amount of reduction in the unemployment rate.

In the next three sections we shall discuss first the natural rate of unemployment and the rational expectations hypothesis, and then integrate these ideas in the augmented Phillips curve.

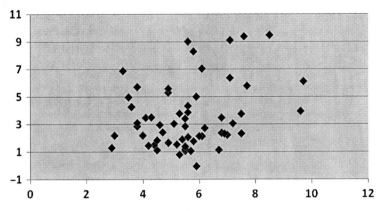

Fig. 4.10 Inflation rate (GDP deflator) vs. unemployment rate 1948–2006

The Natural Rate of Unemployment

Recall that aggregate supply would become vertical at full employment. Thus, near full employment an increase in demand would increase prices while at the same time reducing unemployment. As we get closer to full employment the increase in prices get larger and larger while the decrease in the unemployment rate gets smaller and smaller. Once we reach full employment, prices keep increasing and there is no change in unemployment rate. We could repeat the same argument replacing change in prices with change in inflation rate. But what do we mean by full employment? Does it mean zero unemployment?

In 1945 Sir William Beveridge had posed the question: "What is meant by 'full employment,' and what is not meant by it?" He answered that

> Full employment does not mean literally no unemployment; that is to say, it does not mean that every man and woman in the country who is fit and free for work is employed productively on every day of his or her working life. ... Some frictional unemployment[7] there will be in a progressive society however high the demand for labour. Full employment means that unemployment is reduced to short intervals of standing by, with the certainty that very soon one will be wanted in one's old job again or will be wanted in a new job that is within one's powers.[8]

Edmund Phelps (Nobel laureate 2006) and Milton Friedman argued that, there is a positive rate of unemployment that the economic system would tend to. If unemployment rate is pushed below this *natural rate of unemployment*, we witness accelerating inflation rate while unemployment rate tends to increase. The natural rate

---

[7] He defines *frictional unemployment* as "unemployment caused by the individuals who make up the labour supply not being completely interchangeable and mobile units, so that, though there is an unsatisfied demand for labour, the unemployed workers are not the right sort or in the right place to meet that demand." *Full Employment in a Free Society*, 1945, pp. 408–409.

[8] Op. cit., p. 18.

of unemployment is not a constant magnitude and can be affected by many factors including minimum wage laws, power of labor unions, imperfect information on the part of workers, and other economic agents. In the words of Milton Friedman the natural rate

> is the level that would be ground out by the Walrasian system of general equilibrium equations, provided there is embedded in them the actual structural characteristics of the labor and commodity markets, including market imperfections, stochastic variability in demands and supplies, the cost of gathering information about job vacancies and labor availabilities, the costs of mobility, and so on.

It is not difficult to accept the basic points of natural rate hypothesis; that full employment does not mean zero unemployment but a positive rate; that such a rate is not constant and varies over time; that the natural rate depends on the structure of the economy and the labor market conditions. We may accept that perhaps in early 1970s the natural rate in the United States was around 6% and in the 1990s and early years of the twenty first century it is between 4.5 and 5%.

But if the above description is presented as a technical or formal definition, we have a problem. There is no Walrasian system of equations which embeds all the qualifications that Friedman mentions.

The position we can take is to avoid the pseudo scientific precision and accept the natural rate for what it is: an empirical necessity. Full employment means a small positive rate of unemployment. The economy would revert to this rate. There is no reason to push the unemployment rate below this natural rate as the only result would be the acceleration of inflation. The natural rate of unemployment could be reduced by deregulation and allowing flexibility in the economy. Moreover, better education, retraining programs, and job vacancies information could also help.

Rational Expectations

John Muth[9] used the following model of supply and demand to motivate the concept of rational expectations:

$$Q_t^d = \alpha_0 + \alpha_1 P_t$$
$$Q_t^s = \beta_0 + \beta_1 P_t^e + \varepsilon_t$$
$$Q_t^d = Q_t^s$$

where Q^d, Q^s, P, P^e are respectively, quantity demanded, quantity supplied, price, and expected price, and ε is a random variable with zero mean $E(\varepsilon_t) = 0$. Thus, demand depends on price but supply depends on the expectation of price. This expectation is formed in the period prior to the start of production and therefore embodies only information available up to that point. The model could be thought of as depicting the supply and demand for an agricultural product such as wheat or

---

[9]John Muth (1961), pp. 315–335.

corn. Demand depends on the market price but farmers have to decide on the amount to plant in advance and on the basis of their expectations of price. Furthermore, the supply of an agricultural product is subject to stochastic shocks due to weather and other natural elements.

The question is how the producers are going to form their price expectations. One alternative is to expect the price to be the same as the previous period. That is to set

$$P_t^e = P_{t-1}$$

Combining the equations we end up with the first order non-homogeneous difference equation

$$P_t = \frac{\beta_0 - \alpha_0}{\alpha_1} + \frac{\beta_1}{\alpha_1} P_{t-1} + \frac{\varepsilon_t}{\alpha_1}$$

Since $\alpha_1 < 0$ and $\beta_1 > 0$, the equation is the famous cobweb model, which depending on the magnitude of β_1/α_1 is either converging or diverging. The stochastic term would cause deviations from the cobweb path, although we can expect its effect to be small.

The model implies that when producers are expecting low prices and therefore produce less, the price turns out to be high. On the other hand, when they expect high prices and produce more, they are disappointed because the price turns out low. One might ask, wouldn't these producers figure this repeating pattern and adjust their expectations and behavior? Even if they cannot see this pattern, wouldn't others observe it and make a handy profit by speculating? The model imparts a knowledge that although known to the economist (modeler) no one else is aware of. If the expectation computed from this model is superior to the expectation of the producers p_t^e then there exists an opportunity to make money through the use of this model. One could engage in inventory speculation or at least selling forecasts.

An alternative way of forming expectation is perfect foresight. Producers can figure out the equilibrium price that will prevail in the next period as

$$P_t = \frac{\beta_0 - \alpha_0}{\alpha_1 - \beta_1} + \frac{\varepsilon_t}{\alpha_1 - \beta_1}$$

and set their expectations equal to it.

$$P^e = \frac{\beta_0 - \alpha_0}{\alpha_1 - \beta_1} + \frac{\varepsilon_t}{\alpha_1 - \beta_1}$$

In that case equilibrium will prevail. The problem is that ε is white noise and at time $t-1$ we cannot predict it except to set it equal to its expected value, that is, equal to zero.

Muth suggested the rational expectations. At time $t-1$ producers can estimate the equilibrium price level based on the model except for the stochastic term. This would be the optimal forecast of the price level at time $t-1$ based on the set of all information available to them Ω_{t-1}. Thus,

$$P_t^e = E(P_t \mid \Omega_{t-1}) = \frac{\beta_0 - \alpha_0}{\alpha_1 - \beta_1}$$

That is, the price expectation of economic agents is equal to the mathematical expectation of actual price conditional on the information available at the time. A model with this feature is called a rational expectations model.

Note that if we substitute the above expectation into the model and solve for the equilibrium price level, we get

$$P_t = \frac{\beta_0 - \alpha_0}{\alpha_1 - \beta_1} + \frac{\varepsilon_t}{\alpha_1}$$

Several issues regarding rational expectations need to be emphasized. First, rational expectation is defined within a model. Therefore, a description of rational expectations without reference to a model would become empty generality. For instance, saying that "rational expectations means that in forming their expectations, decision makers take into account all the information available to them" or stating that "on average (and in the long run) expectations are correct (free of systematic bias)" are empty phrases.

Second, the word rational does not refer to actual human behavior, and rational expectations model is not a psychological description of human behavior, it is a feature of the model. If it were a description of human behavior, we may ask: how did the decision makers come to possess such knowledge? At what cost? Since each decision maker may be quite far from the average, what would be the effect of dispersion in expectations and outliers on the market, when these people conclude their transactions?

What rational expectations state is that the modeler or the economist cannot claim to possess a particular knowledge that is denied the economic agents whose behavior she is modeling. This feature is in stark contrast to the paternalistic attitude of Keynes and Keynesians we mentioned in Chap. 1. Without rational expectations, macroeconomic models acquire a mechanical feature. Thus, both in the short and long run there are policies that could be superimposed by the government and would affect the economy. With rational expectations such policies would not work in the long run. Thus, for any macroeconomic policy to be effective in the long run the policymaker should consider people's incentives and persuade them to accept, go along, and help the implementation of the policy. We shall return to these issues again in Chap. 8.

The Augmented Phillips Curve

The original Phillips curve connected inflation and unemployment rates in a mechanistic way. But what was the economic process assumed to be operating to bring about such a relationship. The issue gains even more importance if the economy is operating near the natural rate of unemployment. The usual explanation is that an expansionary monetary policy will increase demand for goods and services. Higher demand causes prices to increase. Producers respond by increasing production which entails hiring more workers. Assuming that prior to the increase in demand the labor market was in equilibrium, to entice workers to increase their supply of labor, employers increase the wage rate. Thus, the higher demand brings with it higher prices, higher wages, and lower unemployment; hence the observed tradeoff between inflation and unemployment rate.

As long as there is unemployment the policy of increasing demand works and the inflationary policy reduces the rate of unemployment. When there is full employment, any increase in demand is reflected in prices with no effect on employment. The question is what do we mean by full employment? As we saw above, Friedman and Phelps argued that full employment is reached not at zero unemployment but at the natural rate of unemployment which, for the United States, would be around 4.5–5.5%. Pushing unemployment rate below this limit would only result in higher rates of inflation.

Thus, close to the natural rate of unemployment an increase in demand increases prices leading firms to demand more labor. But workers are concerned with their real wages, that is, the purchasing power of their remunerations. If both wages and prices are going up then workers will find themselves no better off than before and would have no incentive to offer more labor. The argument is that workers base their wage demands on the expected rate of rise in prices. Close to the natural rate of unemployment the inflation rate accelerates. Workers adjust their expectations and require a larger increase in their nominal wages in return for offering more labor. Thus, it takes a higher rate of inflation to induce employers to demand labor. A larger increase in prices increases inflation expectations and therefore leads to an increase in wage demand. In other words, the Phillips curve has shifted upward. The same rate of unemployment requires a higher rate of inflation. A country that engages in inflationary policies to increase employment ends up in an inflationary spiral with no effects on its long run unemployment rate.

The augmented Phillips curve can be written as

$$\pi_t = \pi_t^e + \gamma(\bar{u}_t - u_t) + \varepsilon_t$$

Thus, the difference between inflation π and the expected inflation π^e is proportional to the distance between unemployment rate u and the natural rate $\bar{u}$, aside from a random term ε which represents the combined effects of all other factors that affect inflation rate and are left out of the equation. If unemployment rate is above the natural rate, then inflation will be decreasing, and if unemployment rate is below the natural rate, inflation will be increasing. We can state the proposition in a different way. If inflation is higher than expected then unemployment will be below the natural rate and if inflation is below its expected rate, unemployment is above the natural rate.

We can write the inflation rate as

$$\pi_t = \pi_t^e + (\pi_t - \pi_t^e)_t = \pi_t^e + \pi_t^u$$

where π_t^u is the unexpected inflation rate. Substituting in the augmented Phillips curve, we have

$$\pi_t^u = \gamma(\bar{u}_t - u_t) + \varepsilon_t$$

In other words only unexpected inflation is connected to unemployment rate. If inflation is expected it cannot affect unemployment. For a policy maker intent on reducing unemployment rate via inflationary policy, there is no choice but to up the ante at every stage and to increase the inflation rate further and further. Indeed it should increase the inflation rate at an increasing speed so people could not forecast the next rate increase.

So far we have made no assumptions regarding the formation of expectations. But let us assume that expectations are rational; then conditional on the available set of information Ω_{t-1} we have

$$E(\pi_t|\Omega_{t-1}) = \pi_t^e + \gamma(\bar{u}_t - u_t) + E(\varepsilon_t|\Omega_{t-1})$$

Since $\pi_t^e = E(\pi_t|\Omega_{t-1})$ and $E(\varepsilon_t|\Omega_{t-1}) = 0$, we have

$$\bar{u} = u$$

To the extent that expectations are rational, in the long-run, that is—when expectations are realized—unemployment rate will stay at the natural rate. And to the extent that the market corrects expectations speedily, there is only a very short time for the tradeoff between inflation and unemployment to be stable.

Income Distribution

The 1960s stand out in terms improving income distribution in the country. Indeed, since 1968 income distribution in the United States, as measured by the Gini coefficient, has become less and less equal (Fig. 4.11). This does not seem to be a short run phenomenon or one that could be blamed on a particular administration or policy.

The starting date of the move toward inequality is instructive. In 1969 the long term growth in manufacturing jobs came to a halt and within a decade a decline in such jobs set in. Since then the US economy has become more and more a service and knowledge economy.

In 1971 the Bretton Woods system was abandoned (see Chap. 6). Adoption of flexible exchange rates, globalization, and deregulation of many industries and activities have disrupted old patterns of business, ushered in a new era, and introduced more challenges. In every sphere of economic activity there is more competition and a wider gap between winners and losers.

Finally, more and more women and minorities have entered the labor force. Families and households with two wage earners have more income and introduce a disparity with one wage earner families. At the same time the magnitude of disparity between two wage earner families at high and low ends has increased.

Fig. 4.11 Income distribution in the United States (the Gini coefficient)

The issue of income distribution is of utmost importance and yet has received insufficient attention in macroeconomics. An economy and society with badly skewed income distribution will face many problems. But in facing this problem, changed characteristics of economy, some of them alluded to above, have to be taken into account. We shall return to this theme in later chapters.

Chapter 5
Macroeconomics of an Open Economy

Moreover, if exchange rates are flexible, an increase in investment or government spending, and a reduction in saving or taxation, will have a substantially different effect on employment than that predicted by the traditional foreign trade multiplier. The reason lies in the fact that equilibrium in the balance of payments is automatically maintained by variations in the price of foreign exchange.

Robert Mundell, "Flexible Exchange Rates and Employment Policy," *The Canadian Journal of Economics and Political Science*, 1961, 509

The dance was very lively and complicated. It was complicated enough without me—with me it was more so.

Mark Twain, *Innocents Abroad*

Up to the 1960s the Keynesian model of macroeconomics pertained to a closed economy. That is, an economy that has no international trade or movement of capital. In modern times no country could be found to conform to such a description. The model was defended on the ground that it was a first approximation. It was argued that in the case of some countries such as the United States, the amount of international trade compared to the GDP was so small as to be negligible for the sake of analysis. For countries such as small European countries exports and imports were a substantial proportion of the GDP. Therefore, the approximation would be off the mark. But it was argued that if somehow the external balance was maintained, the internal macroeconomic issues could be analyzed separately from international problems.

Even if such arguments could ever carry any weight, starting in the late 1960s and especially after the collapse of the Bretton Woods Agreement (see the next chapter), the argument became vacuous. As time has passed, international transactions have played an increasingly important role in the American economy. The same is true for many countries in Asia, Latin America, and other parts of the world. For small European countries with significant international trade sector, the model was never a good approximation. By no stretch of imagination could the United States be considered a closed economy when in 2007, its imports accounted for 16% of the GDP and its annual trade deficit was $700 billion.

K. Dadkhah, *The Evolution of Macroeconomic Theory and Policy,*
DOI 10.1007/978-3-540-77008-4_5, © Springer-Verlag Berlin Heidelberg 2009

In early 1960s Robert Mundell[1] and J. M. Fleming proposed a model to incorporate international trade and capital movement into the macroeconomic model. They added a third equation—the balance of payments equation—to the IS-LM model. The balance of payments consists of two parts: current account and capital account. The current account reflects exports and imports of goods and services, income received from abroad and income sent to other countries, and unilateral payments to and from the country. The capital account shows how much foreigners bought assets inside of the country and how much the citizen of our country bought assets abroad. The word asset is inclusive of both physical assets (direct foreign investment) and financial assets such as government bonds and company stocks. Figure 5.1 depicts the evolution of exports and imports, and Table 5.1 shows a summary of the balance of payments for the United States for the years 2005–2007.

Exports of goods and services bring money into the country; therefore, it is shown as a positive item on the balance of payments. On the other hand imports of goods and services result in the outflow of money from the country, thus the negative sign. This is a general convention in balance of payment accounts. Inflow of money to the country is shown with a positive sign and outflow with a negative sign.

Income earned by Americans abroad and repatriated to the US works like exports and brings in cash. Income is inclusive of wages and salaries of workers who send home their earnings, profit from investment, and interest on loans. Unilateral payments include the US aid to other countries, both economic and military. Since buying of assets abroad entails an outflow of money it is shown with a negative sign. Buying of assets by foreigners brings in money to the country and therefore it is shown with a positive sign.

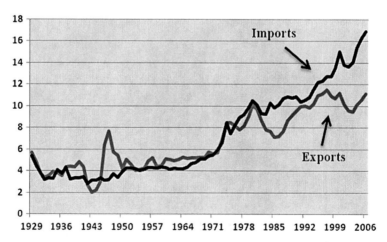

Fig. 5.1 The US exports and imports as a percentage of GDP

---

[1] Robert Mundell won the Nobel Prize in Economics in 1999, "for his analysis of monetary and fiscal policy under different exchange rate regimes and his analysis of optimum currency areas."

Table 5.1 Balance of payments of the United States (in million dollars)

Year	2005	2006	2007
Current account			
Exports of goods and services and income receipts	1,819,016	2,142,164	2,463,505
Exports of goods and services	1,283,753	1,457,015	1,645,726
Income receipts	535,263	685,150	817,779
Imports of goods and services and income payments	−2,458,225	−2,838,254	−3,082,014
Imports of goods and services	−1,995,320	−2,210,298	−2,345,984
Income payments	−462,905	−627,956	−736,030
Unilateral current transfers, net	−89,784	−92,027	−112,705
Capital account			
US-owned assets abroad, excluding financial derivatives (increase/financial outflow (−))	−546,631	−1,251,749	−1,289,854
US official reserve assets	14,096	2,374	−122
US Government assets, other than official reserve assets	5,539	5,346	−22,273
US private assets	−566,266	−1,259,469	−1,267,459
Direct investment	−36,235	−241,244	−333,271
Foreign-owned assets in the United States, excluding financial derivatives (increase/financial inflow (+))	1,247,347	2,061,113	2,057,703
Foreign official assets in the United States	259,268	487,939	411,058
US Government securities	213,334	428,401	230,330
Other foreign assets in the United States	988,079	1,573,174	1,646,645
Direct investment	112,638	241,961	237,542
Financial derivatives, net	n.a.	29,710	6,496
Statistical discrepancy	32,313	−47,078	−41,287
Memoranda			
Balance on goods and services	−711,567	−753,283	−700,258
Balance on current account	−728,993	−788,116	−731,214

Aside from statistical discrepancy (which is inevitable in the balance of payments statistics) the current balance should be equal to capital balance with its sign reversed. Let X denote exports, m imports, and F the net inflow of capital (i.e., the capital balance). For simplicity we subsume the income receipts and payments in exports and imports, respectively, and disregard unilateral payments. We have:

$$X - m = -F \quad \text{or} \quad B = X - m + F = 0$$

To incorporate the analysis of the balance of payments into our IS-LM model, we need to introduce a number of behavioral assumptions. Exports is assumed to be positively related to the exchange rate, e.[2] We define the exchange rate as the price of the foreign currency in terms of domestic currency. For instance, if the United States is the economy under consideration domestic currency would be the dollar. The exchange rate for the euro is stated as $1.30 per euro. That is, to buy one euro we have to pay $1.30. By this convention[3] when the exchange rate increases, the domestic currency (in this case the dollar) is depreciated or devalued. Therefore, domestic goods and services will become cheaper for foreign buyers and foreign goods and services will be more expensive for domestic buyers. Hence, an increase in e will increase X.

In addition, exports depend on the income of other countries, which we represent by one variable Y^*. Since we shall concentrate on one country with the assumption that it does not have an inordinate effect on the world income, we shall assume Y^* to be fixed for the time period of analysis. Thus,

$$X = X(Y^*,e) = X(e),$$

$$X_{Y^*} = \frac{\partial X}{\partial Y^*} > 0, \quad X_e = \frac{\partial X}{\partial e} > 0$$

Imports positively depend on the country's income: the higher the income the higher the demand for goods and services including imported ones. On the other hand, an increase in exchange rates, as defined above, would make foreign products more expensive and, therefore, reduce the imports. We may also note that an increase in the interest rate would reduce the demand for investment goods including machinery and equipment imported from abroad. In all likelihood this last effect would be quite small in magnitude compared to the effect of the interest rate on domestic expenditures. To sum

---

[2] In this chapter and elsewhere we speak of "the exchange rate" when it is well known that there are as many bilateral exchange rates for a currency as there are other currencies. In a fixed exchange rates regime a devaluation or revaluation of a currency would occur with respect to all other currencies. Similarly, depreciation or appreciation of a currency in a flexible regime occurs with respect to all other currencies. It is possible that two currencies are tied together, for example the Chinese yuan (although in recent years China has gradually moved to floating its currency) and the Saudi Arabia's riyal are tied to the dollar and a devaluation or depreciation of the dollar will have no effect on such exchange rates. Nevertheless, since we are interested in macro effects and not on the effects of devaluation on trade with a particular country, we can continue to talk of the exchange rate as a shorthand.

[3] The convention of stating the exchange rate as the number of units of the domestic currency that buys one unit of foreign currency is called the price quotation system. Alternatively, we can express the exchange rate as the number of the units of the foreign currency that buys one unit of the domestic currency. In the example in the text the exchange rate could equivalently be stated as 0.7692=1/1.30 euro per dollar. This convention is referred to as the volume quotation system. For consistency, in this book, we shall adhere to the first system.

$$m = m(Y, e, r),$$

$$m_Y = \frac{\partial m}{\partial Y} > 0, \quad m_e = \frac{\partial m}{\partial e} < 0, \quad m_r = \frac{\partial m}{\partial r} < 0$$

Finally, under the assumption of perfect capital mobility the net inflow of capital to the country will depend on both domestic and international rates of interest denoted, respectively, by r and r^*. Again for our analysis we shall assume r^* to be exogenously determined and constant during the time period under analysis.

$$F = F(r, r^*) = F(r),$$

$$F_r = \frac{\partial F}{\partial r} > 0, \quad F_{r^*} = \frac{\partial F}{\partial r^*} < 0$$

A few points regarding the function F need to be mentioned. First, every country experiences both inflow and outflow of capital. Some investors in country A find some foreign markets more attractive than their domestic market, while at the same time some foreigners prefer to invest in country A. Thus, the function F signifies the net inflow of capital, that is, inflow minus outflow of capital. Hence F could be either positive or negative. Second, rates of interest, domestic and foreign, refer to real, risk adjusted interest rates. Third, if we assume perfect capital mobility, it follows that domestic and foreign interest rates have to be equal. The reason is that if they are different there will be enough inflow and outflow of capital to bring the domestic rate in line with the international rate.

Putting all the elements of the balance of payments together, we can write:

$$X(Y^*, e) + F(r, r^*) = m(Y, e, r)$$

or deleting variables which are taken to be exogenous and fixed

$$B = X(e) - m(Y, e, r) + F(r) = 0$$

Keeping the exchange rate constant, the balance of payment equation is the loci of all combinations of the interest rate and income which result in external equilibrium, i.e., result in the balance of payments being zero. This line is upward sloping (BB lines in Fig. 5.2). To see this, rewrite the equation as

$$X(e) + F(r) = m(Y, e, r)$$

An increase in Y raises the right hand side of the equation. To preserve the equilibrium, r has to increase to raise the left hand side and to lower (albeit with a smaller effect) the right hand side. At points above the BB line there is surplus and at any point below it there is deficit in the balance of payments.

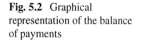

Fig. 5.2 Graphical representation of the balance of payments

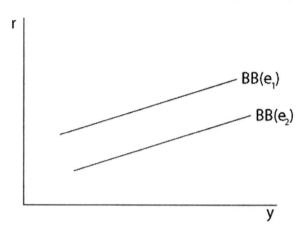

An increase in the exchange rate (devaluation, depreciation) shifts the BB curve to the right and downward.[4] Similarly, a decrease in the exchange rate (revaluation, appreciation) would shift the curve to the left and upward (Fig. 5.2).

Equilibrium in an Open Economy

In a closed economy and assuming prices to be fixed, internal equilibrium is achieved at the intersection of the IS and LM curves, which establishes the combination of income and the rate of interest that result in equilibrium in both goods and money markets. In an open economy we need both internal and external equilibrium. In other words, in addition to establishing equilibrium in goods and money markets, the combination of income and the rate of interest has to be consistent with equilibrium in the balance of payments. Such a point is achieved at the intersection of the three curves: IS, LM, and BB (Fig. 5.3).

In the absence of any adjustment mechanism, there is no reason that such a point is obtained automatically. Mathematically, we have three equations in two unknowns. Unless one of the equations is redundant, the system does not have a solution. We need either to force the BB line to pass through the point of equilibrium by constraining its elements or make a third variable endogenous. The candidate variables are the exchange rate and the money supply . The three options correspond to three different international trade regimes; we shall discuss each in turn.

---

[4] This statement should be qualified. An increase in the exchange rate (devaluation, depreciation) would improve the trade balance if the Marshall-Lerner condition is satisfied, that is, if the sum of the elasticities of imports and exports with respect to the exchange rate is greater than one. The subject, however, is outside the purview of this book and the reader is referred to books on international economics, for example, Giancarlo Gandolfo (2002), Chap. 7.

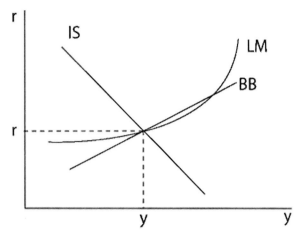

Fig. 5.3 Simultaneous internal and external balance

Fixed Exchange Rates with Capital and Foreign Exchange Controls

During the Bretton Woods regime, exchange rates were fixed and many countries had restrictions on the movement of capital out of the country. Some countries had a balance of trade surplus and some had a deficit. Those who had a surplus were content to accumulate foreign assets, for instance, West Germany. But the deficit countries had to find a way to eliminate their deficit.

Most countries, in addition to capital controls, had restrictions, sometimes quite elaborate, on the purchase and sale of foreign currencies. There were licenses and quotas on imports, requirements of repatriation of foreign currency for the exporters, and limits on how much of a foreign currency travelers could purchase. Still many countries faced a temporary or long term deficit in their current accounts. Under the provisions of the Bretton Woods system, countries facing a temporary deficit could borrow from the International Monetary Fund (IMF) to cover their deficit and hopefully pay back when the situation was reversed and the country experienced a surplus.

But if the deficit persisted the country had to resort to devaluation. Such a move would lower prices of home goods in the international market and increase prices of foreign goods in the domestic market. As a result exports increased and import decreased leading to an improvement in the current account. To elaborate, consider Fig. 5.4. Internal balance is achieved at the point of the intersection of IS and LM curves with the combination of Y_1 and r_1. But this point is below the BB curve signifying a current account deficit. In other words, the internal equilibrium is attained at the expense of external deficit. Devaluation of the currency would move the BB curve down to BB' eliminating the deficit.

The process works as follows: devaluation increases exports and decreases imports leading to an improvement in the balance of trade. But such an improvement causes an increase in income (recall the national income identity where net exports

Fig. 5.4 Devaluation of
currency to eliminate current
account deficit

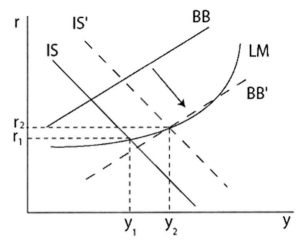

is a component of the GDP). Equilibrium is reached at the point of Y_2 and r_2, where both income and the rate of interest are higher than when only internal equilibrium was obtained. The case of currency revaluation is depicted in Fig. 5.5.

Fig. 5.5 Revaluation of
currency to eliminate current
account surplus

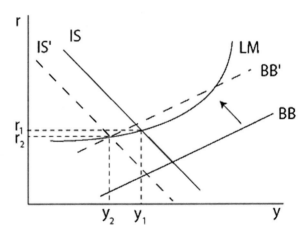

Monetary and Fiscal Policies Under Capital Mobility

In Chap. 1 we discussed the effects of monetary and fiscal policy in a closed economy. The effects of these policies are somewhat different in an open economy and we need to modify our analysis. In the previous section we assumed that all countries exercised capital control. As a result there was a need to balance the current account. This required foreign exchange controls and at times exchange rate adjustments in the form of devaluation and revaluation.

We shall relax this assumption now and allow capital movement between countries. Under such a regime a discrepancy between the interest rates in two countries would result in the movement of capital from the low to high interest country. In principle the inflow and outflow of capital between countries will continue until the interest rates are equalized. Alternatively, we can characterize the system as one for which current account imbalance is a normal occurrence. Normally, continuous current account surplus does not pose a significant problem for a country except that it will come under pressure to appreciate its currency. During the Bretton Woods system, West Germany ran a positive current account for a period of time. In recent years Japan and now China have accumulated large sums of foreign currencies through exports. But aside from the United States no country can run a current account deficit for a long time and expect other countries to buy its financial assets. The United States is an exception, at least for the time being, because the dollar is the international currency and because of its enormous economic power.

In the following analysis we shall abstract from the long term problem of running a current account deficit or surplus. Our comparative static analysis is concerned with comparing the internal and external equilibrium before the policy is put into effect and after all adjustments necessitated by the policy are completed and a new equilibrium is reached. Thus, the country may have a current account deficit or surplus but as long as it stays on the BB line, the external balance conditions are met.

We also need to address the interest sensitivity of the BB curve. If neither the movement of capital F nor import m depends on the rate of interest then the BB curve is a vertical line for any given income level Y. As the sensitivity to interest rate increases, the curve becomes flatter and flatter. In the limit when the domestic rate could not deviate from the international rate, then the BB curve will be a horizontal line at the international rate of interest r^*. In what follows we will assume that the BB line is interest rate sensitive but the elasticity with respect to the interest rate is not infinite. Thus, we shall depict the locus of balance of payments equilibrium as an upward sloping line.

Monetary and fiscal policies have different effects under fixed and flexible exchange rate regimes. In particular, we shall find monetary policy ineffective in raising income under a fixed exchange rate regime but effective under a flexible exchange rate. On the other hand, fiscal policy is effective in increasing income under fixed exchange rates but ineffective under the flexible regime. Therefore, we discuss them separately.

Monetary Policy Under Fixed Exchange Rates

Under the fixed exchange regime, monetary policy is ineffective in increasing income and employment. An expansionary monetary policy results in the loss of foreign reserves for the country. Before describing the process we need to clarify one point regarding the connection between foreign reserves and money supply.

As discussed in Chap. 9 money supply is equal to the product of money multiplier and monetary base. The monetary base itself consists of net foreign assets, net government borrowing, and net commercial banks borrowing from the central bank. Thus, a loss of foreign reserves of the central bank will reduce the amount of money supply. The reader should accept this on faith until Chap. 9 or consult that chapter before going forward.

Now suppose the central bank expands money supply to increase income and employment. An increase in money supply reduces the rate of interest. This leads to higher investment and an increase in income. Given the fact that the exchange rate is fixed an increase in income will lead to an increase in imports without necessarily affecting exports. The result is a deficit in current account. Further, the lowering of the domestic interest rate will bring it below the international rate. Under the conditions of international mobility of capital the gap between the two rates will result in the outflow of capital from the country. The outflow will continue as long as the gap between the two rates persists. As pointed out before, a component of the monetary base is the net foreign assets of the central bank. Outflow of capital will reduce the net foreign assets of the central bank and consequently reduce the monetary base and money supply. The outflow of foreign reserves continues until money supply is reduced to its pre expansion level and the interest rate is equal to the international rate. The reduction in money supply will raise the interest rate, which on the one hand reduces income and on the other closes the gap between the domestic and international rates.

Thus, the economy is back where it started and the only result of the policy is the loss of foreign reserves.

Figure 5.6 illustrates the above process. Suppose the economy is at an internal and external equilibrium point characterized by income Y_1 and the interest rate r_1 which is equal to the international rate r^*. An increase in money supply shifts the LM curve to right, i.e., LM' resulting in a decrease in the interest rate to r_2 which is below the international rate and increases income to Y_2. The new equilibrium is below the BB curve signifying a current account deficit. The disequilibrium

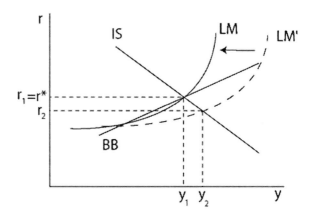

Fig. 5.6 Ineffectiveness of monetary policy under fixed exchange rates

in external balance cannot be remedied through exchange rate depreciation since we have a fixed exchange rate. The result is capital outflow, loss of reserves and a decrease in the money supply. The process continues as long as the domestic interest rate is below the international rate. The process comes to a halt when the economy is back to its old equilibrium.

Fiscal Policy Under Fixed Exchange Rates

Fiscal policy is effective in increasing income and employment. An increase in government spending or a tax cut would increase the demand and, therefore, income and employment. The increase in income will increase demand for imported goods and services, thus causing a current account deficit. On the other hand, the increase in income will also increase the demand for money and consequently its price—the rate of interest. This, in turn, will cause an inflow of capital into the country, thus increasing the foreign reserves of the central bank. As mentioned in the previous section, the monetary base depends on the foreign reserves of the central bank. An increase in the net foreign assets of the central bank increases the monetary base and money supply. The result is a lower rate of interest that brings about the equilibrium at a higher level of income because investment is increased. At the new equilibrium the interest rate is above the original rate but below the rate that brought in foreign capital.

Graphically, the increase in government spending shifts the IS curve to the right and IS′ (Fig. 5.7). The new equilibrium at Y_2 and r_2 is above the BB line signifying surplus in foreign account. Foreign capital will flow in causing the LM curve to move rightward to LM′. The final equilibrium is reached at Y_3 and r_3 where we

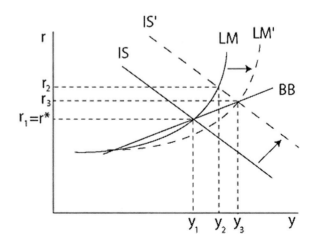

Fig. 5.7 Fiscal policy under fixed exchange rates

observe higher income and interest rate compared to the initial position of the economy. Therefore, fiscal policy is effective in increasing income and employment.

Monetary Policy Under Flexible Exchange Rates

The situation changes when exchange rates are flexible. Today almost all major countries have floating exchange rates and therefore our analysis in this section is more pertinent to the international scene.

An increase in money supply will lower the interest rate and, therefore, increase investment and income. The higher amount of income will raise the demand for both domestic and foreign goods and services thus, causing a current account deficit. Further, a decline in the rate of interest would cause an outflow of capital. All in all, there is a higher demand for foreign currency and a lower supply of it. But now the price of foreign currency, namely the exchange rate, is flexible. It will rise, meaning the domestic currency is depreciated. The depreciation continues until the external equilibrium is restored and supply of and demand for foreign currency are equal.

But the depreciation also cuts the amount of imports because foreign goods and services have become more expensive, and increases the amount of exports because domestic goods and services are cheaper for foreigners. The increase in exports also boosts income. Thus, the final equilibrium is reached at a higher level of income and a lower rate of interest; monetary policy is effective.

Graphically, an increase in money supply shifts the LM curve to the right (LM'). Now the equilibrium is at Y_2 and r_2, which is below the BB line. Thus, we have a deficit in the balance of payments. The deficit causes the depreciation of the domestic currency. As a result the BB curve moves downward to BB'. At the same time the IS curve is moved rightward to IS'. The new equilibrium is reached at a higher income level, lower rate of interest and higher value of foreign currency.

In the case of perfect capital mobility, the depreciation continues as long as there is a discrepancy between domestic and foreign rates of interests. Therefore, the final equilibrium is obtained at the old interest rate with an increase in income and a depreciation of the domestic currency. This is the case depicted in Fig. 5.8.

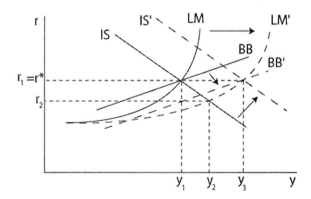

Fig. 5.8 Monetary policy under flexible exchange rates

Fiscal Policy Under Flexible Exchange Rates

Fiscal policy under flexible exchange rate is less effective than under fixed exchange rate. Indeed, under perfect capital mobility, when the domestic and international rates of interest are equal, fiscal policy is ineffective.

Consider an economy with internal and external equilibrium. An expansionary fiscal policy—increase in spending or reduction of taxes—will increase aggregate demand and income. The higher income leads to increased demand for money and a rise in the price of money, i.e., the rate of interest. The higher rate of interest increases the capital inflow. This inflow is, of course, diminished to some extent by an increase in demand for imports. But overall there will be a surplus in the balance of payments which will push the exchange rate downward, that is, the domestic currency will appreciate. The reduction of net exports due to the appreciation of the currency will cause a decline in aggregate demand, negating the early rise in income. Thus, the final equilibrium is characterized by moderately higher income, higher interest rate, and an appreciated currency.

Under perfect capital mobility, the fall of the foreign exchange rate will continue until the domestic and foreign interest rates are equal. Under those circumstances, income has to retract to its initial position. It is perhaps easier to see this more graphically. As a result of expansionary fiscal policy the IS curve shifts to the right but the LM curve stays put. The new equilibrium point has to be on the unchanged LM. Now if r returns to its original value, perforce Y has to return to its initial value as well.

An expansionary fiscal policy shifts the IS curve to the right resulting in r_2 and Y_2 point. The new equilibrium is above the BB curve, signifying an external surplus. The result is an appreciation of the domestic currency which shifts the BB curve upward and the IS curve leftward. The new equilibrium is reached at r_3 and Y_3 (Fig. 5.9).

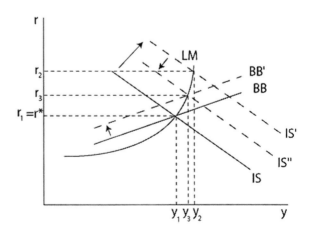

Fig. 5.9 Fiscal policy under flexible exchange rates

The Preeminence of Monetary Policy in the 21st Century

The recent decade has witnessed the process of globalization. More and more economies are connected. This on the one hand has resulted in the preeminence of monetary policy. On the other hand, the connection between economies, unification of financial markets, and the role of interest rates in international flow of capital necessitate some kind of coordination mechanism between central banks. Globalization also requires a stable international currency, perhaps a single world currency. We shall return to these themes in Chaps. 12 and 13.

Chapter 6
The Collapse of Post-War International Economic Order

> *I have directed Secretary Connally to suspend temporarily the convertibility of the dollar into gold or other reserve assets except in amounts and conditions determined to be in the interest of monetary stability and in the best interests of the United States.*
> President Richard Nixon speech of August 15, 1971.
>
> *Good old Watson! You are the one fixed point in a changing age,*
> Sherlock Holmes to Dr. John H. Watson in "His Last Bow."

A New Economic Policy

Throughout history a handful of people can claim that they have changed the world; President Richard Nixon is one of them. Politically one can cite his trip to China. Economically one can cite his epoch making speech of August 15, 1971. The President addressed the nation to announce that "the time has come for a new economic policy for the United States." The goal is "prosperity without war." In particular, "we must create more and better jobs; we must stop the rise in the cost of living; we must protect the dollar from the attacks of international money speculators." To achieve the three goals the following policies were to be implemented.

On the problem of unemployment and job creation, the President said: "Two million workers have been released from the armed forces and defense plants because of our success in winding down the war in Vietnam.[1] Putting those people back to work is one of the challenges of peace." Therefore,

I shall ask the Congress when it reconvenes after its summer recess to consider as its first priority the enactment of the Job Development Act of 1971. I will propose to provide the strongest short-term incentive in our history to invest in new machinery and equipment that will create new jobs for Americans: a 10 per cent job development credit for one year effective as of today with a 5 per cent credit after August 15, 1972.

---

[1] Although the US reduced its troops in Vietnam and was winding down its involvement, the war dragged on until the spring of 1975 when Saigon fell to Communist forces.

K. Dadkhah, *The Evolution of Macroeconomic Theory and Policy*,
DOI 10.1007/978-3-540-77008-4_6, © Springer-Verlag Berlin Heidelberg 2009

Second, I will propose to repeal the 7 per cent excise tax on automobiles effective today. This will mean a reduction in price of about $200 per car.

Third, I propose to speed up the personal-income-tax exemptions scheduled for January 1, 1973, to January 1, 1972, so that taxpayers can deduct an extra $50 for each exemption one year earlier than planned.

I have directed the Secretary of the Treasury to recommend to the Congress in January new tax proposals for stimulating research and development of new industries and new techniques.

To offset the loss of revenue from these tax cuts, which directly stimulate new jobs, I have ordered today a $4.7 billion cut in Federal spending. I have ordered a postponement of pay raises and a 5 per cent cut in Government personnel. I have ordered a 10 per cent cut in foreign economic aid. In addition, since the Congress has already delayed action on two of the great initiatives of this Administration, I will ask Congress to amend my proposals to postpone the implementation of revenue sharing for three months and welfare reform for one year.

To combat inflation, he noted that

One of the cruelest legacies of the artificial prosperity produced by war is inflation. Inflation robs every American, every one of you. The 20 million who are retired and living on fixed incomes—they are particularly hard hit. From the high point of 6 per cent a year in 1969, the rise in consumer prices has been cut to 4 per cent in the first half of 1971. . . . We must do better than that. The time has come for decisive action—action that will break the vicious circle of spiraling prices and costs.

I am today ordering a freeze on all prices and wages throughout the United States for a period of 90 days. In addition I call upon corporations to extend the wage-price freeze to all dividends. I have today appointed a Cost-of-Living Council within the Government. I have directed this council to work with leaders of labor and business to set up the proper mechanism for achieving continued price and wage stability after the 90-day freeze is over. Let me emphasize two characteristics of this action. First, it is temporary. . . . Second, while the wage-price freeze will be backed by Government sanctions, if necessary, it will not be accompanied by the establishment of a huge price-control bureaucracy. I am relying on the voluntary cooperation of all Americans—each of you: workers, employers, consumers—to make this freeze work.

Finally, on the most important issue of protecting the dollar President Nixon said:

In recent weeks, the speculators have been waging an all-out war on the American dollar. . . . Accordingly, I have directed the Secretary of the Treasury to take action necessary to defend the dollar against the speculators. I directed Secretary Connally to suspend temporarily the convertibility of the dollar into gold or other reserve assets except in amounts and conditions determined to be in the interest of monetary stability and in the best interests of the United States.

I am taking one further step to protect the dollar, to improve our balance of payments and to increase jobs for Americans. As a temporary measure I am today imposing an additional tax of 10 per cent on goods imported into the United States.

Thus, the proposed policy consisted of three parts: tax incentives to boost output and employment with concurrent cuts in spending; a temporary incomes policy, that is, a 90 day wage and price control to combat inflation; imposition of a 10% additional tax on imported goods, and closing the gold window, which was expected to result in the devaluation of the dollar. The most important part was the last which

Fig. 6.1 Monthly unemployment rate

effectively amounted to scrapping the Bretton Woods Agreement. The decision had far reaching implications and in the years to come would transform the world economy.

The question is why the United States adopted such policies. To begin with, while inflation had steadily declined since the beginning of the year (Fig. 6.1), there was a genuine fear of inflation. On August 1, the United Steelworkers of America overwhelmingly approved a three year contract that stipulated a 30% wage increase, thus averting a strike. On August 2, the United Transportation Union and railroads reached an agreement that ended a long and damaging strike. The Union agreed to some concessions and received a 42% increase in wages over a 42-month contract. In both instances the Administration had intervened to bring the two sides together. The settlements entailed wage increases that brought with them the fear of inflation. In particular an increase in steel price had followed the steel settlement. The President was under pressure to institute some kind of incomes policy. The Administration did not like that and the Treasury Secretary and the Chairman of the Council of Economic Advisers had spoken against it. Thus, a temporary and voluntary and hence toothless wage and price control was the compromise.

The economy was coming out of a recent recession that had lasted 11 months and had ended in November 1970. Over the 10 months ending in August 1971 unemployment rate had stayed constant at about 6% (Fig. 6.2). The doldrums could not continue. Clearly something had to be done; hence the measures to stimulate investment and increase employment. The tax cuts including income tax, investment tax, and automobile tax would stimulate the economy. The cut in expenditures announced to show fiscal conservatism was basically illusory. Indeed, as Paul Samuelson noted at the time, if both taxes and expenditures are cut dollar for dollar, then not a single job would be created.

Fig. 6.2 Monthly inflation rate

Similarly, the incomes policy was only meant as a window dressing. First, the inflation rate was falling and second, wage and price controls do not work,[2] let alone a toothless one that has no enforcing machinery behind it.[3]

The issues of inflation and unemployment notwithstanding, the real problem was the United State balance of trade. The balance of trade had turned negative in the second quarter of 1971 and there were indications that it would stay negative in the third quarter and beyond. Indeed, the trade balance turned positive only in the second quarter of 1973 (Table 6.1 and Fig. 6.3).

The Bretton Woods system was based on the dollar and on fixed exchange rates. The system would work fine as long as (1) the value of the dollar could be maintained and other countries were willing to accept it, and (2) there was little need for adjustment of parities, or if it was needed, countries would be willing to devalue or revalue. For two decades these conditions held and indeed the system worked well and international trade expanded. But both features of the system could potentially cause problems. First, there was the fundamental problem of adjustment. Countries with a trade deficit had to devalue their currencies. The move on the one hand had an unfounded stigma attached to it[4] and on the other it signified that past economic policies were wrong or had failed. For countries that had a surplus the revaluation meant increasing the price of exports and reducing the cost of imports. This would have negative consequences for the economy. The impact would be worse for nations such as West Germany that were more dependent on exports.

---

[2] Wage and price controls have a long and undignified history. See Robert Schuettinger and Eamonn Butler (1979).

[3] It is interesting to note the conservative *Economist* at the time was advocating an incomes policy noting that "all advanced countries need to bring an incomes policy into effect" (August 21, 1971).

[4] It still has. Witness all the talk about the "weakening" of a currency.

Table 6.1 Quarterly balance of trade of the United States

Year	Quarter	Exports	Imports	Surplus or deficit (−)
1968	I	10,814	10,793	21
	II	11,260	11,041	219
	III	11,784	11,741	43
	IV	11,688	11,717	−29
1969	I	10,352	10,618	−266
	II	12,819	12,830	−11
	III	12,645	12,748	−103
	IV	13,404	12,937	467
1970	I	13,493	13,036	457
	II	14,389	13,456	933
	III	14,290	13,764	526
	IV	14,468	14,132	336
1971	I	14,968	14,324	644
	II	14,965	15,481	−516
	III	15,520	16,032	−512
	IV	14,224	15,142	−918
1972	I	16,306	17,674	−1,368
	II	15,851	17,482	−1,631
	III	16,985	18,117	−1,132
	IV	18,082	19,391	−1,309
1973	I	20,053	20,898	−845
	II	21,940	21,909	31
	III	23,416	22,323	1,093
	IV	25,832	24,212	1,620

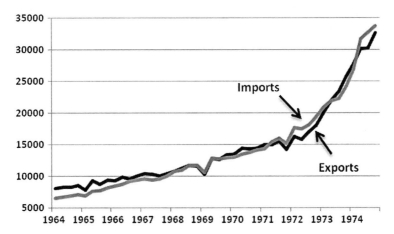

Fig. 6.3 Quarterly exports and imports of goods and services

Thus, in both trade deficit and trade surplus countries the governments were asked to do what was the job of the market. They had to initiate market adjustment moves, with negative consequences, and be blamed for them.

The value of dollar would be no problem as long as the United States had a trade surplus or other countries were willing to accept the dollar. For instance, in the early 1950s the US had payment deficits but other nations were happy to accept the dollar for their reserves.

But the expansionary policies of the 1960s, which led to inflation plus the Vietnam War expenses, resulted in the outflow of the dollar to an extent that other nations were not willing to accept. What made the situation critical were the trade deficit and the realization that the situation could get worse. Hence the dollar had to devalue which meant it had to be decoupled from gold.

In his speech President Nixon implied that currencies of some countries were undervalued and it was hurting the US. The import tax was to counter that unfairness and would be removed when the playing field was leveled. He also noted that the devaluation of the dollar resulting from closing the gold window would slightly reduce the buying power of the dollar abroad, but would not have any effect on domestic prices.

The fact of the matter was that the dollar had to devalue to hopefully eliminate the trade deficit. But the decision had far reaching consequences; it changed the world monetary system. We shall return to this issue below.

The Aftermath

The stock market reacted positively. Despite misgivings about the wage price freeze and the devaluation of the dollar, the tax package was thought to give a boost to the economy. The Dow Jones Industrials registered significant gains. In particular stocks of auto companies General Motors and Ford Motor went up.

Commentators detected a note of nationalism and unilateralism in the decision to sever the connection of the dollar to gold and the imposition of an import tax. The *Wall Street Journal*'s editorial for August 17, 1971 was critical of the rhetoric of the president. *The Journal* worried if the Administration did indeed think as it talked: "If the President and his advisers really think that the present troubles of the dollar are to be blamed on anonymous speculators and on general terms of trade that have treated the United States unfairly, the problems of putting the monetary system back together again could be greatly enlarged." "There is nothing wrong with having greater flexibility in currency parities; in fact, we believe it is desirable. But it must be evident that the more flexible system is a result of cooperative management and not a by-product of conflict and disagreement." Similarly, the *Economist* (August 21, 1971) detected "a distinct and important note of nationalism in President Nixon's announcement of the severing of the link between the dollar and gold."

The *Journal* believed that evidence of discord among the nations could create uncertainty, which in turn would affect international trade. That in turn would damage the economies of the countries that are dependent on international trade such as England, Germany, and Japan. "By combining the dollar move with a 10% import charge, plus a 'buy-America' requirement as a condition of the 10% investment tax credit to industry, the President may have dealt too heavy a blow to the nation's partners."

The *Journal* (August 17, 1971) noted, however, that these were temporary and that the Administration had dispatched Paul Volcker, the Under Secretary of Treasury, to London in order to confer with foreign money men. It seems that the *Journal* was fuzzy about the future international monetary system. "What most likely will emerge is something very much resembling what has existed in the past, with the dollar remaining as the base, with some new parities for major currencies but without a link to gold, which was partly a fiction anyway."

But gradually the idea of flexible exchange rates was being discussed. The *Journal* (August 19, 1971) noted the dollar had been under pressure and the dollar had to float freely. Moreover, the Western nations were to forge a new international monetary system and "if the new arrangement is to have much chance of success, it will have to include more flexibility than its predecessor." But even in August 21 the *Economist* hadn't got the message that the era of Bretton Woods was over and the world would have a new system of flexible exchange rates. Instead it kept harking at the idea of the devaluation of the dollar.

Whether or not people, policy makers, and the media saw it or not, the Bretton Woods era had come to an end. The international monetary system entered a new age in which nothing was fixed. Indeed, from now on all economic variables would display much more volatility than before.

The End of Bretton Woods

For 26 years the world had lived with fixed exchange rates. It had been a nice ride; international trade had expanded, and the advanced economies had experienced stability and prosperity. Developing countries too had had impressive economic growth and improvement in their standards of living. But all things good or bad come to an end. The Bretton Woods era was over.

In Chap. 2 we noted that every international monetary system has four components: an international currency, the mechanism by which exchange rates are determined, a central authority to manage the system and if necessary back the currency, and a mechanism for correcting disequilibrium. In the post Bretton Woods system, the international money became the dollar (but with no connection to gold or any other commodity). Exchange rates would be determined by market forces and through the interaction of supply of and demand for each currency. The managing authority was now the market backed by the United States economic might. Any disequilibrium will be reflected in the supply of and demand for a currency. Thus, the disequilibrium would be corrected by market forces which would balance the supply of and demand for each currency. Currencies of countries with trade deficit would depreciate and those of countries with surplus would appreciate.

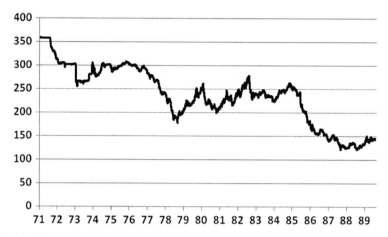

Fig. 6.4 Daily exchange rate of Japanese yen per dollar

While today we are accustomed to this system and take it for granted, it took people, the business and financial community, and politicians some time to get used to it. It took time to get used to ups and downs in foreign exchange markets instead of dealing with fixed exchange rates.

To be sure the dollar started a downward trend against major currencies, for instance the Japanese yen and the German mark (Figs. 6.4 and 6.5). Economic variables had to adjust to these realities (see the discussion regarding oil prices below). The situation was further complicated because in the past 26 years everything had been kept in place by thwarting, to some extent, the market forces. Now these forces were asserting themselves with a vengeance.

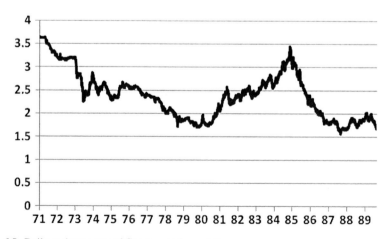

Fig. 6.5 Daily exchange rate of German mark per dollar

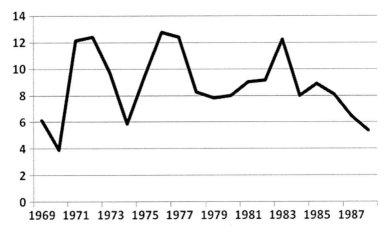

Fig. 6.6 Annual growth of M2 in the United States

In November 1973 the US economy went into a recession which lasted until March 1975. The date is significant since the recession started before the oil price increase. But despite the change in circumstances old remedies were applied. Money supply was increased. Indeed, between August 1971 and December 1979, money supply (M1) increased by more than 60% and M2 more than doubled. Figure 6.6 shows annual growth rate of M2 from 1969 to 1989. In the years 1971 and 1972 as well as 1976 and 1977, the growth rates were above 12%. It is no wonder that the United States and most of the world experienced an inflationary period.

Milton Friedman and Flexible Exchange Rates

Long before President Nixon ended the Bretton Woods Agreement and ushered in the era of flexible exchange rates, Milton Friedman had persuasively argued for flexible exchange rates.[5] He noted that for a market economy and a free trade system to bring its utmost benefits exchange rates have to be allowed to float freely.

Exchange rates are relative prices and like all other prices have to be determined by the market. To illustrate consider the price of oil in the United State and in Europe. The price in the dollar was about $90 per barrel at the end of 2007. In the euro the price was about €60. The two prices imply that one euro should be traded for 1.50 dollars. The price of the euro or any other currency is determined by supply of and demand for that currency, which depend on all other relative prices. Allowing the market to freely determine the exchange rates will eliminate any excess demand or supply. Thus, monetary and fiscal authorities would be able to base their decisions on domestic conditions without worrying about balance of payments consequences.

---

[5] Milton Friedman (1953a).

On the other hand, only by accident, and then only for a short period could a fixed exchange rate bring about market equilibrium for a currency. Sooner or later changes in economic circumstances would result in either excess demand or excess supply. Policy makers have two choices: to institute controls and quotas or tailor their domestic policies to maintain external equilibrium (see Chap. 5). Either way fixed exchange rates would be an impediment to economic health and prosperity.

Controls and quotas are detrimental to free flow of goods and services. Also if the price of foreign currency is below its equilibrium value, it will engender a shortage of that currency. This in turn could create a black market for the currency and, with it, the concomitant corruption.

Alternatively, monetary and fiscal authorities may have to adjust their policies to attain and maintain external equilibrium. The restriction on monetary and fiscal policies would hamper the achievement of domestic goals such as price stability or reducing unemployment rate. When exchange rates are market determined the government need not worry about the external balance and can concentrate on its domestic objectives.

The Oil Shocks

The decade of 1970s was an eventful time. The 1973 Arab-Israeli War, Watergate and the resignation of Richard Nixon, the end of Vietnam War, Anwar Sadat's trip to Israel, and the Iranian revolution are only a sample of the most important events. But perhaps the economic events that will be remembered from that era are the oil shocks of 1974 and 1979 (Fig. 6.7).

Before talking about the shocks, however, we need to clarify what we mean by the price of oil. There are many prices of oil depending on their quality and the

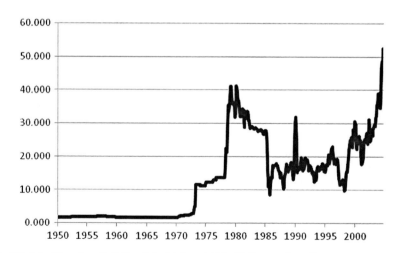

Fig. 6.7 Monthly price of oil: Saudi Arabia's arab light (dollars per barrel)

place of delivery. Based on its chemical content oil is classified as light, medium, heavy, and extra heavy. The light crude, also called sweet, is more desirable. The classification is based on the API of the oil which is computed using the special gravity of the crude. The industry defines oil as light if its API is more than $31.1°$, medium if it is between $22.3°$ and $31.1°$, heavy if it is between $22.3°$ and $10°$. If the API is less than $10°$ oil is classified as extra heavy. Thus, the lighter the oil the higher is its price.

To illustrate, consider three average oil prices. In January 2005 Iran light with API of $34°$ and delivery at Kharg Island in the Persian Gulf was \$39.87 per barrel, Arab light with the same API but delivery FOB at Ras Tanura in Saudi Arabia was \$38.26, and West Texas Intermediate with the API of $39.6°$ and delivery in Cushing Oklahoma was \$46.85. The oil price quoted in the media usually refers to WTI. Trade of WTI contracts in the New York Mercantile Exchange (NYMEX) started in April 1983.[6] Thus, in order to speak of oil prices during the 1970s we need to choose another crude but remembering that all crude prices are related and move together. For our purpose we have chosen the Arab light with API of $34°$ FOB delivery in Ras Tanura in Saudi Arabia.

For a long period of time oil prices had stayed constant.[7] From September 1960 to January 1971 the price of Arab light had stayed constant at \$1.80 per barrel. Even then the change was very slight, and in August of that year when the connection between the dollar and gold was severed it was \$2.86 per barrel. But in the new era of changing exchange rates all prices were in flux and oil prices were no exception. What makes the analysis somewhat complicated is that the Yom Kippur war started in September 1973 and the Arab oil producers decided on an oil embargo against the United States for its support of Israel. Thus, it has become the received wisdom that the Organization of Oil Exporting Countries (OPEC), characterized as an oil cartel, engineered the price increase. The facts of the case are somewhat different. But first, let us learn something about OPEC.

OPEC

The Organization of Petroleum Exporting Countries (OPEC) was formed in September 1960 at the Baghdad Conference by five oil exporting countries: Iran, Iraq, Kuwait, Saudi Arabia, and Venezuela. Later on, Qatar (1961), Indonesia, Libya (1962), the United Arab Emirate[8] (1967), Algeria (1969), Nigeria (1971), Ecuador

---

[6] See Kamran Dadkhah (1992), pp. 207–219.

[7] To understand the oil business the reader could do no better than to start with Daniel Yergin (1991).

[8] In 1967 Abu Dhabi joined the Organization. In the early 1970s the seven states on the Persian Gulf: Abu Dhabi, Ajman, Dubai, Fujairah, Ras al-Khaimah, Sharjah, and Umm al-Quwain formed the United Arab Emirates (UAE). In 1974 the UAE replaced Abu Dhabi in the OPEC.

(1973)[9], Gabon (1975–1994), and Angola (2007) joined the Organization. Since 1965 the OPEC Secretariat has been located in Vienna, Austria.

While sometimes it is implied that OPEC has some kind of monopoly in the crude market and can manipulate its price at will, the fact is that OPEC supplies about 37% (slightly more than one thirds) of the world oil crude. What gives OPEC its aura is the reserves of its members. It is estimated that OPEC members hold half of the reserves of crude and natural gas liquids.

The stated goal of the Organization is "to co-ordinate and unify petroleum policies among member countries, in order to secure fair and stable prices for petroleum producers; an efficient, economic and regular supply of petroleum to consuming nations; and a fair return on capital to those investing in industry." However, the main objective has always been to protect the interest of oil producing countries against giant oil companies. In all member countries governments own the oil reserves. Thus, oil policy advocated by each member is dependent on its government's outlook and policies. For this reason the OPEC members do not see eye to eye on every issue. The Organization may try to project a picture of a unified group of countries, but discord on matters of production and pricing has been the norm.

Still it is possible that one or more country be capable of influencing production and price of oil. Such a country needs to have excess capacity so it can increase output and reduce prices and it has to have enough financial reserves to cut output and increase prices without financial hardship at home and its concomitant political risk. In today's world only two countries fit the bill: Saudi Arabia and Russia.

It is convenient to find a culprit and blame economic ills on it. As we saw President Roosevelt blamed "the unscrupulous money changers" and President Nixon the speculators. But if OPEC had the power to determine the price of oil why did it take 13 years to get its act together and increase the price? If it really could keep the price high why did it allow the price to fall so low from 1986 to 1998?

The fact of the matter is that the supply of and demand for oil determine its price. If a nation is serious about energy independence and the environment then the solution is straightforward. Oil prices should be kept high by taxation to curtail demand and encourage the development of alternative sources of energy and technologies that increase energy efficiency.

The Sources of Oil Shocks

To understand the oil shocks of the 1970s we should consider the two episodes separately. The price increase of 1974, however, was a necessary market adjustment. For many years the Bretton Woods Agreement had pinned down the price of gold. Thus, the real value of a barrel of oil in terms of gold remained constant. With the end of the Gold Exchange Standard, the price of Gold rose from around $40 per troy ounce to around $160 in 1974. Other prices had to adjust and oil was one of them.

---

[9]Ecuador suspended its membership in the Organization from December 1992 to December 2007.

Table 6.2 A comparison of post Bretton Woods prices of gold and oil

Year	Price of gold ($ per troy ounce)	Price of crude oil ($ per barrel)	Price of gold / Price of oil
1969	41.51	1.80	23.06
1970	36.41	1.80	20.23
1971	41.25	2.19	18.80
1972	58.60	2.47	23.73
1973	97.81	3.30	29.67
1974	159.74	11.58	13.79
1975	161.49	11.53	14.00
1976	125.32	12.38	10.13
1977	148.31	13.33	11.13
1978	193.55	13.66	14.17
1979	307.50	30.73	10.01
1980	612.56	36.44	16.81
1981	459.64	34.54	13.31
1982	375.91	32.08	11.72
1983	424.00	28.96	14.64
1984	360.66	28.16	12.81
1985	317.66	27.52	11.54
1986	368.24	13.64	27.00
1987	447.95	17.23	26.00
1988	438.31	13.44	32.61

Table 6.2 and Fig. 6.8 show that following the suspension of the dollar convertibility the price of gold increased dramatically. This meant that while in 1971 less than 19 barrels of oil bought one ounce of gold, in 1973 more than 29 barrels were needed. Further, had the price of oil in 1974 stayed at the 1973 level, it would have

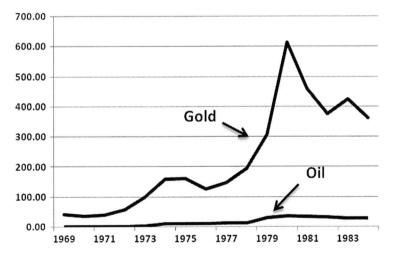

Fig. 6.8 Annual gold and oil prices

taken more than 48 barrels to buy one ounce of gold, and had the price stayed at the 1971 level the number of barrels required would be slightly less than 73.

Thus, adjustment of oil prices was a natural consequence of the end of the Bretton Woods Agreement. But as Figs. 6.7 and 6.8 show the increases in gold and oil prices were dramatic.

The oil shock of 1979 was a political event and was due to the Iranian revolution. As can be seen in Fig. 6.7 the shock was short lived and soon the price of oil returned to its previous level.

Chapter 7
The New Classical Revolt Against Activist Economic Policy

*An expectation acquires explanatory value only if we are made
to understand why people expect what they expect. Otherwise
expectation is a mere deus ex machina that conceals problems
instead of solving them.*
      Joseph Schumpeter, "Review of Keynes's General Theory."

*If, for example, you come at four o'clock in the afternoon, then
at three o'clock I shall begin to be happy. I shall be happier and
happier as the hour advances. ... But if you come at just any
time, I shall never know at what hour my heart is to be ready to
greet you.*
      Antoine de Saint Exupèry, *The Little Prince.*

In the 1970s macroeconomics witnessed a counterrevolution, or perhaps more aptly
an insurgency, against Keynesian orthodoxy. The insurgency targeted the entire Keynesian economics: theory, empirical validity, and policy. The New Classicals argued
that the Keynesian model lacked microfoundations, that is, the posited macro relations had no grounding in microeconomics of optimizing individuals and firms.
They also argued that econometric analysis does not validate Keynesian macro relationships; at best it shows that the reduced form of the Keynesian model corresponds to the data. Worse, the New Classicals argued, Keynesian models do not
perform well against simple time series forecasting models such as Box-Jenkins
method (see below). A consequence of ad hoc modeling is that the estimated relationships are not stable over time. Lucas criticized activist economic policy on the
ground that it is based on a misperception. The policy is based on an estimated
econometric model, which according to Lucas, would not be stable and whose estimated coefficients would change once the policy goes into effect. As a result what
would have been an optimal policy would not be so anymore. We already saw in
Chap. 5 how the Phillips curve on which macroeconomic policy during the 1960s
was based shifted over time. The upshot was that well-intentioned policies resulted
in simultaneous rise of unemployment and inflation. But the *Lucas critique* went
beyond this and extended the instability to all reduced forms.

   New Classicals questioned the effectiveness of Keynesian policies. They claimed
that monetary policy was ineffective unless it was sprung as a surprise on an

K. Dadkhah, *The Evolution of Macroeconomic Theory and Policy*,
DOI 10.1007/978-3-540-77008-4_7, © Springer-Verlag Berlin Heidelberg 2009

unsuspecting public. Any increase or decrease in money supply or government expenditures that are anticipated by the public would not have any effect on real variables such as the GDP.

The New Classicals premised their theories on three pillars: rational expectations, natural rate of unemployment, and instantaneous market clearing in the economy. They should also be credited with explicitly including the stochastic element into economic models. This helped the recent developments in time series analysis to gain wide acceptance and applications in economics. The record of New Classicals, however, is mixed. They had a great impact on the profession of economics: rational expectations, the natural rate, and incorporation of stochastic elements in economic models have all found their way into economic models. But their models as advocated by Lucas, Sargent, Wallace, and Barro have given way to New Keynesian and real business cycles models. The New Classicals had an impact on the environment of economic policy formulation. They definitely helped the Reagan revolution of the 1980s. But their main policy conclusions, that is, the policy ineffectiveness proposition, and the Lucas critique, seem to be topics having the nature of academic curiosity than serious propositions regarding economic policy formulation.

In previous chapters we have discussed the rational expectations hypothesis and the concept of natural rate of unemployment. The idea of instantaneous market clearing proved to be the Achilles' heel of the New Classical models. The concept is well known to economists and can be observed in organized financial markets on a daily basis. But the question is: to what extent is such a concept applicable to the housing market? Or to the labor market for skilled workers such as engineers? Thus, the idea of instantaneous market clearing in the economy or approximating the economy with a Walrasian model is both ludicrous and unproductive.

In this chapter we review the New Classical critic of the Keynesian economy, discuss the main propositions regarding economic policy and make a digression on time series analysis as applied to macroeconomics.

Microfoundations

It is contended that any macro relationship, for instance, consumption, investment, or demand for money functions, should be based on the assumption of optimizing agents. Thus, we should start with a utility function and perhaps a constraint. Optimizing the utility subject to the constraint will result in a behavioral relationship. Aggregating the relationship over all economic agents one gets a macro relationship. Usually it is assumed that all economic agents are identical or equivalently we are dealing with a representative agent, so the macro relationship is the same as the micro.

The New Classicals argued that macro relations in Keynesian models were ad hoc and were not based on micro relationships stemming from behavior of optimizing agents. In other words, Keynesian models did not have microfoundations. Despite their advocacy of microfoundations and the necessity of deriving macro relations from micro behavior of optimizing agents, the New Classicals did not provide such models and did not advance economics along this line. Later Kydland and Prescott building the real business cycles models started from such foundations.

The fact of the matter is that the microfoundations issue is more a matter of rituals than a theoretical exercise. Such models do not end up with a refutable hypothesis that can be subjected to empirical tests. Consider the utility maximization of a consumer subject to a budget constraint. We end up with demand for a product depending on income and the price of all commodities in the utility function. Now suppose that income increases, would that entail an increase in the demand for that product? Not necessarily. If the demand for a product increases, it is called a normal good and if declines it is called an inferior good; so much for a testable hypothesis. On the other hand, would an increase in the price of a good or service reduce its demand? Well, we don't know unless we compensate for the change in income because of the change in price. Thus, the hypothesis is difficult if not impossible to test.

If a theory is to be useful it has to start with verifiable conditions or come up with testable constraints on coefficients or variables of interest. Microeconomic theory does not comply with either condition. What economic theory tells us, however, are that (1) incentives are important, (2) there are constraints facing every decision maker, and (3) there are tradeoffs; you cannot get something for nothing. While these considerations are rather general, they are important in understanding economic conditions and in designing policies. Hence, instead of being hung up on rituals, perhaps it is better to be cognizant of these general guidelines.

Coordination Mechanism

Every economy consists of a very large number of decision makers each making several decisions a day. In an economy such as the United States the number of decisions easily reaches a few billion a day. An important theoretical issue is that, given the limited amount of resources and constraints on the amount of information each decision maker possesses, how are these decisions coordinated and reconciled with each other? One answer is the working of the Walrasian general equilibrium model.[1] Léon Walras (1834–1910), one of the great Neoclassical economists, conceived the idea that the economy coordinates supplies and demands for all goods and services in the same way that a stock market brings about the equality of supply and demand for different stocks by gradually moving (the tatonnement process) toward the equilibrium prices that clear the market. This is the idea of general equilibrium as opposed to partial equilibrium of Alfred Marshall.

---

[1] During the middle years of the twentieth century and all the way to the demise of the former Soviet Union an alternative answer was "central planning." Given the bankruptcy of that idea today, there is no reason to devote any time to discussing it.

The idea of partial equilibrium is that in each market, given initial endowments of the participants, the price of a good or service adjusts to equilibrate supply and demand of that product. The general equilibrium theory extends this to all goods and services whose prices adjust to bring about simultaneous equilibrium of supplies and demands in all markets.

As a metaphor for understanding the interdependence of different markets whether they are in or out of equilibrium the Walrasian theory is useful. If we understand it as a description of a long run process according to which markets tend toward equilibrium and large deviations would set in motion correcting mechanism, again Walrasian general equilibrium is beneficial. But that is all. On the negative side, during the second half of the twentieth century a large number of economists wasted their time and talents elaborating on a theory that could only be applied to lalaland. Any time the enterprise was questioned the standard answer was that the model was in the process of being developed and it provides "insight" in the working of the economy.

The New Classicals took the general equilibrium scheme too seriously and based their theory and policy recommendations on instantaneous market clearing. This was in contrast to the Keynesian premise that due to many imperfections in the market, equilibrium may not be attained and even if it attained may not be at full employment. In particular, issues of downward rigidity of wages, monopolistic powers, incomplete information, and gestation period to increase supply (as in skilled manpower, housing, and other markets) were central to Keynesian theory. Due to these imperfections the economy would be in disequilibrium and the process of groping for equilibrium may be lengthy. Furthermore, the corrective mechanisms may not always work or worse they may work in a perverse way. For instance, a drop in aggregate demand may cause layoffs which in turn will reduce demand further. Or an increase in price of certain items may cause panic or hoarding which would aggravate the situation. Thus, general equilibrium may be a long run and somewhat elusive destination.

The New Classicals did not address these issues. They simply assumed away market imperfections and premised their theory on instantaneous market clearing and general equilibrium.

While one cannot accept the New Classicals market clearing at face value, it was perhaps a good antithesis against the Keynesians disregard of market forces. It seemed at times that many Keynesians believed that markets and the price system would not work. Government intervention was needed at all times. Somehow bureaucrats knew better than all the market participants. The New Classicals broke this myth. Neither assuming market clearing at all times nor assuming that markets do not work and government intervention is needed at all times are plausible postulates. The issue is which one do we take as norm and which as exception. Something like whether we assume everyone is innocent till proven guilty or we assume everyone guilty till proven innocent. The New Classical contribution was to help the Reagan-Thatcher revolution in persuading most of the people that markets work unless there is evidence that something is amiss and government intervention is needed.

Empirical Validity of the Keynesian Model

The attack on the empirical validity of the Keynesian model progressed in two fronts. First, Keynesians claimed that, with or without microfoundations, their equations forecast macro variables quite well. The validity of a theory is not measured by whether it is derived from some preordained postulates. Rather a theory has to correspond to facts, and the Keynesian model passes this test with flying colors. The New Classicals could not dispute this but they argued that the forecasting ability of the reduced form[2] models do not validate the structural models because a reduced form model could correspond to more than one structural model .

Second, Keynesians had devised large econometric models such as the famous FRB-MIT-PENN model with hundreds of variables and equations. In 1972 Charles Nelson published an article showing that simple ARIMA models would beat these gigantic models. In other words, perhaps there was less information and insight in some Keynesian equations than could be found in a simple time series model.[3]

Below we will discuss the question of identification of structural models from reduced forms. But macroeconomics is intimately tied to time series analysis. Later in this chapter we shall have a brief discussion of time series analysis with reference to its use in macroeconomics. There we should discuss the ARIMA models.

The Identification Problem

Consider the following structural model where y_1 and y_2 are endogenous variables, x and z are exogenous, and u and v stochastic terms.

$$y_1 = \alpha_1 x + \alpha_2 y_2 + u$$
$$y_2 = \beta_1 z + \beta_2 y_1 + v$$

The reduced form for this model would be

$$y_1 = \frac{\alpha_1}{1 - \alpha_2 \beta_2} x + \frac{\alpha_2 \beta_1}{1 - \alpha_2 \beta_2} z + \frac{u + \alpha_2 v}{1 - \alpha_2 \beta_2}$$
$$y_2 = \frac{\alpha_1 \beta_2}{1 - \alpha_2 \beta_2} x + \frac{\beta_1}{1 - \alpha_2 \beta_2} z + \frac{\beta_2 u + v}{1 - \alpha_2 \beta_2}$$

and with obvious change of notation

$$y_1 = \pi_{11} x + \pi_{12} z + \varepsilon_1$$
$$y_2 = \pi_{21} x + \pi_{22} z + \varepsilon_2$$

We cannot consistently estimate the parameters of the structural model directly. But we can consistently estimate the parameters of the reduced form. In the above model both equations are identified; therefore, we can recover the structural

---

[2]See Chap. 3 for a brief discussion of structural and reduced form models.
[3]Charles Nelson(1972), pp. 902–917.

parameters from the estimated reduced form parameters. The estimates thus obtained are consistent because they are functions of consistent estimates. For instance,

$$\hat{\alpha}_2 = \frac{\hat{\pi}_{12}}{\hat{\pi}_{22}}, \text{ and } \hat{\beta}_2 = \frac{\hat{\pi}_{21}}{\hat{\pi}_{11}}$$

and once we have $\hat{\alpha}_2$ and $\hat{\beta}_2$, estimation of $\hat{\alpha}_1$ and $\hat{\beta}_1$ would be straightforward.

$$\hat{\alpha}_1 = \pi_{11} - \hat{\pi}_{21}\frac{\hat{\pi}_{12}}{\hat{\pi}_{22}} \text{ and } \hat{\beta}_1 = \hat{\pi}_{22} - \hat{\pi}_{12}\frac{\hat{\pi}_{21}}{\hat{\pi}_{11}}$$

But the problem is that the reduced form of the following model would also be the same as the above reduced form:

$$y_1 = \alpha_1 z + \alpha_2 y_2 + u$$
$$y_2 = \beta_1 x + \beta_2 y_1 + v$$

Thus, is $\hat{\alpha}_1$ the effect of x on y_1 or the effect of z on the same variable? The New Classicals argued that the identification of α_1 is obtained by excluding z from the first equation. But since this exclusion (and the exclusion of x from the second equation) has no basis in economic theory, the fact that estimated coefficients correspond to the Keynesian stipulation does not confirm the Keynesian model. Indeed, since based on economic theory we cannot easily exclude any variable from any equation, the forecasting ability of an equation cannot be taken as evidence for the validity of any theory.

The New Classical Criticism of Keynesian Policies

The New Classicals' objections to the activist policies advocated by Keynesians had already been made by others notably by Keynes's contemporaries whom he referred to as classicals and by Milton Friedman. What Lucas, Sargent, Wallace, Barro and others brought to the table was restating these criticisms in mathematical and technical form and with reference to the stochastic nature of economic processes.

Policy Ineffectiveness

The policy ineffectiveness debate that raged among economists for a time could best be characterized as much ado about nothing. The debate started with the 1976 paper by Sargent and Wallace.[4] What readers and the profession took from that paper—something perhaps the authors did not intend—was that monetary policy was ineffective in affecting aggregate output and income. Sargent and Wallace were concerned with the optimality of monetary policy that followed a set rule—as

---

[4]Thomas Sargent and Neil Wallace (1976).

Milton Friedman had proposed—and the policy rule based on considering all possible information regarding the economy—as advocated by Paul Samuelson. They start by noting that "it is widely agreed that monetary policy should obey a rule, that is, a schedule expressing the setting of the monetary authority's instrument (e.g., the money supply) as a function of all the information it has received up through the current moment." Thus, "if by remote chance, the same circumstances should prevail at two different dates, the appropriate settings for monetary policy would be identical."

As a preliminary exercise they posit the following model:

$$y_t = \gamma_0 + \gamma_1 m_t + \gamma_2 y_{t-1} + u_t$$
$$m_t = g_0 + g_1 y_{t-1}$$

where y_t is the deviation of real GDP form potential GDP, m_t the rate of growth of money supply , and u_t is white noise. Note that the first equation maintains that the output gap depends on output gap in the previous period and the rate of growth of money supply. The second equation is the policy rule followed by the central bank. Specifically, the rate of growth of money supply is determined by the output gap in the previous period. If the above model characterizes the economy and if the objective of the central bank is to minimize the variance of y, then g_0 and g_1 could be set in such a way to achieve this goal. Under such circumstances Friedman's rule would not be optimal.

But now suppose that the economy is characterized by the following model

$$y_t = \gamma_0 + \gamma_1 \left[m_t - E(m_t|\Omega_{t-1}) \right] + \gamma_2 y_{t-1} + u_t$$
$$m_t = g_0 + g_1 y_{t-1} + \varepsilon_t$$

It follows that

$$E(m_t|\Omega_{t-1}) = g_0 + g_1 y_{t-1}$$

where $E(m_t|\Omega_{t-1})$ is the conditional expectation of m given all the information available at time $t-1$, all variables are as defined before, and ε_t is also white noise.

Sargent and Wallace engage in some algebraic manipulations, which could potentially confuse the reader, but most importantly confused the authors themselves. They conclude that the "proof of the inferiority of a rule without feedback is fallacious. The argument for the 'look at everything, respond to everything' view is correspondingly vitiated." Thus, "the simple model above is one in which there is no scope for the authority to conduct countercyclical policy by suitably choosing g_0 and g_1 so as to minimize the variance of y." But if we substitute m_t and its conditional expectations in the first equation of the model, we shall have:

$$y_t = \gamma_0 + \gamma_1 \varepsilon_t + \gamma_2 y_{t-1} + u_t$$

Thus, by assumption, money supply does not figure in the equation so the conclusion is not surprising. Note that in mathematics one cannot deduce something that is not already in the formula. Sargent and Wallace first assume that only the unanticipated growth of money appears in the GDP equation, that is, only a white noise ε affects y. Since a white noise can neither be anticipated nor manipulated, they conclude that policy is ineffective. This resembles a magician who does not put a rabbit in the hat and then is surprised that the hat does not produce a rabbit. If money supply is not in the equation then it cannot possibly have any effect on the output gap. In other words, they *assume* that policy is ineffective.

Perhaps Sargent and Wallace did not mean to say policy is ineffective but only under such circumstances is it ineffective. Thus, the question becomes an empirical issue.

Robert Barro[5] showed that indeed a model where only unexpected rate of growth of money supply affects unemployment and the price level fit the United States data well. Pesaran showed that Barro's conclusion was valid if there were no contenders. Using a test of non-nested hypothesis, Pesaran showed that the Keynesian model in which the actual rate of growth of money supply affects unemployment is superior to the New Classical model.[6]

All in all policy ineffectiveness seems to have been much ado about nothing.

The Lucas Critique

The "Lucas critique" is one those chic phrases that can be dropped in the middle of a discussion with some effect. It is something like the name of a director of the New Wave French cinema or a particular act in an opera. There is no doubt that it has logical validity. There is no doubt either that it served to warn economists from assuming mechanical relationships and basing policies on them. What may be doubted is its empirical and policy significance.

The critique is directed at the theory of economic policy proposed by Jan Tinbergen (1903–1994). The idea is to represent the structure of the economy with a set of equations whose parameters are estimated using past data. An objective function which represents the priorities of the policy makers is agreed upon. For instance, the objective function may have a quadratic form and involve inflation and unemployment rates:

$$W = (u - \bar{u})^2 + \beta(\pi - \pi^*)^2$$

where u and $\bar{u}$ are, respectively, actual and natural rates of unemployment and π and π^* are actual and target rates of inflation.

Minimizing the objective function subject to the constraint of the structure of the economy would determine the time path of the policy variables such as money supply , government expenditures, and the like. Lucas noted that the structure of the economy changes over time and so do the parameters of the model. Moreover, even if the structure and the parameters were constant, econometricians rely on a finite number of past observations to build a model. Such a model may be successful for

---

[5]Robert Barro (1977, 1978).
[6]See Hashem Pesaran (1982). See also Kamran Dadkhah and Santiago Valbuena (1985).

short run forecasting, in particular because forecasters may give a higher weight to more recent observations and adjust constant terms in their equations to reflect recent trends. But such a model would not be appropriate for simulating the effects of a policy change in the long run. Over a long period of time the estimated coefficients will be out of line with "true" parameters and would not be useful in assessing the effects of a policy.

The main objection to the Tinbergen model, however, rests on the instability of the estimated coefficients of reduced form because these coefficients depend on expectations which in turn depend on people's perception of government policies. Once these policies change, expectations change, and therefore coefficients of the model change. Lucas noted that these coefficients are possibly nonlinear functions of the structural model. The latter in turn are dependent on people's and firms' expectations. Now suppose under a particular regime economists estimate the reduced form. A policy is found optimal on the basis of such estimates. But once this policy is put into effect, expectations of consumers and producers change because they are dependent on a certain perception of government policy, which is now changed. Once the expectations are changed, coefficients of structural models change, which in turn change the reduced form coefficients. Thus, the policy which was optimal on the basis of the old coefficients will not be optimal with the new parameters. In Lucas's words, "the features [of econometric models] which lead to success in short-term forecasting are unrelated to quantitative policy evaluation, that the major econometric models are (well) designed to perform the former task only, and that simulations using these models can, in principle, provide *no* useful information as to the actual consequences of alternative economic policies."[7] The cause is the change in the "true" structure of the system as a result of implementing a new policy.

The main example where policy makers relied on a relationship that shifted over time is the case of the Phillips curve and policies based on it (see Chap. 4). But the problem was known and accepted long before Lucas wrote his paper. Lucas gives other examples but none really persuasive.

Consider Friedman's consumption function where permanent consumption c_{pt} is a function of permanent income y_{pt}

$$c_{pt} = k y_{pt}$$

and where the actual or observed values consist of permanent and transitory parts:

$$c_t = c_{pt} + u_t$$
$$y_t = y_{pt} + v_t$$

The permanent income is defined as

$$y_{pt} = (1 - \beta) \sum_{i=0}^{\infty} \beta^i E (y_{t+i} | I_t)$$

---

[7]Robert Lucas (1981), emphasis in the original. The paper was first published in 1976.

where β is the discount factor. Lucas assumes that the actual income consists of three parts: a constant, a sum of independent increments each of which has zero mean and constant variance, and a transitory income:

$$y_t = a + w_t + v_t$$

The minimum variance estimator of y_{t+i} is shown by Muth to be:

$$y_{t+i} = (1 - \lambda) \sum_{j=0}^{\infty} \lambda^j y_{t-j}, \forall i$$

where λ depends on the relative variances of v and w. Substituting this into the consumption function, we get

$$c_t = k(1 - \beta)y_t + k\beta(1 - \lambda) \sum_{j=0}^{\infty} \lambda^j y_{t-j}, + v_t$$

Lucas points out that an econometrician would estimate the above equation using past data on actual consumption and income. Now suppose the model is used for policy evaluation. For example, the policy may entail additions to the income of consumers over an extended period. We can think of several scenarios: (1) every year a fixed amount $\bar{x}$ is added to the consumer income, (2) the addition may be in the form of $\bar{x}a^t, 1 < a < 1/\beta$, or (3) it could be in the form of a sequence of independent random variables with zero mean and constant variance. Lucas shows that the prediction of the estimated model would deviate from the "true" model and, except for the case (1), the two do not converge as t goes to infinity. To illustrate, consider the second case and assume that the consumer knows the policy in advance. Then the "true" change in consumption in t-T would be

$$\Delta c_t = k\bar{x}\frac{(1 - \beta)a^t}{1 - \alpha\beta}$$

But the econometrician estimates it as

$$\Delta c_t = k\bar{x}\left\{(1 - \beta) + \beta(1 - \lambda)\sum_{j=0}^{t-T}\left(\frac{\lambda}{a}\right)^j\right\}a^t$$

and as t tends to infinity the ratio of the forecast to the true effect does not tend to unity.

Lucas also works out an example on taxation and investment demand. But perhaps a better example would have been tax revenues. Consider a government that taxes the citizen at the rate θ, given an aggregate income of y, the total government revenues would be

$$T = \theta y$$

It would be tempting to try to increase the tax rate for all citizens but particularly for higher income groups to collect even more revenues. Suppose the following tax scheme is proposed: (1) all citizens with income below a certain threshold will pay taxes at θ_1 and those above the threshold at the rate θ_2 where both rates are higher than before: $\theta_2 > \theta_1 > \theta$. Further suppose that α is the ratio of the taxpayers with higher income. The estimated revenues with the new scheme would be:

$$T = (1 - \alpha)\theta_1 y + \alpha\theta_2 y = \theta_1 y + \alpha(\theta_2 - \theta_1)y$$

which is clearly much higher than before. But the calculation is based on two assumptions: First, the same amount of income will be generated as before, and second the percentage of individuals with higher income will stay the same. In other words, people do not change their behavior. But they indeed do. First, there will be less incentive to work or invest, and second many higher income individuals may choose to leave the country. The latter has been happening in Europe, particularly France, where the rich and professionals leave the country. This option is not available to Americans since they are taxed on the basis of citizenship rather than residence. Further, those with higher levels of income will find ways to evade taxes or hide their income. The net result most likely would be that in the long run the government would have less revenue.

Here lies the main lesson of the Lucas critique: economic policy cannot be formulated on the basis of mechanical relationships. There are still do-gooders who think that they can change the society using preconceived ideas, that is, they believe in social engineering. For those and anyone who still has an illusion of economics being physics, the Lucas critique is an important antidote. Beyond this the argument of Lucas critique cannot be taken too seriously in formulating actual policies.

The main issue regarding the Lucas critique is its empirical significance. If indeed the only source of deviation of the model from reality was the change in the coefficients of the reduced form due to a change in public perception of policy then we should have been very concerned. Even then, we needed to gauge the extent of the deviation from optimality due to this change. But there are other sources of deviations from reality. First, the model itself is an approximation and like any approximation, it is subject to error and deviation from the actual behavior of the economy. The situation would be worse if through omission of relevant variables, inclusion of irrelevant variables, or the choice of functional form, the model is misspecified. Second the coefficients are estimated and as such they do not necessarily coincide with the "true" parameters. Thus, any policy that may figure optimally for the model may not necessarily be optimal in reality.

Econometric models are constantly updated and they provide valuable benchmarks to assess the effect of policy changes. But it is also important to note that econometric models, while the most important tool, are not the only tool of policy evaluation. A range of sources are consulted for devising and evaluating policies.

The fact of the matter is that researchers have not found empirical evidence to support the Lucas critique. As a result some have resorted to saying that econometric tools may not be able to detect it. It is unfortunate that some economists make a religion or ideology out of economics and therefore show an antagonism to econometrics and indeed any empirical investigation. We shall return to this subject and discuss it extensively in the next chapter.

Time Series Analysis

During the 1970s and 1980s time series analysis gained prominence in econometric analysis. Not only were several new techniques discovered for dealing with times series data, but the outlook and scope of econometrics underwent a revolutionary transformation. Although not specifically a result of the New Classical macroeconomics, the two trends shared so many intersections that it is appropriate to discuss these developments in the present chapter. The techniques and discoveries included the Box-Jenkins or ARIMA method due to George E. P. Box and G. M. Jenkins, causality test proposed by Clive W. J. Granger (Nobel laureate 2003), spurious regression discovered by Granger and Paul Newbold, vector autoregression (VAR) modeling by Christopher Sims, unit root analysis by David A. Dickey and Wayne A. Fuller, and cointegration analysis by Engle (Nobel laureate 2003) and Granger. These are highly specialized subjects requiring detailed mathematical treatment. But even a brief discussion of these developments is well beyond the scope of this book. Here I shall allude to these issues and highlight their influence on the development of macroeconomic theory and policy.

Statistical techniques for the analysis of time series data are different from those of cross section or sample survey data. Statisticians and econometricians have always been cognizant of the special issues related to time series analysis. For instance, the high correlation between two time series may simply be due to trends in the variables involved. Or it is quite natural to suspect serial correlation among the error terms in a regression model involving time series. Hence Durbin-Watson (1950–1951) proposed a statistics to detect serial correlation and Cochrane-Orcutt (1949) and Hildreth-Lu (1960) devised techniques to "correct" for it. But the new techniques proposed in the 1960s onward were not concerned with extending regression analysis to time series data or correcting the least squares methods to be applicable to such cases. Rather they took the viewpoint of how to model and understand time series data.

For ease of exposition in what follows we first talk about modeling stationary time series (to be defined below). As we shall see most economic time series are not stationary. Therefore, we also discuss the tests for stationarity and how to make non-stationary series stationary. Finally, we discuss the modeling of non-stationary series.

Stationary Series and ARIMA Models

Intuitively, a stationary series is such that if we look at any extended segment of its graph it would look like any other segment. In other words, the series do not show trend. Consider the next four graphs of the logarithm of the GDP, its first difference, the logarithm of the CPI, and its first difference (Figs. 7.1 to 7.4) Trends in the original series are quite apparent, while the first difference series are stationary. As can be seen stationary series return to their mean while non-stationary series do not have a mean and they are always increasing (series with positive trend) or declining (when there is a negative trend).

A stationary series y_t has the following properties:

$$E(y_t) = \mu \ \forall t$$

$$E(y_t - \mu)^2 = \sigma^2 \ \forall t$$

$$E(y_t - \mu)(y_s - \mu) = \gamma(t - s) \ \forall t \neq s$$

In other words, the mean and variance of a stationary process do not change; they are constant over time. Moreover, the covariance of the stationary process between any two points in time depends only on the time difference between those two points.

A special case of a stationary process is white noise, which has the following properties:

$$E(\varepsilon_t) = 0 \ \forall t$$

$$E(\varepsilon_t^2) = \sigma^2 \ \forall t$$

$$E(\varepsilon_t \varepsilon_s) = 0 \ \forall t \neq s$$

Wold's Theorem

An important theorem in time series analysis is due to Herman Wold. Consider the stationary process y_t and let $E(y_t) = \mu$ and

$$z_t = y_t - E(y_t) = y_t - \mu$$

The Wold Theorem (or Wold decomposition) states that z_t consists of two parts:

$$z_t = u_t + \eta_t$$

η_t is completely predictable from the past values of z_t and indeed it is the least squares projection of η_t on z_t. In economics we assume η_t to be equal to zero. u_t on the other hand could be written as the weighted sum of white noise processes:

$$u_t = \sum_{i=0}^{\infty} \lambda_i \varepsilon_{t-i}, \lambda_0 \equiv 1, \sum_{i=0}^{\infty} \lambda_i^2 < \infty$$

Recall the lag operator L which is defined as

$$Lx_t = x_{t-1}, L^2 x_t = x_{t-2}, \text{ and } L^i x_t = x_{t-i}$$

Using the lag operator we can write:

$$u_t = \sum_{i=0}^{\infty} \lambda_i L^i \varepsilon_t$$

Now we can define a lag polynomial as

$$\Lambda(L) = \lambda_0 + \lambda_1 L + \lambda_2 L^2 + \cdots = \sum_{i=0}^{\infty} \lambda_i L^i$$

Thus,

$$u_t = \Lambda(L)\varepsilon_t$$

Fig. 7.1 Logarithm of the US quarterly GDP

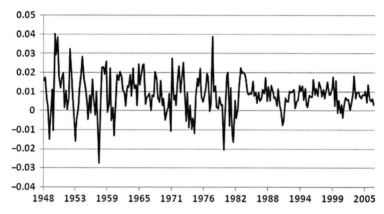

Fig. 7.2 First difference of the logarithm of the US quarterly GDP

An infinite lag polynomial could be approximated by a finite rational lag polynomial. That is, we can write:

$$\Lambda(L) \simeq \frac{\Theta(L)}{\Phi(L)} = \frac{1 + \theta_1 L + \theta_2 L^2 + \cdots + \theta_q L^q}{1 - \varphi_1 L - \varphi_2 L^2 - \cdots - \varphi_p L^p}$$

Applying the above to either stationary economic time series or series rendered stationary by differencing, we can write:

$$\Phi(L)u_t = \Theta(L)\varepsilon_t$$

Or in the expanded form:

$$u_t = \varphi_1 u_{t-1} + \varphi_2 u_{t-2} \cdots + \varphi_p u_{t-p} + \varepsilon_t + \theta_1 \varepsilon_{t-1} + \theta_2 \varepsilon_{t-2} + \cdots + \theta_q \varepsilon_{t-q}$$

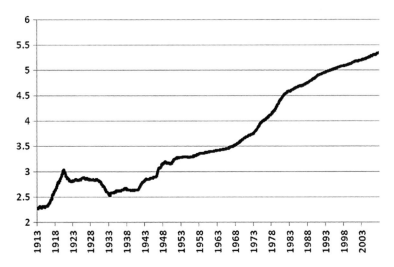

Fig. 7.3 Logarithm of the monthly US CPI

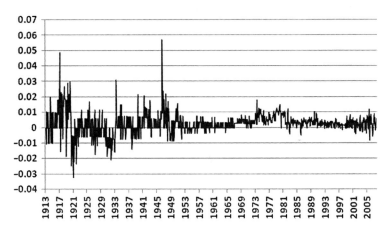

Fig. 7.4 The first difference of the logarithm of the US monthly CPI

Therefore, for y we can write:

$$y_t = (1 - \varphi_1 - \varphi_2 - \cdots - \varphi_p)\mu + \varphi_1 y_{t-1} + \varphi_2 y_{t-2} \cdots + \varphi_p y_{t-p}$$
$$+ \varepsilon_t + \theta_1 \varepsilon_{t-1} + \theta_2 \varepsilon_{t-2} + \cdots + \theta_q \varepsilon_{t-q}$$

Generally speaking, for economic data the values of p and q are usually low. As an example consider the monthly US consumer price index. The Dickey-Fuller test (see below) shows that the logarithm of the CPI is not stationary but its first difference is. Estimating different ARIMA models, the best fit turns out to be:

$$\Delta \ln (CPI_t) = 0.003 + 0.964 \Delta \ln (CPI_{t-1}) + \varepsilon_t - 0.582\varepsilon_{t-1} - 0.181\varepsilon_{t-2}$$

with AR=1 and MA=2. Thus, we have the inflation rate (change in the logarithm of the CPI) explained by the inflation rate in the previous month and two white noise shocks that occurred in the past two months.

Spurious Regression

When dealing with time series, one has to be wary of spurious regression. Granger and Newbold[8] showed that two randomly generated time series with no connection could show a high degree of correlation. The reader could perform the following experiment to convince herself about this possibility. On an Excel sheet (or on any statistical program) create the following series:

$$y_t = y_{t-1} + \alpha\varepsilon_{1t}, \ y_0 = c_1$$
$$x_t = x_{t-1} + \beta\varepsilon_{2t}, \ x_0 = c_2$$

where ε_1 and ε_2 are white noise and parameters α and β as well as initial values c_1 and c_2 are arbitrary. One can generate sufficiently large numbers of observations, for example, 50 or 100 for each series. If we use Excel we can generate these series as

	A	B
1	3	4
2	=A1+2.1*RAND()	=B1+1.5*RAND()
3	=A2+2.1*RAND()	=B2+1.5*RAND()
4	=A3+2.1*RAND()	=B3+1.5*RAND()
5	...	...
6	...	...

Instead of 3 and 4 you can choose any initial values and instead of 2.1 and 1.5 you can choose any coefficients.

Needless to say, the two generated series are independent of each other. Yet a regression of y on x will produce an R^2 of more than 0.9. At the same time the Durbin-Watson statistics would be very low indicating positive serial correlation. On the other hand, a regression of $\Delta y_t = y_t - y_{t-1}$ on $\Delta x_t = x_t - x_{t-1}$ will produce a very low R^2 and a DW statistics around 2. The outcomes described above are sure signs of spurious correlation: two unrelated time series showing high correlation. Macroeconomists should be particularly wary of not falling into the trap of taking similarities between two time series or their correlation as causal connections.

---

[8]Clive Granger and Paul Newbold (1974), pp. 111–120; see also their book *Forecasting Economic Time Series*, 2nd ed., 1986, pp. 205–215.

Causality

It is a well known fact that correlation does not imply causation. In a sample survey, we may find that college graduates have a higher income compared to those who did not go to college or did not finish it. In general, we may find a positive correlation between the number of completed years of schooling and income. But such a finding neither implies that more schooling causes higher income or higher income causes more schooling. In experimental sciences, all variables are kept constant and then variable x is changed. If variable y responds and it too changes, we conclude that x is causing y. No such device is available to economists.

Clive Granger noted that a necessary, but not sufficient, condition for causality is that knowledge of past values of x should improve the forecast of y. Surely if we can reject causality in the Granger sense then definitely we can reject causality in the more strict experimental sense. But failure to reject causality in the Granger sense does not mean causality in the strict sense cannot be rejected.

The test of causality involves estimating the following equations:

$$y_t = \beta_0 + \beta_1 y_{t-1} + \cdots + \beta_k y_{t-k} + u_t$$
$$y_t = \beta_0 + \beta_1 y_{t-1} + \cdots + \beta_k y_{t-k} + \gamma_1 x_{t-1} + \cdots + \gamma_m x_{t-m} + v_t$$

and testing the joint hypothesis that $\gamma_1 = \cdots = \gamma_m = 0$ against the alternative that at least one of the coefficients is different from zero. If we are not able to reject the null hypothesis then we should conclude that x does not cause y. Rejecting the null hypothesis means that we have accepted that the necessary condition for x causing y exists.

In the 1970s and 1980s a large number of studies purported to test causality between different economic variables including growth and exports, money and inflation, and others. Some of these studies used a small number of observations and concluded that there was no causality between these variables. It should be noted that the Granger test of causality is valid asymptotically. Therefore, we need a large number of observations before we can be confident in the results.

VAR Modeling

We already encountered the Wold Theorem in the case of univariate time series. The same theorem holds for a vector of time series. Let $\mathbf{z}_t$ be a k-vector of stationary variables. Using the Wold Theorem, and neglecting the MA part (hence *Vector Autoregression* or VAR) we can write:

$$\mathbf{z}_t = \mu + \mathbf{A}_1 \mathbf{z}_{t-1} + \mathbf{A}_2 \mathbf{z}_{t-2} + \cdots + \mathbf{A}_k \mathbf{z}_{t-p} + \varepsilon_t$$

where μ is a vector of constants, $\mathbf{A}_i$'s are $k \times k$ matrices of coefficients, and ε_t is a vector of white noise. For example, suppose the $\mathbf{z}_t$ vector to contain three elements: y the rate of growth of the GDP, g the rate of growth of government expenditures, and m the rate of growth of money supply . We can write the VAR model as

$$\begin{bmatrix} y_t \\ g_t \\ m_t \end{bmatrix} = \begin{bmatrix} \mu_1 \\ \mu_2 \\ \mu_3 \end{bmatrix} + \begin{bmatrix} A_1(L) \ A_2(L) \ A_3(L) \\ B_1(L) \ B_2(L) \ B_3(L) \\ C_1(L) \ C_2(L) \ C_3(L) \end{bmatrix} \begin{bmatrix} y_t \\ g_t \\ m_t \end{bmatrix} + \begin{bmatrix} \varepsilon_{1t} \\ \varepsilon_{2t} \\ \varepsilon_{3t} \end{bmatrix}$$

where $A_i(L)$, $B_i(L)$, $C_i(L)$, $i = 1, \ldots, 3$ are lag polynomials with the first term set equal to zero. One could estimate different VAR models and tests for different restrictions. For instance, if a statistical test shows that $B_1(L) = B_3(L) = 0$, then the growth rate of government expenditures is exogenous to the system. On the other hand, if we can show that $C_3(L) \neq 0$ then monetary policy is effective in increasing the growth rate of the GDP.

Since VAR models do not put any a priori restrictions on the system, they are not open to the criticism of being ad hoc. Rather they start from the data to see what kind of restrictions on the connections between macro variables is empirically supported by data. For this reason some have talked of *atheoretical macroeconometrics*. Definitely VAR models are a powerful tool for forecasting and for testing causal connections between different variables.

Deterministic vs. Stochastic Trend

Statistical inference is based on random sampling. But economic time series, like history, are unique or one shot deals. We cannot go back and resample the GDP of the United States. To solve this problem, we can consider the GDP for each year as the "realization" or the random sample from all possible values of the GDP for that year.

Statistical inference also assumes that the mean and the variance of the population sampled are constant. Most economic time series show trend, that is, usually an upward movement. For example, if we look at the graph of the United States GDP we notice that it has been on the rise. This creates a problem for statistical analysis. While we can consider each observation as a sample or realization of a distribution with constant mean and variance, the whole series cannot be assumed to have constant mean and variance.

Three questions arise here: (1) how can we model a trend? (2) How can we determine if a series is stationary? And (3) should a series have trend, how can we turn it into a stationary variable so we can utilize time series methods that have been designed for the analysis of stationary series?

Two types of trend (as well as a combination of them) are observed: deterministic and stochastic. A deterministic trend is of the form

$$y_t = \alpha_0 + \alpha_1 t + \varepsilon_t$$

where t denotes time and ε_t is white noise. A stochastic trend is of the form:

$$y_t = \rho y_{t-1} + \varepsilon_t$$

where $|\rho| \geq 1$. This is a crucial assumption since a ρ less than one in absolute value would not result in trend because the process would be stationary. A test of the existence of stochastic trends would be a statistical test of the null hypothesis $|\rho| \geq 1$ vs. the alternative hypothesis of $|\rho| < 1$. This a test of *unit root* and is called the Dickey-Fuller test. Dickey and Fuller also suggested a test to distinguish between stochastic and deterministic trends.

Taking the first difference of the series we have:

$$\Delta y_t = \alpha_1 + \varepsilon_t - \varepsilon_{t-1}, \text{ Deterministic}$$
$$\Delta y_t = (\rho - 1)y_{t-1} + \varepsilon_t, \text{ Stochastic}$$

As can be seen when the series with deterministic trend is differenced, we obtain a stationary series albeit it has a moving average component. An alternative way of detrending a series with deterministic trend is to regress y on time and then take the residuals of the regression as detrended series.

Regarding the series with stochastic trend, it is clear that if $\rho = 1$ then the first difference of series would be white noise. But even when $1 < |\rho| < 2$, the differenced series would be stationary.

In appearance, the two trends are quite similar. Figure 7.5 shows two generated series one with stochastic and the other with deterministic trend . They were created with the following formulas:

$$y_t = 100 + 0.9t + 2\varepsilon_t, \text{ Deterministic}$$
$$y_t = y_{t-1} + 2\varepsilon_t, \ y_0 = 100 \text{ Stochastic}$$

As can be seen it is difficult to distinguish one from the other and this is reflected in the low power of the Dickey-Fuller test for distinguishing between the two (but not the test for determining the unit root). Nevertheless, the two trends have different implications, which are quite significant for economic analysis.

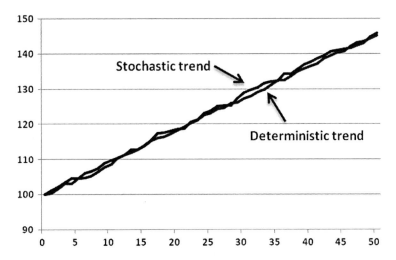

Fig. 7.5 Deterministic vs. Stochastic trend

In the deterministic trend model the effect of a shock to the system ε is limited to one period and would not have an effect on the future values of y. If, for example, y represents the GDP the effect of any disturbance is short lived. Furthermore, the system has a long term trend. Stabilization policy would make sense because the system is stabilized around its long term trend.

By comparison we can write the variable with stochastic trend, through successive substitutions, as

$$y_t = \rho^t y_0 + \sum_{i=0}^{t-1} \rho^i \varepsilon_{t-i}$$

First, the effects of shocks to the system are permanent. Indeed, the variable y is nothing but the accumulated shocks. Second, the system does not have a long term trend around which it could be stabilized. It seems that the deterministic model matches the Keynesian model of the demand side of the economy while the stochastic trend is a more appropriate reflection of the Schumpeterian vision of the supply side. We shall come back to this issue in the next chapter when discussing the real business cycle theory. According to this model, trends and cycles have a common source and it is the accumulation of technological shocks that produces a long term trend as well as short run fluctuations around it as represented in the above equation.

Cointegration and Error Correction

There are time series that are non-stationary and yet move together. For instance, quantity supplied and demanded of a particular good move together over time. If demand exceeds supply an error correction mechanism is set in motion to increase supply and reduce demand. Thus, the two quantities stay close to each other and their difference hovers around zero sometimes negative and at other times positive. Similarly, we may see such a relationship between domestic price level, foreign price level, and the exchange rate, i.e., the purchasing power parity (PPP) theory. International economists agree that the PPP is a long run equilibrium relationship. If so then any deviation from it would set in motion changes (error correction mechanism) that would bring back the parity. Another example would be the relationship between the fundamental value of a financial asset (such as a stock) and its market price.

Technically, when a linear combination of two or more variables is stationary, we say that they are cointegrated. Note, however, any combination of two or more stationary variables would also be stationary. Therefore, the existence of equilibrium or cointegration among variables cannot be statistically tested unless at least two of the variables involved exhibit nonstationarity. Thus, first we need to establish that variables involved are integrated of order one, denoted by I(1), that is, they will become stationary after differencing. Suppose that we have tested using Dickey-Fuller test that x and y are both I(1). Then we could run the following regression:

$$y_t = \alpha + \beta x_t + \varepsilon_t$$

If the two variables are cointegrated, then the residual from the regression would be stationary based on Dickey-Fuller test. For this purpose the Dickey-Fuller test will have different critical values from the test of stationarity on the original variables. Such a test could also detect if the relationship is spurious correlation because in that case the residuals would not be stationary. If two variables are cointegrated they have a common trend. When the correlation is spurious, there is no common trend. If we confirm the cointegrating relationship between x and y, then we have also ascertained (although we need to test it too) that an error correction relationship exists between them:

$$\Delta y_t = \phi_0 + \phi_1 \hat{\varepsilon}_{t-1} + \xi_t$$

Thus, a discrepancy in the equilibrium $\hat{\varepsilon}_{t-1}$ would set in motion in the next period a correction mechanism equal to Δy_t to bring back the equilibrium. Of course the error correction mechanism could be more complicated and involve inertia.

The existence of cointegration and error correction also implies causality between the two variables. Consider that we can write the above equation as

$$\Delta y_t = \phi_0 + \phi_1 (y_{t-1} - \hat{\alpha} - \hat{\beta} x_{t-1}) + \xi_t$$

In other words, information on the past values of x helps in forecasting changes in y.

Finally, we should note that there may be more than one cointegrating relationship between a set of variables.[9] The ideas of cointegration and error correction have made it possible to test certain macroeconomic relationships and changed our perception of the nature of some of them. In the late 1980s and early 1990s many macro relationships, including consumption function and money inflation nexus, were subjected to such tests.

---

[9]There can only be at most $k-1$ cointegrating relations between k nonstationary variables. But there may be several stationary variables in each equation.

Chapter 8
Business Cycles: Evidence, Theory, and Policy

But another indictment stands against the vast majority of the economists of that period [1870–1914] if it be indeed proper, considering the analytic situation in which they worked, to call it an indictment: with few exceptions, of which Marx was the most influential one, they treated cycles as a phenomenon that is superimposed upon the normal course of capitalist life and mostly as a pathological one; it never occurred to the majority to look to business cycles for material with which to build the fundamental theory of capitalist reality.
Joseph Schumpeter, *History of Economic Analysis*, 1954,
p. 1135

Like waves of the sea, our rest is our extinction
We are alive because we are restless
Kalim Kashani

Ups and downs in an economy are a natural occurrence, similar to periods of health and activity or times of slowdown or even sickness in a human body. This feature of the economy has for decades been a preoccupation of economists and many theories have been suggested to explain them. Many also have tried to devise methods for forecasting the onset of a recession or the beginning of a recovery. As discussed in Chap. 1, since the Great Depression many economists have tried to come up with policies that could avoid recession or at least ameliorate its effects so that the economy would experience a soft landing (presumably as opposed to a crash landing).

First we should ask what is a recession and what are its characteristics? In the United States the National Bureau of Economic Research (NBER) dates the peaks and troughs of the economy and maintains a chronology of business cycles. Table 8.1 shows the chronology of business cycles in the United States as compiled by the NBER.

The NBER uses a variety of measures to come up with the dates. As a simplification or a rule of thumb a recession is defined as when in two consecutive quarters the aggregate output, the GDP, has negative growth. The NBER declarations are ex-post in the sense that the determination is made several months after a peak or trough has happened. The value of NBER's work is mostly of the nature of bookkeeping. By the time they announce that there is a recession, only inhabitants of

K. Dadkhah, *The Evolution of Macroeconomic Theory and Policy*,
DOI 10.1007/978-3-540-77008-4_8, © Springer-Verlag Berlin Heidelberg 2009

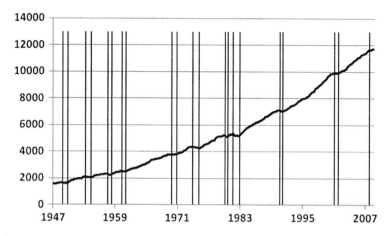

Fig. 8.1 Business cycles and the real GDP in the United States

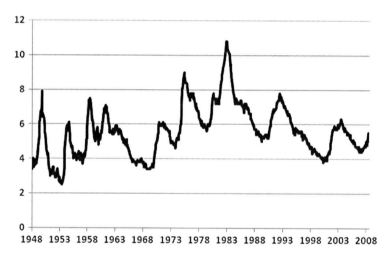

Fig. 8.2 Monthly unemployment rate

Mars don't know it. In November 2001, the NBER announced that the US economy has been in recession since March of that year. But November was the month when the recession ended. Similarly, in November 2008, the NBER announced that since December 2007, the economy had been in recession. Compare this to your physician calling you and saying "by the way, you got sick six months ago."

Figure 8.1 depicts the movement of the GDP during the periods of recession and recovery in the United States since 1947. Perhaps a better depiction of the cyclical nature of the economy could be found in Fig. 8.2 which shows the unemployment rate in the United States since 1948.

Before turning to the issue of forecasting and theories of business cycles, it is important to observe certain features of the cycles which will have bearing on any theory or policy dealing with business cycles. The first feature is that cycles are

Table 8.1 Business cycles in the United States*

Recessions			Expansions		
Beginning	End	Duration (months)	Beginning	End	Duration (months)
1918 August	1919 March	7	1919 March	1920 January	10
1920 January	1921 July	18	1921 July	1923 May	22
1923 May	1924 July	14	1924 July	1926 October	27
1926 October	1927 November	13	1927 November	1929 August	21
1929 August	1933 March	43	1933 March	1937 May	50
1937 May	1938 June	13	1938 June	1945 February	80
1945 February	1945 October	8	1945 October	1948 November	37
1948 November	1949 October	11	1949 October	1953 July	45
1953 July	1954 May	10	1954 May	1957 August	39
1957 August	1958 April	8	1958 April	1960 April	24
1960 April	1961 February	10	1961 February	1969 December	106
1969 December	1970 November	11	1970 November	1973 November	36
1973 November	1975 March	16	1975 March	1980 January	58
1980 January	1980 July	6	1980 July	1981 July	12
1981 July	1982 November	16	1982 November	1990 July	92
1990 July	1991 March	8	1991 March	2001 March	120
2001 March	2001 November	8	2001 November	2007 December	73
2007 December					

*Source: The National Bureau of Economic Research (www.nber.org/cycles.html)

irregular (see Table 8.1). Some recessions have lasted no more than 6 or 8 months and one as long as 43 months. There have been periods of recovery as short as 10 months or a year and as long as 9 and 10 years. Even if we confine ourselves to the post World War II era still we observe the irregularity in cycle duration. This feature rules out any deterministic theory of cycles and perforce we have to have stochastic elements in any theory of business cycles. Mathematically, trigonometric functions can generate fluctuations. Such functions can emerge as solutions to second order difference and differential equations with complex roots. But such cycles will be regular and predictable.

Forecasting Recessions and Recovery

Given the impact of business cycles on the economy and the life of citizenry it makes sense to develop statistical measures that would warn in advance of the impending recession, much in the same way that meteorologists warn of coming hurricanes. The first efforts in this direction dates back to the early years of the twentieth century. Roger Babson[1] and James Brookmire[2] proposed constructing series as barometers for economic conditions. Both developed services for businesses, bankers, and

---

[1] Roger W. Babson (1910), pp. 111–134.
[2] James H. Brookmire (1913), pp. 43–58.

investors based on statistical indices that could be used for forecasting economic conditions. After the economic crisis of 1907 the French government set up a commission for finding ways of ameliorating the effects of periodic economic crises. The commission made some recommendations and also named eight statistical series as most significant in studying business conditions, but did not come up with a single index.[3]

Perhaps the most significant work at the time was done by Warren Persons at Harvard University. He constructed three curves: A-speculation, B-Business, and C-Money. The A curve was meant to be a leading indicator, the B curve coincident, and C a lagging index. For different periods different time series were used to build these indices. But at the end the following series were settled on[4]:

A– Speculation
   New York City bank clearings
   Shares traded on New York Stock Exchange
   Price of industrial stocks
B– Business
   Bank clearings outside New York City
   Bradstreet's indices of commodity prices
C– Money
   Rate on 4–6 months paper
   Rate on 60–90 day paper

The A-curve was the leading indicator because stock market investors were forward looking; the B-curve was coincident indicator because it reflected commodity prices which were tied to production. Finally, the C-curve was lagging indicator as it reflected the cost of borrowing. The work on the ABC curve came to an end after a failure to foresee the Great Depression, although this may have been more the fault of the optimistic outlook of those who interpreted the indices.

The modern index of leading indicators, however, dates back to the work of Wesley Mitchell and Arthur Burns at the National Bureau of Economic Research. In 1937 while the country was slowly recovering from the Great Depression the economy experienced another recession. The Secretary of Treasury, Henry Morgenthau, Jr. asked the NBER to come up with indicators that could predict business cycles.[5] The result was a system of leading, coincident, and lagging indicators. In 1961 the task was transferred to the Bureau of the Census. In 1972 the task was transferred to the Bureau of Economic Analysis. Finally, in 1995 the Bureau of Economic Analysis transferred the compilation of business cycles indicators to the Conference Board, a non-governmental organization. It should be noted that throughout its history the series used to construct these indices have changed as researchers have found some series more useful than others or because of the availability of new data or discontinuation of old series. Components of the current indices are listed in Table 8.2.

---

[3]Warren M. Persons (1916), pp. 739–769.
[4]Warren M. Persons (1920), pp. 39–48; (1927), pp. 20–29; see also the reference in footnote 3 above.
[5]Geoffrey H. Moore (1975), pp. 17–23.

Table 8.2 Components of the indices of leading, coincident, and lagging indicators*

Index of Leading Indicators
 1. Average weekly hours, manufacturing
 2. Average weekly initial claims for unemployment insurance
 3. Manufacturers' new orders, consumer goods and materials
 4. Vendor performance, slower deliveries diffusion index
 5. Manufacturers' new orders, nondefense capital goods
 6. Building permits, new private housing units
 7. Stock prices, 500 common stocks (S&P)
 8. Money supply, M2
 9. Interest rate spread, 10-year Treasury bonds less federal funds rate
10. Index of consumer expectations

Index of Coincident Indicators
 1. Employees on nonagricultural payrolls
 2. Personal income less transfer payments
 3. Index of industrial production
 4. Manufacturing and trade sales

Index of Lagging Indicators
 1. Average duration of unemployment
 2. Inventories to sales ratio, manufacturing and trade
 3. Change in labor cost per unit of output, manufacturing
 4. Average prime rate charged by banks
 5. Commercial and industrial loans outstanding
 6. Consumer installment credit outstanding to personal income ratio
 7. Change in consumer price index for services

*Source: Conference Board, *Business Cycles Indicators Handbook.*

For a time, it was said that by using a simple rule of 3 months or 4 months the Index of Leading Economic Indicators could be used to forecast recessions and recoveries. In other words, if the Index of LEI declined for 3 or 4 consecutive months then the economy would slip into a recession. Similarly, 3 or 4 consecutive increases in the index heralded a recovery. The problem was that the system produced many false alarms, which prompted Paul Samuelson to observe that the Index of Leading Economic Indicators has forecasted 9 out of the past 5 recessions. Moreover, even when it forecasted correctly, the lead time between the third or fourth decline and the onset of recession was almost nonexistent. As to recovery, the rules missed many recoveries. Nevertheless, the index of LEI could be used as an input into a Bayesian probability model to enhance the accuracy of the probabilities attached to the forecasts of recession or recovery.

Frisch's Theory of Cycles

The first model of business cycles was proposed by Ragnar Frisch who noted that

> The majority of the economic oscillations ... seem to be produced by the fact that certain exterior impulses hit the economic mechanism and thereby initiate more or less regular oscillations. ... [t]he length of the cycles and the tendency towards dampening are

determined by the intrinsic structure of the swinging system, while the intensity (the amplitude) of the fluctuations is determined primarily by the exterior impulse.[6]

As far as the propagation is concerned he posits a number of deterministic relations. First, let I_t be the amount of new orders for capital goods and Z_t the amount of capital goods produced at time t. Thus, following an idea of Aftalion,[7] assuming that production of capital goods takes a length of time equal to ε and

$$Z_t = \frac{dK}{dt} = \frac{1}{\varepsilon} \int_{t-\varepsilon}^{t} I_s ds$$

we can write

$$\varepsilon \frac{dZ}{dt} \approx I_t - I_{t-\varepsilon}$$

On the other hand the production of capital goods depends on the amount of consumption and the change in consumption:

$$I_t = mC_t + \mu \frac{dC}{dt}$$

Finally the change in consumption linearly but inversely relates to the value of money needed for the transaction on both capital and consumption goods. It is assumed that when the amount of money needed for this transaction increases but the supply of money in circulation does not increase, the result is a decrease in consumption.

$$\frac{dC}{dt} = C_0 - \lambda(\alpha C_t + \beta Z_t)$$

Now we have three equations which form a system of mixed difference and differential equations. Frisch considers the solution of the system and its properties.[8] To illustrate the behavior of the system, he calibrates his model using the available data and informed guesses. In all, the system is stable with damping fluctuations. But then how could we explain oscillations that are not damped and in a way characterize the system? The answer is "erratic shocks" to the system. Each shock may not be large or effective in causing and maintaining oscillations in the economic system, but their accumulated effect would produce fluctuations that are not damping. Thus, erratic shocks are impulses to the system and the system of difference-differential equations propagates the fluctuations.

---

[6]Ragnar Frisch (1933), reprinted 1967, pp. 171–205.

[7]Albert Aftalion (1927), pp. 165–170.

[8]Later on Frisch and Harold Holme published "The Characteristic Solutions of a Mixed Difference and Differential Equations Occurring in Economic Dynamics," *Econometrica*, 1935, pp. 225–239 to help readers with the technical points in the previous article.

One can speak of erratic shocks in a mathematical model but then what are their economic counterparts? Frisch identifies them as innovations as presented in the Schumpeterian theory of growth (see Chap. 11). These innovations are both sources of fluctuations and long term growth. In many respects, including his ideas on the cause of economic fluctuations, Frisch anticipated later work on the real business cycles model.

Incidentally this is the paper in which Frisch for the first time introduced the word macro as distinguished from micro. He noted that in order to analyze the essential problems of business cycles on a macro-dynamic basis and explain the movement of the system in its entirety

> we must deliberately disregard a considerable amount of details of the picture. We may perhaps start by throwing all kinds of production into one variable, all consumption into another, and so on, imagining that the notions "production," "consumption," and so on, can be measured by some sort of total indices. At present certain examples of micro-dynamic analyses have been worked out, but as far as I know no determinate macro-dynamic analysis is yet to be found in the literature.[9]

Ragnar Frisch (1895–1973) was a great economist and one of the founders of the discipline of econometrics.[10] He won the first Nobel Prize in economics together with Jan Tinbergen in 1969.

Samuelson's Model of Interaction Between Multiplier and Acceleration

Some economists have proposed business cycle models, which are in the Keynesian tradition. That is, their starting points are the basic relationships of the IS-LM model, but in some equations one variable responds to the other with time delay. By this device the models are made dynamic, which means that time plays an essential role in them. In this section we consider Samuelson's, and in the next, Hicks's model.

Consider the following Keynesian model where consumption depends on lagged income, investment is proportional to increase in consumption, and government expenditures stay at a preset level.

$$C_t = \alpha Y_{t-1}$$
$$I_t = \beta(C_t - C_{t-1})$$
$$Y_t = C_t + I_t + G_t$$

Substituting the first two equations in the last equation, we get the following second order non-homogenous difference equations.[11]

---

[9] Ibid., p. 173.

[10] For an appreciation of his work see Kenneth Arrow (1960), pp. 175–192; and Leif Johansen (1969), pp. 302–324.

[11] For a discussion of difference equations and their solutions see Dadkhah (2007), Chap. 14.

$$Y_t = \alpha(1 + \beta)Y_{t-1} - \alpha\beta Y_{t-2} + G_t$$

The solution to this equation will have complex roots and cyclical behavior if

$$\alpha < \frac{4\beta}{(1 + \beta)^2}$$

For example, let us suppose that $\alpha = 0.7$ then if $\beta \geq 0.3$ we shall observe cyclical behavior.

Hicks's Model of Two Limits

An alternative Keynesian model is suggested by John Hicks. The basic model is the same as the multiplier acceleration model but Hicks added two limits to the amount of output in the economy. First, aggregate output Y could not go above what could be produced with full employment. Second, the amount of net investment could become negative but can never go below the amount of depreciation. Recall that—given the consumption function and the amount of government expenditure—the engine of change in the Keynesian model is investment. Thus, in the upswing investment increases to the point that the output reaches full employment level. On the downswing investment decreases to the point that it is negative and in absolute value equal to the amount of depreciation. We can revise the multiplier-accelerator model as follows:

$$C_t = \alpha Y_{t-1}$$

$$I_t = \begin{cases} \beta(C_t - C_{t-1}) & \text{if} \quad \beta(C_t - C_{t-1}) > -\delta K_{t-1} \\ -\delta K_{t-1} & \text{if} \quad \beta(C_t - C_{t-1}) \leq -\delta K_{t-1} \end{cases}$$

$$Y_t = \begin{cases} C_t + I_t + G_t & \text{if} \quad Y_t \leq Y_t^f \\ Y_t^f & \text{if} \quad C_t + I_t + G_t > Y_t^f \end{cases}$$

Hicks posits that the system is inherently unstable. In other words, the resulting second order difference equation has complex roots. But the oscillations in the system are contained within the two bounds: the full employment output and output resulting from negative investment equal to the depreciation of the capital stock. Suppose the economy is in equilibrium but then due to an increase in investment or government expenditures, income and consumption increase and, as a result, the economy starts on an upward path. The economy will be on the upswing till it reaches full employment output, beyond which it cannot go. At that point income and consumption stay constant; as a result investment decreases to zero. Lack of investment sets in motion the downturn in the economy. Lower income means lower consumption and lower consumption means negative investment. Nevertheless, investment cannot go below the amount of natural depreciation of capital.

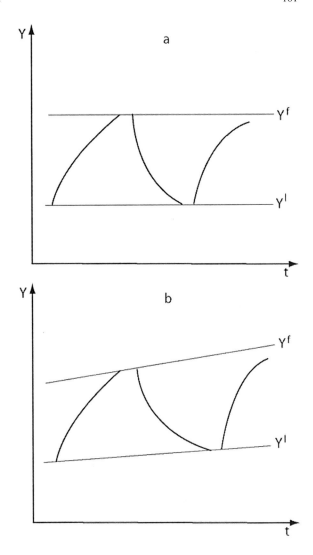

Fig. 8.3 Hicks's two-limits model of business cycles

Therefore, income has a lower level below which it cannot go. For a time the economy may travel at this level, and then some event such as an increase in government expenditures or investment by entrepreneurs who observe the decline in capital stock will set in motion an upward movement in the economy. Hicks's theory can be presented in the context of a static economy where the full employment level of output and capital stock remain constant (Fig. 8.3a).But, the model is also applicable to an expanding economy where capital stock and full employment output are increasing over time (Fig. 8.3b). In this case, however, as time passes the amplitude of oscillations will be on the rise.

A Critique of Keynesian Models of Business Cycles

Keynesian models of business cycles are at best ad hoc. The idea is that if you want a model to exhibit cyclical behavior, then you need to have a second order difference equation with complex roots. The easiest way to achieve this is to introduce lags into the behavioral equations of the model. For instance, Samuelson makes consumption dependent on lagged level of income and investment dependent on lagged consumption. The same device is employed by Hicks.

While these models show the possibility of fluctuations within a Keynesian model, it is difficult to reconcile their characterization of cycles with empirical facts. Empirical evidence shows that business cycles are anything but regular. It is hard to find any two cycles that are similar. Yet Samuelson's model produces cycles that are all of the same duration. This also implies that cycles are perfectly predictable, which again contradicts empirical evidence.

Hick's model allows for the economy to stay an unspecified period of time either at full employment or at the trough with negative investment equal to the amount of capital depreciation. Thus, the length of the cycles and the timing may not be exact. But it still predicts regular behavior during the cycles.

It is possible to superimpose several cycles on each other and obtain complicated behavior. But still the patterns will be predictable. It seems that in order to obtain a model of business cycles that correspond to empirical evidence, we have no choice but to introduce random shocks to the system, and this is what Kydland and Prescott did in their real business cycles model.

Real Business Cycles Theory

The real business cycles theory has its origin in the seminal work of Kydland and Prescott, who shared the Nobel Memorial Prize in economics in 2004. Their work ushered in three innovations in macroeconomics: dynamic stochastic general equilibrium models (DSGE) as a vehicle for the analysis of aggregate economic phenomena, calibration as a means of quantifying macro models, and the real business cycles theory. Below we first present a simple model that captures the essence of the real business cycle theory. Then we shall discuss the structure of dynamic stochastic general equilibrium models, and finally review the calibration method.

A Simple Model of Real Business Cycles

The model posits a Cobb-Douglas production technology but abstracts from consumer preferences. Similarly issues such as monetary and fiscal policy are not dealt with. But the resulting model combines features of Keynesian and Frisch's models. The production function is

$$Y_t = K_t^\alpha (A_t L_t)^{1-\alpha}$$

where Y, K, A, and L denote, respectively, output, capital stock, technology, and labor. It is assumed that the stock of capital is equal to the previous period saving. This, of course, is a quite unrealistic assumption. Perhaps a better choice is to set the additional capital equal to last period saving less depreciation. But that will make the model more complicated.

$$K_t = Y_{t-1} - C_{t-1} = sY_{t-1}$$

where C is consumption, and s marginal propensity to save. It is assumed that population (N) grows at the rate η and the labor force participation rate $\bar{l}$ is constant. We have

$$N_t = N_0 e^{\eta t}, \quad L_t = \bar{l}N_t = \bar{l}N_0 e^{\eta t}$$

Thus,

$$\ln L_t = \ln \bar{l} + \ln N_0 + \eta t$$

Technology progresses over time both deterministically (γt) and stochastically (u)

$$A_t = A_0 \exp(\gamma t + u_t)$$

and

$$\ln A = \ln A_0 + \gamma t + u_t$$

Taking the logarithm of the production function and making the substitutions we end up with the following first order non-homogeneous difference equation:

$$\ln Y_t = \alpha \ln Y_{t-1} + [\alpha \ln s + (1 - \alpha)(\ln A_0 + \ln N_0 + \ln \bar{l})]$$
$$+ (1 - \alpha)(\eta + \gamma)t + (1 - \alpha)u_t$$

where the non-homogeneous part involves a stochastic element. It would not have been difficult to have a second order difference equation. For instance, we could have written the equation for the evolution of capital stock in a more realistic way as

$$\frac{K_t}{K_{t-1}} = s\frac{Y_{t-1}}{Y_{t-2}}$$

Going back to our first order equation and letting

$$B = \alpha \ln s + (1 - \alpha)(\ln A_0 + \ln N_0 + \ln \bar{l})$$

the solution to the equation is

$$\ln Y_t = \left(\ln Y_0 - \frac{B}{1 - \alpha} + \frac{\alpha(\eta + \gamma)}{1 - \alpha} \right) \alpha^t + \frac{B}{1 - \alpha} - \frac{\alpha(\eta + \gamma)}{1 - \alpha}$$

$$+ (\eta + \gamma)t + (1 - \alpha) \sum_{i=0}^{t-1} \alpha^i u_{t-1}$$

The GDP consists of a deterministic part but also the accumulation of technological shocks to the system. Thus, at least part of the trend in the economy and its short term fluctuations are indistinguishable. If such a model represents the economy then stabilization policies would be pointless.

As can be seen, however, while the model generates fluctuations, at least in the above form it cannot account for downturns in the economy. If we introduce consumption and incorporate changes in consumer tastes that are random, there could be more ups and downs in the economy. But the fact of the matter is that a model lacking a monetary sector and an explicit demand side cannot account for the crisis of 2007–2009, let alone provide any guidance to counteract it (see Chap. 13).

Later researchers have added money, international trade, and other features to DSGE models. They have become more complicated, but they also do not necessarily lead to the same conclusions as Kydland and Prescott reached.

Dynamic Stochastic General Equilibrium Models

Dynamic stochastic general equilibrium (DSGE) models are great tools in economic analysis and policy evaluation. Their modern origin is the work of Finn Kydland and Edward Prescott. They are different from the previous generation of macroeconometric models in three aspects. First, they are based on optimizing agents and neoclassical growth theory and, therefore, they can claim some kind of microfoundations. Second, stochastic elements are explicitly introduced and are an integral part of the model. This sets them apart from a deterministic model that is made stochastic by addition of an error term. While this is an advance over the older model where the random variable is an afterthought, we are still a way from a fully worked out stochastic model. Third, the models are dynamic through intertemporal optimization, gestation period in capital formation, and autocorrelation of stochastic terms. The models are flexible and different features of the economy could be incorporated. More recent work using DSGE models have incorporated money, international trade, and even rigidities in wages and prices.

Yet there seems to be some controversy surrounding them, and recently Mankiw has complained that the recent advances in macroeconomic modeling and theory have not found their way into policy making. While a lag between theoretical innovation and policy application is natural, other factors have influenced the delay in a wide acceptance and application of these models. We can distinguish between DSGE as a tool of economic analysis and as shorthand for a particular creed with a dogmatic view in macroeconomics. The following is a stripped down version of the original model proposed by Kydland and Prescott.[12] Its usefulness as a tool of economic policy will be taken up in a later section.

The first relationship of the model is an aggregate production function relating output to technology growth, capital, and labor:

$$Y_t = A_t F(K_t, L_t)$$

A is the technology level and grows at a random rate. Output is divided between consumption C and investment I. Therefore,

$$Y_t = C_t + I_t = w_t L_t + r_t K_t$$

where w and r are, respectively, compensation of labor and capital. The evolution of capital and technology are governed by the following dynamics

$$K_{t+1} = (1 - \delta)K_t + I_t$$
$$A_{t+1} = \rho A_t + \varepsilon_{t+1}$$

where δ is the depreciation rate, $0 < \rho < 1$, and ε_t's are identically and independently distributed stochastic terms representing technological shocks. The amount of labor supplied is determined by utility maximizing households with intertemporal utility functions.

$$E \sum_{t=0}^{\infty} \beta^t U(C_t, 1 - L_t) = E \sum_{t=0}^{\infty} \beta^t \frac{\left(C_t^\theta (1 - L_t)^{1-\theta} \right)^{1-\gamma}}{1 - \gamma}$$

Thus, utility depends on consumption and leisure, that is, the time not worked. The consumer faces a restriction in that there is a tradeoff between income that would be consumed and the time people would have for non-market activities such as entertainment, family affairs, and social activities; hence, L appears with a negative sign in the utility function. For simplicity, the total amount of time available to the household is normalized to one. β is the discount factor and it is assumed that the average household lives forever.

Values of different variables are determined under the condition of general equilibrium. These conditions, for instance, specify that the remuneration of labor and capital are equal to their marginal product. Similarly they specify the intertemporal rate of substitution between consumption as well as between consumption and leisure. Using information available in empirical research, parameters of the model

---

[12] The original model of Kydland and Prescott (1982) is much more elaborate. It includes gestation lags in capital formation, production depends on inventories, technology shocks are of three different varieties, and leisure appears in the utility function in a distributed lag format. The present model is based on their expository paper: "The Computational Experiment: An Econometric Tool," *Journal of Economic Perspectives*, 1996, pp. 69–85.

are calibrated to produce a path of variables similar to those observed in the economy. Then using equilibrium conditions and dynamic programming one can come up with a solution to the model.

The model presented above contains only basic relationships. Over time researchers have added money, government budget, and international trade to the model. While such additions complicate the model and its computation they are essential if the DSGE models are to be used for policy analysis.

Calibration

To understand calibration and its limitations let us start with an example. We know from experience and empirical work that people respond to incentives. There will be more labor supply for higher wages. Now from the point of view of workers it is real, after tax wages that count. Thus, a lowering of the tax rate should increase labor supply, output, and income. But by how much? Furthermore, some have argued that a reduction of tax rate would increase total tax revenues of the government. Is that true? To answer we set up a model of production, labor supply, and tax revenues. We make several simplifying assumptions to make our computation easy.

Consider the production function

$$Y = AK^\alpha L^\beta$$

Thus, we have assumed a Cobb-Douglas production function and have abstracted from technological progress. We shall also assume that capital stock is fixed. If we further assume that the price level is equal to one, then Y represents both output and income.

Profit maximization requires expanding output to the point that the wage rate W is equal to the marginal product of labor.

$$W = \beta AK^\alpha L^{\beta-1}$$

Note that because we assumed the price level to be equal to unity, real wage is equal to nominal wage. We posit the following labor supply function:

$$\ln(L) = \ln(\bar{L}) + \gamma \ln(W(1 - \theta))$$

where θ is the tax rate. The function implies that at a wage rate equal to zero there will be no supply of labor. Solving the equations, we have

$$\ln(L) = \frac{1}{1 - \gamma(\beta - 1)}[B + \gamma \ln(1 - \theta)]$$

where $B = \ln(\bar{L}) + \gamma \ln(\beta) + \gamma \ln(A) + \gamma\alpha \ln(K)$. Needless to say a lowering of the tax rate would increase employment and, therefore, output and income.

Now consider the total tax revenues

$$T = \theta Y$$

On the one hand the tax rate is declining and on the other the income is increasing; what is the net effect? Recall that a good economist is the one who makes an assessment of all forces involved to come up with the net effect. One way is to put some reasonable numbers on parameters and constants and pronounce a verdict. Let us try the following numbers: $A = 100$, $\alpha = 0.2$, $\beta = 0.7$, $K = 500$, $\bar{L} = 150$, $\gamma = 1$, and $\theta = 0.35$. Using these numbers we get $Y = 78517.98$ and $T = 27481.29$. Now suppose that we reduce the tax rate to 0.30 and recalculate income and tax revenues. We get $Y = 81714.54$ and $T = 24514.36$. Thus, the increase in output as a result of the tax cut is consistent with this model but the assertion that tax revenues will increase is not borne out. We may also change the numbers to see if there are any circumstances under which we can arrive at different conclusions. In sum, we can tease out the implications of the model under reasonable assumptions about the magnitude of the parameters. Furthermore, we can get an order of magnitude regarding the effects of a tax cut on income and tax revenue.

So far most if not all reasonable people will go along and have no objections. Nevertheless, the same reasonable people would ask two questions: (1) where did these numbers come from? And (2) how do we know that the model is a reasonable representation of the economy under consideration and an appropriate model to answer the question at hand?

It is in answering these questions that the controversy starts. An acceptable answer to everyone is to estimate the model using econometric techniques and ascertain that the model is the best model for the economy. By the best we mean it fits the past data and can predict the future changes better than any other proposed nested or non-nested model. Better fit is determined by statistical measures. Kydland and Prescott instead chose the numbers for their parameters from a variety of sources and based on whether the resulting model would mimic certain aspects of the economy under consideration. For instance, in our example one could look at the labor share in total income to ascribe a value to α or use labor market studies to come up with an estimate of the elasticity of labor supply with respect to wage rate. The initial values of parameters could be changed to fine tune the model to better mimic the actual data. Indeed, a sensitivity analysis could be performed.

Calibration as described above is used in physics. The difference is that physics has many constants, the ranges of parameters are limited, and there are ironclad laws of physics verified by many experiments around the world. None of these features exist in economics. There are no constants in economics, free parameters populate our discipline, and even when a range is specified—for example, in the case of marginal propensity to consume—it is quite wide. It would be a horrendous search if we simultaneously look for the best fit for each and every parameter in an economic model. Kydland and Prescott didn't do that and if anyone tries that, the result would not be different from econometric estimation except that standard errors would be missing. Finally, there are hardly any ironclad laws in economics.

The upshot is that calibration and the resulting model is researcher-specific. Indeed, the research program is based on a particular philosophy regarding the nature and role of economics. According to this view economic theory is not a set of statements about an actual economy. Rather it is a set of instructions as to how to build an artificial economy. Then specific questions will be answered with reference to this artificial economy. We shall return to this issue below.

To sum, Kydland and Prescott introduced a new tool to the toolbox of economists, which would be useful in working out the implications of the model. But they also used the tool in a way that could only cause controversy or strip economic theory from its connection to reality. When values for parameters of the model are chosen by researcher instead of estimated and the predictions of the model are not subject to statistical testing, the whole enterprise reduces to statements of preconceived policies and ideas and of not much use for serious work.

A Bayesian Interpretation of Calibration

Perhaps to best understand the ideas of calibration and its critics, we can present it in a Bayesian framework. We can estimate the parameters of a model using data and a method such as maximum likelihood. Alternatively, we may believe or have external evidence that the parameters of the model have certain values. This belief or information could be formalized in the form of a prior distribution of the parameter vector θ. The Bayes Theorem allows us to combine our prior information with the information from data.

Suppose we have the data set $\mathbf{X}$ on the variables of the model, then we can write:

$$P(\theta|\mathbf{X}) = \frac{P(\mathbf{X}|\theta)P(\theta)}{P(\mathbf{X})}$$
$$\propto P(\mathbf{X}|\theta)P(\theta)$$

The left hand side is the posterior distribution of the parameter vector which is proportional to the likelihood function times the prior distribution. Thus, the Bayes Theorem allows us to combine information from other sources with that contained in the data. However, if the researcher is certain that the value of the parameter vector is θ_0 and holds this belief with probability one, then

$$P(\theta|\mathbf{X}) = P(\theta_0)$$

But then the result is acceptable only to that particular researcher and those who hold similar beliefs.

We can think of econometric analysis as the case where no prior is specified, and the posterior distribution is determined by the likelihood function alone. That is, the researcher relies on the data and economic theory to determine the parameters of the model. Alternatively, we may think that the researcher has some non-informative prior and, therefore, allows the data to be the sole determinant of the parameters.

The pure case of calibration coincides with having a prior that is concentrated on one parameter point. In other words, the researcher believes that $\theta = \theta_0$ and holds this belief with probability one. Many will find it difficult to defend such a position. An alternative is to introduce information gathered from different sources on the parameters of a model into computation, but to specify a range for each parameter and define a probability distribution over it. Such a distribution need not be uninformative and diffused nor does it need to be concentrated on one point.

Recent work indeed suggests that a Bayesian approach to the estimation of DSGE models is becoming the norm.[13]

New Keynesian Models with Nominal and Real Rigidities

The basic question left unanswered by the New Classicals and by the real business cycles theory is why demand shocks change quantities rather than prices. Why do we observe quantity adjustments when the general equilibrium theory predicts that prices adjust and bring about a new equilibrium? In the same vein, why does an increase in nominal quantities, such as a change in money supply, affect employment and output?

Let us illustrate the point with two examples. You are the manager of a car dealership that sells 10 cars per week. Therefore, you have a standing order for the delivery of 10 cars per week from the factory. Now last week you sold 5 cars, and it seems that this week you are going to sell another 5. In other words, you are left with 10 unsold cars and 10 more on the way and your lot is getting full. What is going to be your reaction? Most likely you ask the factory to send 5 or even less cars for the time being. That is quantity adjustment as opposed to the prediction of the theory that you discern a drop in demand and lower the price. The same is true in the business upswing. If demand for cars increases, the first reaction would be to order more cars rather than increase price.

Similarly, consider a small manufacturing industry. You have 50 workers who are more or less adequate to produce the amount of output you have been able to sell. Now suppose that there is a 20% increase in demand for your product. The first reaction of the manager would be to pay overtime and produce more or hire more workers. The last thing that occurs to the manager is to immediately raise the price of his/her product. The same is true in the downswing of business. The first reaction is to wait out the reduction in demand but if that doesn't work to lay off workers.

In the examples above we see quantity rather than price adjustment. We need a theory to explain this behavior and answer the questions posed at the beginning of this section. The answer to these questions by a group of economists, who have

---

[13] See for example, Thomas Lubik and Frank Schorfheide (2004), pp. 190–217; Frank Smets and Rafael Wouters (2005), pp. 422–433; Malin Adolfson et al. (2005), pp. 444–457; and Jean-philippe Laforte (2007), pp. 127–154.

become known as New Keynesian, is rigidities in different markets. But to better understand the New Keynesian ideas, let us review the background.

For a time, that is from the early 1940s to mid-1970s, there was an uneasy compromise between micro and macroeconomics. The paradigm was labeled *the neo-classical synthesis* and consisted of optimizing households and firms at the micro level. The individuals maximized their utilities and the firms their profits. Both responded to market signals. The market was generally competitive although certain monopolies were not ruled out. Decisions at the micro level were coordinated through the market mechanism, which was captured by a general equilibrium model. But the analysis stopped here and it was argued that at macro level due to market rigidities and imperfections, we observe involuntary unemployment and cycles as captured by the Keynesian theory and the IS-LM model. There was a schizophrenic dichotomy and everyone knew it. The dichotomy was even reflected in elementary textbooks like Samuelsson's. Yet no one came up with a scheme to reconcile the two parts of the theory.

In the 1970s, the New Classicals simply assumed the problem away by declaring that all markets cleared instantaneously. This was a theory without, or perhaps in spite of, facts. But the reality prevailed. The New Keynesians came up with a number of reasons why there are rigidities at the micro level and prices and wages are sticky.[14] These elements have been incorporated in many models including the dynamic general equilibrium models discussed above.[15]

The sources of rigidities include monopolistic competitive power at the firm level, labor contracts, asymmetric information, menu cost, and efficiency wages.

Convergence in Macroeconomics: DSGE Models with New Keynesian Features

If we consider DSGE models as a tool of analysis, there is nothing to prevent us from introducing money, international trade, government budget, and New Keynesian features in them. Indeed, this is what has been happening since Kydland and Prescott ushered in such models into economics literature.

Examples of such models are many:

i. Christiano, Eichenbaum, and Evans[16] studied the effects of exogenous shocks to monetary policy within a DSGE model with Keynesian feature.
ii. Clarida, Galí, and Gertler[17] analyzed different aspects of monetary policy using a DSGE with Keynesian features.

---

[14]For a more detailed discussion of the New Keynesian models see Olivier Blanchard and Stanley Fischer (1989), Chaps. 8 and 9; Gregory Mankiw and David Romer (1991); and David Romer (2006), Chap. 6.

[15]See Michael Wickens (2008), Chap. 9.

[16]Lawrence Christiano et al. (2005), pp. 1–45.

[17]Richard Clarida et al. (1999), pp. 1661–1707.

iii. Altig, Christiano, Eichenbaum, and Linde set out to reconcile the macro observation that inflation shows inertia with the micro level observation that "firms
re-optimize prices on average every 1.5 quarters." For this purpose they use a
dynamic general equilibrium model with nominal rigidities.[18]

Woodford[19] points out that different strands of macroeconomics have converged
in these models although there is more work to be done. Of course, some are less
sanguine.[20]

Business Cycles and Economic Policy

There are two outlooks regarding business cycles. One considers business cycles as
natural occurrences that are useful for the proper functioning of a decentralized capitalist economy, something akin to brush fires that get rid of dead woods and leaves
and maintain the overall health of the forest. Or like a natural predator that plucks
out the weak of a species and leaves the healthy flock to thrive on the available food
source. In the same manner a recession weeds out inefficient firms, wipes out excess
investment and cleans the slate for future growth. This point of view is supported by
the real business cycles theory or theories that posit that unemployment is caused
by misperception of the real wage rate by workers. Proponents of this point of view
usually go one step further and claim that even if the cycles are detrimental to the
overall welfare of the society still nothing can be done about them. Any action by
the government would be counterproductive; indeed, it would cause more harm than
the cycle itself.

From the time of the Great Depression to mid-1970s such views were in the
minority both in academia and in policy circles. Since then there has been a resur-
gence of such views among academics with little influence on policy. One reason is
that during crises proponents of no action are usually in hiding. It is hard to find an
editorial or a lecture by them proposing the government refrain from doing anything
and let the cycle takes its course. Of course, once the crisis is over, it is easy to come
out and claim that the recession would have been over anyway and the government
action was superfluous.

Another point of view is that at every moment we may have either too much
investment because entrepreneurs are too optimistic or too little because pessimism
is the order of the day. Furthermore, the coordination mechanism in a decentralized
economy does not always work perfectly. As a result many individual plans may
not be compatible with each other and could not be realized. Finally, government
policies could be stimulus for disequilibrium that would result in a recession.

---

[18] David Altig et al. (2005).

[19] Michael Woodford (2009), pp. 267–279, who argues that the DSGE models are being used for
policy analysis by the IMF, the European Central Bank, and other European banks.

[20] V. Chari et al. (2009), pp. 242–266.

Consider the US economy after it had weathered the mini recession of 2001. In order to make sure that the economy would keep its footing, the Federal Reserve lowered the federal funds rate and kept it low for quite a long time. On the other hand, the September 11, 2001 terrorist attack on the United States demanded appropriate response. The United States opened two fronts against terrorists in Afghanistan and Iraq. This in turn, caused an increase in the total government expenditures and budget deficit. After President Bush's victory in 2004—given that the economy was growing—perhaps it was time to bring the budget deficit under control. But that was not to be.

Increased income and increased credit created a boom in the housing market. Some argued that the credit market was discriminatory against minorities. Hence some banks did not ask for documentation of income or any evidence that the borrower could pay back the loan, because low income minorities were the one who could not provide documentation. There was also predatory lending. The idea was that even if the borrower could not pay back the loan, the collateral in the form of the house would be worth more than the loan and the bank can recoup its money.

When the housing bubble burst, all these calculations were turned upside down. Some found that the value of their home was less than the amount of loan. Those who tried to refinance found that the credit was not available because their house wasn't worth enough. Some abandoned their home. Banks who foreclosed and took possession of the houses found that they could not sell them in the weak market. We shall return to this story in Chap. 13.

There was a danger of the banking and financial system going down and taking with it the rest of the economy. Some argued that those who took the risk or were not prudent should be punished. But suppose you try to punish the banker and housing speculator; what about all the construction workers, plumbers, electricians, factory workers producing construction material, real estate agents, and others? What about the rise in unemployment in general?

Since the Great Depression the general understanding is that the government could and should interfere in such situations. Indeed, since World War II government intervention to thwart the onset of recessions or ameliorate its effects has been the official and actual policy of all governments around the world. Duration and severity of recessions in post WWII compared to pre War years have been reduced. Furthermore, the expansion periods have been longer than during the pre War years. These have been taken as evidence that indeed countercyclical policies are effective.

Policies to counteract business cycles are of two types. First, there are automatic stabilizers. When the economy is on the downswing, the progressive tax system ensures that the total tax collection is reduced faster than the decline in income. Similarly, some government expenditures such as unemployment benefits, welfare payments, and the like are increased. In other words, there is an automatic fiscal stimulus to the economy. The reverse happens when the economy is expanding; taxes increase faster than income rises and there will be less social payments.

The second type are those discussed in Chap. 1: expansionary monetary and fiscal policy. Increasing money and liquidity in the market lowers interest rates.

To the extent that investment and consumer expenditures are affected by interest rate, its lowering would increase aggregate expenditures, income, and employment. Similarly, increase in government expenditures or reduction of taxes would be a fiscal stimulus for the economy, increasing aggregate demand.

Regarding the economic troubles of 2007–2009, the Federal Reserve lowered the interest rate and later the Congress passed a bill to send rebate checks totaling $168 billion to taxpayers below certain income levels. In other words, the government resorted to expansionary monetary and fiscal policy to stimulate the economy (see Chap. 13).

Economic Model as a Means of Communication

Economic theory is the way we organize our thoughts about economic processes and issues. Economic models make them more specific and amenable to empirical validation. But they also are a means of communication between economists, the next generation of economists to whom the ideas are transmitted, policy makers, and most importantly the public who should understand and support a policy if it is to succeed. The old IS-LM model and its extensions did that job. The model was simple, and the sign and order of magnitude of its parameters were agreed upon by most economists. It was easy for economists to say that if the economy was operating below full employment an increase in government expenditures would increase income and output. This is not to say that there was no dissent or all policy makers and members of the public understood the implications of the model or the proposed policies. There was, however, a consensus that lasted for a long time. Even today it seems to be the main vehicle of economic discourse. How else can we interpret the passage of the stimulus packages by the US Congress in 2008 and 2009 and support for them from the majority of decision makers excluding hard-line free marketers?

Even when economists or policy makers did not agree among themselves, they were speaking the same language. The differences could be narrowed down to either difference in objectives—avoiding inflation vs. avoiding recession or a slowdown in the economy—or the order of magnitude of the coefficients.

The consensus came under attack in the 1970s and soon was asunder at least in academic circles. Despite more sophisticated models proposed, nothing quite replaced the old IS-LM. The model that today comes closest to such a communication device at least in a part of the profession is the DSGE model. But the model and its results are more often researcher specific. One researcher can specify the model, choose her own parameters and come up with the conclusion that the stimulus package is effective. But another researcher could change the structure of the model or calibrate it differently or simply delete government expenditures from the model and conclude that the package would have no effects. It is difficult to communicate the results between economists; the discussion boils down to "my model" vs. "your model." To convey the conclusions to policy makers and the public is even more difficult. During the recession of 2007–2009 we hardly heard the conclusions and recommendations of the proponents of DSGE models. Some economists have expressed concern over disconnection between academic macroeconomic research and macroeconomic policy making.[21]

Nor it is easy to pass the wisdom to the next generation. The IS-LM model was taught to students in the United States and indeed around the world thanks to Samuelson's now classic textbook. On the contrary, current macroeconomics textbooks, both at graduate and undergraduate levels, either shun the subject of the DSGE models or give it a perfunctory treatment. Makiw's *Macroeconomics* (6th edition) and Gandolfo's *International Finance and Open-Economy Macroeconomics* do not mention DSGE. Blanchard's *Macroeconomics* (5th edition) and Romer's *Advanced Macroeconomics* (3rd edition) give it scant coverage. Perhaps the new book, *Macroeconomic Theory, A Dynamic General Equilibrium Approach* by Michael Wickens is the vanguard of the future crop of textbooks using DSGE models as the main analytic vehicle.

It may be argued that large Keynesian macroeconometric models had the same problem. Economists, let alone policy makers and the public, hardly knew what the several hundred equations were about. But there was a significant difference with the present models. There were no disputes regarding the core of the models. Once forecasts of the main macro variables such as the GDP, rate of interest, consumption, and others were complete the results were fed into other equations to forecast housing starts or inventory change of the auto industry. Such results were of importance to a group of people who had other means of checking the results.

What macroeconomics needs now is a more advanced and sophisticated model with the tractability and communicability features of the IS-LM. But that may be a tall order.

An Anti Empirical Trait Among Economists

From Keynes to Hayek to Lucas and Kydland and Prescott one notices a tendency to shield their theories from empirical falsification. The tendency is understandable. Consider a Marxian economist who all of his/her life has expounded on the theory that capitalism is doomed and shall be replaced by socialism. Indeed the transition is around the corner, only as far away as the next recession. The whole theory is based on a vague concept called surplus value and the proposition that the rate of profit is declining. Now an assistant professor or a graduate student shows up, collects data, and runs a regression and shows that not only the rate of profit is not decreasing but indeed is increasing. What is our prominent Marxian economist supposed to do? Of course, the honest thing to do is to say: "I have been wrong all these years."

---

[21] For example Gregory Mankiw (2006), pp. 29–46. See also Woodford, op. cit., who argues that the DSGE models are being used for policy analysis by the IMF, the European Central Bank, and other European banks.

But not everybody is that honest or brave. There are several ways to hide behind ostensibly philosophical or technical statements: (1) I don't "believe" in this data, (2) the test is inappropriate, (3) the whole econometrics practice is irrelevant, and (4) the theory (i.e., my theory) is not subject to empirical test. The last statement in particular makes a religion out of economics and potentially is the most dangerous one. If you look for such statements you will be surprised how frequently they show up. Below are a few examples.

In his Nobel Prize lecture Friedrich Hayek stated:

> But because we, the observing scientists, can thus never know all the determinants of such an order, and in consequence also cannot know at which particular structure of prices and wages demand would everywhere equal supply, we also cannot measure the deviations from that order; nor can we statistically test our theory that it is the deviations from that "equilibrium" system of prices and wages which make it impossible to sell some of the products and services at the prices at which they are offered.

And later he added

> Its effect has been that what is probably the true cause of extensive unemployment has been disregarded by the scientistically[22] minded majority of economists, because its operation could not be confirmed by directly observable relations between measurable magnitudes, and that an almost exclusive concentration on quantitatively measurable surface phenomena has produced a policy which has made matters worse.

And even later

> I confess that I prefer true but imperfect knowledge, even if it leaves much indetermined and unpredictable, to a pretence of exact knowledge that is likely to be false. The credit which the apparent conformity with recognized scientific standards can gain for seemingly simple but false theories may, as the present instance shows, have grave consequences.

But if you just haven't come down from the mountain, how do you know which is the "true" and which is the "false" theory?

Kydland and Prescott say that by Lucas's definition a theory is

> an explicit set of instructions for building an imitation economy to address certain questions and not a collection of assertions about the behavior of the actual economy. Consequently, statistical hypothesis testing, which is designed to test assertions about actual systems, is not an appropriate tool for testing economic theory. One way to test a theory is to determine whether model economies constructed according to the instructions of that theory mimic certain aspects of reality.[23]

This corresponds to Keynes's view that considered economic theory a collection of tools. But also note two points. First, "instructions" would be practitioner specific and therefore, as mentioned above, precludes communications among economists. Second, "mimic[ing] certain aspects of reality," is in the eye of the beholder, further precluding consensus.

Incidentally, an early and scathing criticism of this kind of theorizing comes from Milton Friedman. In reviewing Oscar Lange's work, Friedman noted: "The approach

---

[22] This is not a typo, it is the way Hayek used it.

[23] Finn Kydland and Edward Prescott (1996), p. 83.

that is standard in the physical sciences is to use theory to derive generalizations about the real world."[24] "A theory that has no implications that facts, potentially capable of being observed, can contradict is useless for prediction."[25] He added:

> For the most part, the crucial question, "What observed facts would contradict the generalization suggested, and what operations could be followed to observe such critical facts?" is never asked; and the theory is so set up that it could seldom be answered if it were asked. The theory provides formal models of imaginary worlds, not generalizations about the real world.[26]

Finally, in its abstract Jesper Lindé describes his article thus

> I use a real-business-cycle model to verify that Lucas critique is quantitatively important in theory, and to examine the properties of superexogeneity test, which is used to detect the applicability of the Lucas critique in practice. The results suggest that the superexogeneity test is not capable of detecting the relevance of the Lucas critique in small samples.[27]

Let us paraphrase this and say that a believer in the existence of otherworldly angels sets up a model in which angels do exist and runs a physical or chemical test that is incapable of detecting the angels. Does that mean angels exist? Here lies the danger of making macroeconomics into some kind of religion with different sects and cults.

We have been here before. For a long time economists elaborated on general equilibrium theory. No one claimed that the model corresponded to any economy. Indeed, some crucial features of modern economies such as money, government, and international trade were absent. Yet the work continued in the belief (or pretension) that the exercise would provide "insight" into the working of the economy. Moreover, since many economists were working on it, at some point in the future a more complete model with money and everything would be built. The enterprise did not bear fruits that we can speak of.

To see how such attachment to a model could cause the analysis to become irrelevant, consider the issue of difference in unemployment rates between the United States and Europe. During the 1950s all the way to early 1980s Europe had a lower unemployment rate than the United States. This situation has changed in the recent decades and the US has a lower unemployment rate. A legitimate question for economists to answer is what caused this reversal of fortune. Chari and Kehoe[28] describe the answer offered by Prescott.

> Prescott (2002) cleverly sidestepped [the issue of how taxes are spent] by noting that in a general equilibrium model, the details of the expenditures are captured by their effects on consumption. ... Assuming that both the utility function and the production function have unit elasticity of substitution between consumption and leisure, and using long-term

---

[24] Milton Friedman (1953b), p. 282.

[25] Op. cit. p. 283.

[26] Ibid.

[27] Jesper Lindé (2001), pp. 986–1005.

[28] V. Chari and Patrick Kehoe (2006), pp. 3–28.

averages to pin down share parameters, Prescott showed that this simple theory works sur-
prisingly well in accounting for employment observations for the G-7 countries (that is,
the United States, Canada, France, Germany, Italy, Japan, and the United Kingdom) for
the 1970s and the 1990s. The Prescott analysis works well in a comparison of the early
1970s and the mid-1990s, in part because tax policies clearly changed dramatically during
this time. His analysis works less well in a comparison of the 1950s and the 1970s. . . . As
Prescott has acknowledged, his analysis does not work well for the Scandinavian countries,
which generally have both high tax rates and high employment.

In other words, we have a cleverly constructed theory that only works if you
compare early 1970s to mid-1990s and even then it does not work for the Scandinavian countries. Incidentally, if you look up the table in Chari and Kehoe's paper you
notice that the theory doesn't work well for Japan and Italy either.

Chapter 9
Money, Monetary Policy, and Monetarism

We suffer from the longest and one of the worst sustained inflations in our national history. It distorts our economic decisions, penalizes thrift and crushes the struggling young and the fixed-income elderly alike. It threatens to shatter the lives of millions of our people.
The inaugural speech of President Ronald Reagan,
January 20, 1981

Every empirical study rests on a theoretical framework, on a set of tentative hypotheses that the evidence is designed to test or to adumbrate. ... That framework is the quantity theory of money—a theory that has taken many different forms and traces back to the very beginning of systematic thinking about economic matters. It has probably been "tested" with quantitative data more extensively than any other set of propositions in formal economics—unless it be the negatively sloping demand curve.
Milton Friedman. "A Theoretical Framework for
Monetary Analysis"

But down these mean streets a man must go who is not himself mean, who is neither tarnished nor afraid.
Raymond Chandler, "The Simple Art of Murder"

Early in 1979 inflation rate in the United States reached 10% and there were no signs of let up on the horizon; indeed, it would reach 14% in 1980 before subsiding (Fig. 9.1). If one relied on estimates of the Phillips curve, another Great Depression would be needed to get rid of inflation. Past expansionary policies were bearing fruit. [1]

Then in August 1979 President Jimmy Carter appointed Paul Volcker as the Chairman of the Board of Governors of the Federal Reserve. Volcker had wide government and banking experience; he had been Under Secretary of the Treasury Department, vice president of Chase Manhattan Bank, and president of the Federal

---

[1] Robert J. Samuelson recounts the history of inflation of the 1960s and 1970s, which was brought down in the 1980s and discusses its transforming effects on the American society in *The Great Inflation and Its Aftermath*, 2008.

K. Dadkhah, *The Evolution of Macroeconomic Theory and Policy*,
DOI 10.1007/978-3-540-77008-4_9, © Springer-Verlag Berlin Heidelberg 2009

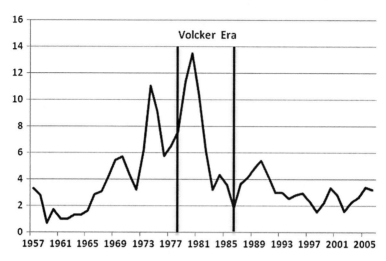

Fig. 9.1 Inflation rate in the United States

Reserve Bank of New York. He was reappointed by President Reagan to another term and left the Fed in 1987.

During his tenure at the Fed, Volcker used monetary policy to effectively bring down the inflation rate. His success enabled the US economy to enjoy a long period of growth without inflation or serious fear of inflation. He deserves much credit and praise. He raised the federal funds rate to restrain credit and money. In December of 1978, the federal funds rate reached 10%. The rate was kept up and in April 1980 was just under 18%. After that there was an easing of monetary policy, perhaps because the presidential election was around the corner. However, in October of that year the tightening of money was resumed and the rate reached the unprecedented level of above 19% (Fig. 9.2). The contraction of the money supply, in turn, caused high rates of unemployment that were unprecedented in the post War era. For instance, in September 1982 the unemployment rate reached 10.1% and for ten months stayed above 10% (Fig. 9.3).

Ultimately, the inflation was tamed. The country paid a heavy price in terms of lost employment and output. But perhaps there were no alternatives. Inflation and expectation of inflation had to be eradicated so that the economy could grow. Indeed, for the next two and a half decades, we have witnessed growth without serious inflation.

Nowadays, the idea that inflation is caused by increased money supply seems to be universally accepted. Yet it was not always so. For many years, particularly in the 1980s, imported inflation and structural inflation were named as causes of domestic inflation.[2] Moreover, there has been the talk of money being endogenous, that is, a

---

[2]Even today in some countries, usually those prone to conspiracy theories, the idea of imported inflation is frequently floated to deflect the attention of the population from the government's mismanagement of the economy.

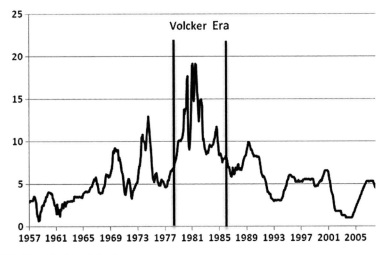

Fig. 9.2 Monthly federal funds rate

Fig. 9.3 Monthly unemployment rate

passive element responding to changes in other economic variables. Thus, money would not be the cause but a symptom or side-effect.

The experience of the United States in the 1980s and other countries that fought inflation are convincing evidence that money is the cause and that the conduct of monetary policy is of great importance for the health of the economy. It is not surprising that many countries have made their central banks independent and charged them with keeping the value of domestic currency stable.

Intellectually, these developments owe a lot to monetarists and particularly to Milton Friedman. In this chapter we shall explore issues of monetary policy and central banking. We shall also discuss monetarism. Needless to say, not all ideas of monetarists were accepted or plausible.

The Quantity Theory of Money

We start the discussion of monetarism with the Fisher (sometimes called Newcomb-Fisher) equation of exchange.[3] Let T denote the total volume of trade, M the amount of money in circulation, P the general price level, and V the velocity of circulation, that is, the average number of times money changes hands. Then the equation of exchange is

$$MV = PT$$

We can consider this equation as an equilibrium condition. Suppose that the volume of trade is given; furthermore assume that either V is constant or that its value is determined by factors such as interest rate and income. Then once the amount of money in circulation is determined by the central bank, the equation of exchange determines the general price level that equates both sides of the equation. Hence, a doubling of money supply would bring about, after a period of adjustment, an equilibrium general price level that is twice its previous value.

While the above description is an elementary textbook caricature of the monetarist position, it contains an important proposition of monetarism, namely that the cause of inflation is monetary growth. This conclusion is incontrovertible, in that around the world and in all recorded instances, inflation has had monetary cause.

The equation, however, raises many questions. These include definitions and measurement of the variables involved, the constancy or stability of V, and the nature of the relationship. These issues were discussed from the early days of the theory. In particular, the choice of a price index and the definition of money were contentious issues. Presumably the volume of trade should encompass all transactions including financial assets and resale of goods and assets. Such a measure is not compiled by any statistical office and its usefulness can be questioned. It is replaced by the aggregate output as measured by the GDP in constant prices. Thus, we can write the equation as

$$MV = Py$$

Now P is the implicit GDP deflator and Py represents nominal GDP. Both M1 and M2 are used as measures of the money supply.[4] Again suppose that V is constant

---

[3] Although we start with Fisher's equation, the theory and the equation have a much longer history dating back to David Hume and Copernicus.

[4] The Federal Reserve defines money in three different ways: M1 consists of currency, travelers checks, demand deposits, and other checkable deposits; M2 is equal to M1 plus retail money market

or somehow determined, then the amount of money in circulation determines the nominal value of the GDP in the short run and the long run. Further, if in the long run, the value of the real GDP settles at the amount commensurate with the natural rate of unemployment, M would determine the level of P. These are the two main propositions of monetarism as expounded by Milton Friedman.

The policy implication is clear: if the central bank wants to control the inflation rate, it has to control the growth rate of the money supply. Note that the equation implies that in the long run the rate of growth of the money supply is equal to the growth rate of GDP plus inflation rate:

$$\frac{dM/dt}{M} = \frac{dP/dt}{P} + \frac{dy/dt}{y}$$

For instance, in the United States the long run growth rate is about 3.3% per year, and if we assume that the desirable rate of inflation for the economy is 2%, then the Fed should keep the growth rate of money supply at 5.3%. Friedman went further and said that the Fed should be compelled, perhaps through a Constitutional amendment, to adhere to a preset rate for the growth of money supply. In our example, the Fed should follow the rule that money supply should grow at 5.3%, no more and no less. In other words, the Fed should not have a discretionary power.

Friedman's policy prescription raises two questions. First, is V constant or stable to the extent that we can base the nation's monetary policy on the equation of exchange? Second, is the central bank able to control money supply to a reasonable degree of certainty?

The answer to the first question is important. If like the early advocates of the Fisher equation, we state that the velocity of circulation is determined by several factors including the interest rate and expected rate of inflation and the like, then the equation of exchange turns into a special case of the LM curve. To see this, let $V = V(i)$ and rewrite the Fisher equation as

$$\frac{M}{P} = V(i)^{-1}y = L(i,y)$$

The new version of the equation brings up the more important issue of the nature of the relationship. Note that we have one equation with four variables. Therefore, three variables have to be either constant or determined outside this equation. If we consider it as an equilibrium condition for the economy as a whole—a position taken by the originators of the theory—then it determines the aggregate price level, given that the other variables are already determined. The output is at its long run level (consistent with the natural rate of employment), money is determined by the central bank, and the velocity is either constant or a function of the interest rate, which itself is determined through another equation. However, it is possible to interpret

---

mutual funds, and savings and small time deposits. In the past the Fed defined M3 to consist of M2 plus large time deposits, repurchase agreements (RPs), euro-dollars, and institutions' money market mutual funds. In recent years the Fed has stopped compiling M3.

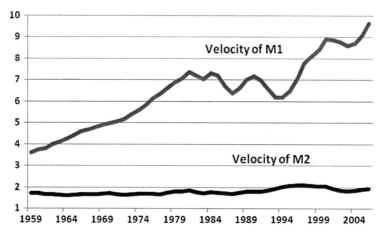

Fig. 9.4   Velocity of circulation

the equation as the demand for money function. In this case, we need a few more equations to determine output, interest rate, and the price level. The issue of the nature of this relationship doesn't seem to have been adequately discussed in the literature.

Figure 9.4 shows the evolution of the velocity in the United States over time. It is clear that the velocity of circulation for M1 is quite volatile especially after 1981. Thus, the monetary policy based on M1 is at the mercy of God. On the other hand, the velocity of M2 seems to be reasonably stable, and it is on this observation that Friedman based his recommendation to use M2 as the policy instrument for the United States. We should note that in another country and at another historical time it may be M1 or even currency in circulation that has a stable velocity.

The second issue—the ability of the central bank to control money supply effectively and in a timely fashion—faces two problems. First, unlike the federal funds rate that is continuously observable as a market variable, compilation of data on money supply takes time. Thus, the Fed's information on the money supply lags behind actual developments in the money market. But more important, as we shall show below in the section on the process of money supply, the Fed does not have complete control over money supply. The central bank's decisions are an important factor in determining the money supply, but there are other variables that are as important and are not under the control of the central bank.

The Money Supply Process

Monetary policy is conducted by the central banks, which in the United States is the Federal Reserve System. Monetary policy refers to the manipulation of money supply thereby affecting the interest rates lenders charge borrowers, depositors receive from banks, and government pays on its debt. Since these rates affect decisions to consume, save, and invest, monetary policy has far reaching effects on the economy. Too much liquidity in the economy could cause and accelerate inflation, and tight money could bring about recession.

The central bank has several instruments for affecting money supply and thereby interest rates: required reserve ratio, discount rate, and open market operation.

The required reserve ratio is the percentage of deposits that banks have to keep with the central bank. The central bank can require commercial banks to deposit a certain portion, say, 8% or 10% of their deposits with the central bank. Increasing this ratio would restrict commercial banks ability to extend credit and increase liquidity. Reducing it would have the opposite effect. In recent decades the Fed has refrained from manipulating this ratio to adjust the money supply in order to achieve short term policy goals.

Commercial banks under certain conditions can borrow funds from the central bank. The interest rate the banks are charged for the use of this facility is called the discount rate. By reducing the discount rate, the central bank encourages commercial banks to borrow and extend credit to their customers. The reverse would restrict credit and liquidity.

In many elementary textbooks M is *determined* by the Fed. Some critics of monetarist ideas have argued that money is endogenous or passive and, therefore, cannot be an exogenous variable and tool of the policy. Both are partially correct. Or more precisely, the process of money supply is somewhat more complicated than either declares.

Let us start with the definition of money in the narrow sense:

$$M = C + D$$

where C is currency in circulation and D the demand deposits. Let cu denote the currency deposit ratio

$$cu = \frac{C}{D}$$

Then we have

$$M = (cu + 1)D$$

We define *the monetary base* or *high powered money*, B, as the sum of currency in circulation plus the required reserves, Rr; that is, the part of commercial banks' demand deposits that they are required to keep as reserves with the central bank. The rationale for this definition will become clear below.

$$B = C + Rr$$

Let x be the required reserve ratio

$$x = \frac{R}{D}$$

Then

$$B = (cu + x)\,D \quad \text{or} \quad D = \frac{1}{cu + x}\,B$$

Combining the above with the equation for money supply, we get

$$M = \frac{cu + 1}{cu + x}\,B$$

$(cu + 1)/(cu + x)$ is called the money multiplier. Thus, money supply equals money multiplier times the monetary base.

But now we may ask why did we define the monetary base as we did? Consider a stylized balance sheet of a central bank.

Assets	Liabilities
Foreign assets	Foreign liabilities
Government borrowing (bonds)	Government deposits
Commercial banks' borrowed reserves	Commercial banks' excess reserves
	Commercial banks' required reserves
	Currency in circulation

We have neglected a few items but their inclusion would not have affected the result. The sum of assets should equal the sum of liabilities. Therefore, rearranging terms, we can see that the monetary base (the sum of the last two items in the liabilities column) should equal the sum of net foreign assets (assets less liabilities), net government borrowing (borrowing minus deposits), and net borrowed reserves.

By excess reserves we mean commercial banks, deposits with the central bank in excess of the required reserves, and by borrowed reserves, we mean commercial banks, borrowing from the central bank. Their difference or net borrowed reserves is a function of market interest rate and the central banks' discount rate. An increase in the rates of interest in the market would encourage banks to borrow more reserves. Increasing the discount rate would discourage banks from borrowing from the central bank thereby limiting their ability to extend credit. Thus, we may write the net borrowed reserves H as a function of the difference between market rate of interest, i, and the discount rate, i^d

$$H = H(i - i^d)$$

We can summarize the arguments above in the following formula:

$$M = \frac{cu + 1}{cu + x}[F + G + H(i - i^d)]$$

where F is net foreign assets, and G net government borrowing.

The above formula shows that the Fed can effect changes in the money supply through three channels or instruments: the open market operation (buying and selling government bonds) which affects G, changes in the required reserves ratio, and the discount rate. In recent years, the discount rate has lost its place as an important policy instrument.

In the meantime, the formula shows that the Fed does not have absolute control over money supply. The public as well as banking technology can change the currency deposit ratio and through it the money multiplier. An increase in that ratio would reduce the money multiplier and would counteract the Fed's intentions. Similarly, H would be affected if the public changes its behavior regarding its demand for credit or banks change their reactions to interest rates in regards to the supply of credit.

The lack of total control is even more pronounced in the case of broadly defined money. Consider M2 which is composed of currency in circulation plus checking, savings, and time deposits. The money supply is determined as

$$ M = \frac{cu + 1}{cu + \alpha x_1 + (1 - \alpha)x_2}[F + G + H(i - i^d)] $$

where x_1 and x_2 are, respectively, required reserve ratios for checking and savings and time deposits and α is the share of demand deposits in total deposits.

There are other reasons for uncertainty with respect to the central bank's ability to control the money supply particularly in developing countries. Consider the oil producing countries such as Saudi Arabia or Russia. A huge amount of foreign assets is acquired through oil exports. That would increase F and, therefore, the money supply unless some countermeasures are taken by the central bank. After the oil price increase in 1973, several members of the OPEC including Saudi Arabia, Iran, and Algeria experienced unprecedented inflation. Saudi Arabia was able to stop the inflation due to its extraordinarily large resources.

The Federal Funds Market

Commercial banks are required to keep a percentage of their deposits with the Federal Reserve banks. These are called required reserves. Banks sometimes keep with the Fed reserves in excess of what is required. They also keep reserves to clear financial transactions. Some banks may have a shortfall in their reserves and others may have excess reserves. It seems natural that those who have a shortfall borrow from those who have excess reserves and pay an interest on their loans. Indeed, this is what banks started to do as far back as the summer of 1921 in New York City.

In addition to banks, participants in the federal funds market include thrift institutions, agencies and branches of foreign banks in the United States, federal agencies, and government securities dealers. Transactions are usually for overnight. But the parties could agree on long term contracts whereby overnight transactions are automatically renewed until the agreement is terminated by either the borrower or lender.

At any moment the amount of funds available in the market is fixed and the transactions between participants would not increase or decrease it. Thus, the interest rate prevailing in the market, that is, the Federal Funds rate reflects the value market participants put on the use of available funds. The Federal Reserve Board of Governors, however, could increase or decrease the available funds, thus changing the prevailing rate. This is done through the open market operation conducted by the Federal Open Market Committee (FOMC).

Open Market Operation and FOMC

By far the most important instrument is the open market operation which is conducted by FOMC. The Federal Open Market Commission has 12 members; the seven members of the Board of Governors of the Federal Reserve System, the president of the Federal Reserve Bank of New York, plus four out of 11 presidents of regional Federal Reserve Banks. The regional banks are divided into four groups: Boston, Philadelphia, and Richmond; Cleveland and Chicago; Atlanta, St. Louis, and Dallas; and Minneapolis, Kansas City, and San Francisco. From each group one president serves one year on a rotating basis. The FOMC has eight regularly scheduled meetings every year. The other seven presidents could attend and participate in discussions, but do not vote.

The decisions are based on an assessment of the economic conditions of the country. If there is a fear of inflation or its acceleration, the FOMC may decide to reduce liquidity in the economy. By selling government bonds, money supply is reduced and the federal funds rate is increased. Conversely, when the Fed concludes that the economy is moving toward recession, FOMC orders buying government bonds, thus providing banks and other participants with more money. Such a move would reduce the federal funds rate. The selling or buying of government bonds is called open market operation. As described above, an instance of the Fed fighting inflation by contractionary monetary policy happened during the chairmanship of Paul Volcker in 1979–1987, which resulted in reducing inflation and eliminating inflationary expectations in the US economy. Similarly, in 1987 the stock market took a nosedive prompting a fear that the economy would go into recession. The Fed stepped in to announce that it would provide liquidity to the economy, thereby averting a repetition of 1929.

The federal funds rate is determined by market forces of supply and demand. The Fed staff have to estimate how much additional reserves would bring the rate to the desired level. Since the rate is observable on a daily basis, the Fed can make adjustments through trial and error. It may be asked why the federal funds rate, why not the prime rate, Treasury bills or even mortgage rates. The fact is that all interest rates are connected[5] and changing one would affect all the rates. The federal funds rate has the advantage of being affected by the FOMC decisions most directly and fastest.

Targeting Money Supply vs. the Federal Funds Rate

Monetarists have argued that the Fed or any central bank should simply target the money supply, for example M2, and not concern itself with anything else. In particular the growth rate of money supply should be kept constant and the Fed should refrain from manipulating the rate of interest. The Fed adopted such a policy in 1979 and a few years later determined that it did not work and chose to target the federal funds rate.

There are several reasons for the Fed to prefer working with the Federal funds rate rather than the money supply. First, as mentioned above, while the Fed has many instrument to affect money supply it does not have full control over it. The situation is aggravated by a second factor. It takes time to collect and compile money supply data. Information from banks has to be collected, collated, and aggregated. This takes time but so does data collection for each bank. Thus, there is always two weeks lag in the preliminary data for the money supply becoming available and about four weeks lag for the final estimates. Thus, it may happen that the central bank perceives the money supply is on the rise and tries to curb it. By the time final figures are available, it may be that the money supply was not rising at all and the Fed's intervention could cause problems. The Fed's decisions are supposed to steer the course of the economy in the future. But neither is the present state of affairs free of uncertainty nor can the future effects of the decisions taken be predicted with reasonable confidence.

The federal funds rate is observable on a regular basis without any uncertainty. Moreover, the Fed can decrease the rate by providing more funds to the market through open market operations. Alternatively, it can increase the rate by selling bonds. In either instance, the Fed's intention would not be thwarted by the public or financial institutions.

Paul Volcker points out another reason for the Federal Open Market Committee (FOMC) preference for the federal funds rate. He notes that the members do not completely trust the chairman. As mentioned above, there is a two weeks lag in availability of data regarding the magnitude of money supply. Other members of the FOMC are suspicious that the chairman might use this small leeway to produce results that are slightly different from what the committee wants.

---

[5]Later in this chapter we discuss the term structure of interest rates, that is, the connection between rates for bonds with different maturities. In general rates are connected through arbitrage.

Central Bank's Credibility

Some years ago on a CBS 60 Minutes program a police chief reminisced about his youth growing up in Harlem in New York City. He recalled that every week a frail old woman would carry two bags full of money in plain sight of everyone. Yet despite the neighborhood being rough no one bothered the woman. Because everyone knew that she was carrying the money for the mob and if anything happened to her within a space of time there would be retribution. Now this is credibility. Everyone believes you and you need not threaten anyone or take any action.

In this regard it is instructive to remember that on July 15, 2008 Treasury Secretary Henry Paulson told the Senate Banking Committee "if you have a bazooka in your pocket and people know it, you probably won't have to use it." He was talking about rescuing Fannie Mae (the Federal National Mortgage Association) and Freddie Mac (the Federal Home Loan Mortgage Corporation), which were in trouble due to the housing and credit crisis of 2007–2009. The Treasury Secretary was seeking broad powers to extend credit to the mortgage giants, buy their preferred stocks, or take them over. He hoped that such a potential backing would cause investors and lenders to buy stocks and bonds of the two corporations and the government wouldn't have to do much. Market response was not what was expected. On September 7, 2008 Paulson announced that the government was taking over Fannie Mae and Freddie Mac.

A central bank in conducting monetary policy needs to convince the financial community, investors, and consumers that it means business and will stick to its guns. Suppose the central bank announces that it intends to hold inflation rate around two percent. If everyone thinks that the bank under pressure will budge and "this too shall pass," no one will have a reason to adjust the expectation of inflation. The bank will have a hard time convincing everyone to fall in line. On the other hand, a credible central bank need not persuade anyone. Its statements are as good as gold.

This is important in that on occasion the economy may experience a shock that would increase prices temporarily. For instance, there may be storm in the sea cutting oil production, or a frost affecting agricultural products, or some political event causing turmoil in the market. When the financial sector, firms, and consumers believe that the central bank is committed to a policy of stable prices there is no reason to panic or fan the flames of inflationary expectations. Thus, the central bank has to deal with the particular event or simply let the shock work itself out.

Two necessary, though not sufficient, conditions for a central bank to be credible are independence and transparency.

Central Bank's Independence

Central bank independence has been a hot topic for both researchers and policy makers. It is argued that an independent central bank can effectively control inflation and ward off political pressure to increase liquidity and aggregate demand. At the time of elections in developed and democratic countries the party in power may pressure the central bank to lower the interest rate and give a boost to the economy. In developing countries an undemocratic government may ask the governor of the central bank—who usually is a government employee and an appointee of the finance minister—to print money and extend credit to the government and government owned companies.

An independent central bank has a board of governors whose members are appointed for a set period with the approval of the parliament and whose members cannot be removed at the whim of the executive branch. Moreover, the mission of such a board is clearly spelled out and the board is answerable to the public. In a democratic country such a central bank can stand up to political pressure and carry out its mission to keep inflation rate within certain bounds. In addition, the bank may be charged with promoting economic activity and economic stability. Then the bank has to consider the tradeoff between the goals.

The independence of central banks is a qualitative characteristic and is a matter of degree. It is said to depend on the following[6] four criteria:

1. The board members of the central bank including its chairman need to be insulated from political pressure. This can be achieved when the management of the bank is appointed by the approval of both executive and legislative branches of the government and is guaranteed a set period of tenure.
2. The board should be able to make decisions without interference or participation from any branches of the government. Moreover, a bank's decisions have to be final and not subject to revision or annulment by the government.
3. The mandate of the bank should clearly define its duties and objectives. A bank with a single objective—for example, the European Central Bank (ECB) which is charged with maintaining price stability—is more independent than a bank with multiple objectives—for example, the US Federal Reserve which is charged with maintaining price stability and maximum employment.
4. There have to be limits on the lending to the government. Without such limits government can borrow extensively from the central bank thus throwing monetary policy into a tailspin. See the section on the money supply process where the effect of government borrowing on money supply is discussed. The stricter the limits on government borrowing from the central bank the more effectively it can carry out its policy mandate.

Borrowing from the literature of fuzzy logic we may say that the membership function in the set of independent banks is not a binary variable. Rather it is like membership in the set of tall people or large cities. Having any of the following attributes adds to the independence of the central bank and the stronger the attribute the higher is the membership score. A bank that has all the characteristics to the

---

[6]Christopher Crowe and Ellen E. Meade (2007), pp. 69–90.

highest level has a membership function of one and a bank that lacks all of them a membership score of zero.

There has been an extensive literature on the connection between central bank independence and inflation. The conclusions of this literature are mixed.

Inflation Targeting

In the 1990s a number of central banks around the world adopted a framework called inflation targeting for the conduct of monetary policy.[7] The idea is straightforward: the central bank announces an inflation target for the economy and tries to keep the actual rate close to it. Thus, when the inflation rate shows a sign of increasing, the bank raises the interest rate and restricts credit to bring down the inflation. Conversely, when inflation is low, the bank would lower the interest rate and ease credit.

Such a framework would best suit central banks that have independence and have a single mandate, namely, the stability of the internal value of the currency. Thus, the European Central Bank (ECB) which is charged with maintaining price stability has adopted inflation targeting. The United States Federal Reserve, however, has to pursuit "maximum employment, stable prices, and moderate long-term interest rates." These goals are not always compatible, and therefore, the Fed cannot set a single inflation target and commit itself to its attainment and maintenance.

Price stability does not mean zero inflation and the central bank should not aim for zero inflation. Usually the target is 2–3% inflation rate. The reason is that nominal wages are downwardly rigid. Most employees, except in extraordinary circumstances, would not agree to lower their wages. Yet because of changes in economic conditions and because of different rates of productivity gains not all businesses can grant wage increases and some need to cut the real wage of their employees. If the economy as a whole is experiencing, say, 2% inflation, then by default all employees will have a 2% cut in their real wages unless they get pay increases. This allows the employers whose business is doing all right and experiencing productivity gains to grant wage increases of 2% and more. On the other hand those businesses that are having a hard time can keep wages constant and indeed reduce their real costs.

The alternative for the latter group of businesses is to lay off workers. The choice of zero inflation rate as a target, therefore, would increase the natural rate of unemployment. For this reason it is prudent to have a target rate of about 2% and indeed all central banks which practice inflation targeting have chosen rates of no less than 2%.

It is easy to see that a requirement for adopting inflation targeting is the central bank's independence. Furthermore, transparency would make the job of inflation targeting much easier. Indeed it is difficult to see how a central bank can pursue inflation targeting and maintain vagueness or secrecy about its goals and policies.

---

[7] A good reading on this subject is Ben Bernanke and Frederic Mishkin (1997), pp. 97–116.

Monetarism Program for Monetary Stability

A group of economists including Milton Friedman, Alan Meltzer, Karl Brunner and others came to be known as monetarists, that is, those who advocate the monetarist understanding of the economy and the set of policies implied by it. But it should be noted that there are not one but several brands of monetarism.[8] All of them share in the view that money is the source of fluctuations in the economy and accuse Keynes and Keynesians as having downplayed its role. They share the view that a decentralized capitalist economy is inherently stable and should be left to itself. Some fluctuations in the economy are natural and would work themselves out. Tampering with the economy would result in amplifying these fluctuations. Indeed, they accuse the Federal Reserve System of aggravating perhaps a normal business cycle into the Great Depression. In general they are suspicious of government meddling in the economy.

Going back to the process of money supply, recall that money supply equals monetary base times money multiplier. According to monetarists the Fed can and should control the monetary base and allow it to grow at a steady rate in accord with the needs of the economy. Furthermore, in order to eliminate the sources of fluctuations in money multiplier they propose requiring 100% reserve banking. Thus, banks will not be found illiquid. If this is implemented there would be no reason for a shift in currency deposit ratio. The combined effect would be a stable velocity of circulation and the elimination of all fluctuations due to monetary factors.

Note that the 100% reserve requirement for banks eliminates their role in financial intermediation, because money creation by banks is nothing more than borrowing short term from depositors and lending long term to investors. Monetarists suggest that financial intermediation should be carried out in capital markets where both lenders and borrowers are clear about what they are doing and make their decisions based on risks and returns.

As noted earlier some monetarists are quite suspicious of the power of state. They believe, with some justification, especially in the case of developing countries, that an unconstrained central bank will impose inflationary tax on the citizens by printing money and allowing the government to pay for its expenditures without (explicit) taxation. In all countries a central bank can become an instrument of the political party in power. For instance, the bank will be under pressure to help the government at election times. Thus, instead of serving the interest of the people and the economy it will serve the politicians and bureaucrats. Worse, if the management is incompetent it can seriously hurt the economy.

Rules vs. Discretion

Friedman went further than prescribing the Fed control money supply. He argued that we don't know enough about the working of the economy, and there are enough lags and leads in the effects of money supply that the Fed's discretionary

---

[8]For more on the subject of monetarism see J. Bradford De Long (2000), pp. 83–94.

intervention may be counterproductive and aggravate the situation. To see his point let us assume that the economy follows a cyclical path similar to a trigonometric function. If the central bank can pinpoint the exact low and high points of the function and intervene at the exact moment, then it may be able to reduce the amplitude of the function and produce a smoother path for the economy. But suppose it cannot pinpoint such points or by the time it gets its act together and intervenes it is too late, then it only increases the amplitude of the function and causes more fluctuations.

Underneath such seemingly practical considerations lie Friedman's and Chicago school's suspicion of government and an aversion to allowing the government to have discretionary power over economic affairs. Their argument is quite general and extends to all manners of control. Consider a government agency charged with controlling utility rates. The agency on the one hand has to deal with a small number of utility companies with extensive resources. A small rate increase would benefits these companies tremendously. Needless to say, the companies are ready to spare no expense, lobby, bribe, and persuade the top brass of the agency to vote their way. On the other side are the mass of consumers each having a small stake in this affair. Usually they are not organized and many may shrug their shoulders over the rate increase. Thus, the regulating agency turns into an instrument of utility companies.

In the case of the central bank, political temptation is too much. Consider election time. A president could persuade the central bank to increase the supply of money and create a mini boom. Once the election is won, of course, the bank can go back and try to mitigate the inflationary effects of its easy monetary policy.

While in many respects Friedman's argument won the day and countries and central banks became more conscious of the role of money and controlling inflation, in a significant way the apparatus of monetary policy evolved in an opposite direction. Friedman and monetarists wanted a powerless Fed that would follow a set rule. Instead, we have an independent Fed with authority over monetary policy. The same has happened around the world. Friedman advocated a central bank that had control neither of the objectives nor of the instruments of monetary policy. As Alan Blinder has noted the central banks are bound by their mandates to follow certain objectives but they are free in their choice of instruments.

Time Inconsistency of Optimal Plans

It is a bad idea to build houses on flood plains, where they could be washed away within a few years. It seems reasonable for the government to declare that it will not build dams and levees to protect houses in a flood plain and anyone who does so is on his/her own. This policy would be optimal for the society. But suppose some go ahead and build such houses. Now maximizing social welfare calls for building dams and levees to protect such houses, and if houses are washed away, helping the owners. Simply put, the policy that was optimal yesterday isn't optimal anymore.

What makes such plans not optimal is the fact that rational decision makers figure out that the government will not stick to the plan. Should there be some law or strong commitment by the government not to change its policy, rational individuals would adjust their expectations, and there would be no need to change the plan. This is the gist of the argument forwarded by Kydland and Prescott in their seminal paper.[9]

There are other examples, where the government may decide on an optimal policy and then find it expedient or beneficial to the society to renege on it. Research and development benefit the society. The government may give a long term tax break or grant patent rights to pharmaceutical companies that invest in research for new drugs. But once drugs are discovered and the company is making large profits, the government may think it fair to revoke the tax exemption, or force the company to give up its patents or sell the drugs at a considerable discount to poor countries.

Another example would be a government that encourages capital formation through tax incentives. But, once savings are made and factories are built, the government may feel that it would be good policy to tax capital and spend it on social programs.

In both these cases, if firms and individuals suspect that the government will change course, they will adjust their expectations of the future and, therefore, their present behavior.

We already have discussed the argument against activist monetary policy to lower the unemployment rate by increasing money supply and thus inducing a higher rate of inflation. The policy works as long as individuals have not anticipated the policy and, therefore, have not adjusted their expectations of inflation. Once the public is onto the central bank's scheme, they will anticipate higher inflation rate and the policy will become ineffective. The only outcome of the monetary policy would be higher rates of inflation with no lasting effects on unemployment.

This argument is different from Friedman's in favor of rules vs. discretion. Yet it strengthens the case for the government and central banks to be constrained to follow a predetermined policy. What is important is the credibility of the government and central bank.

The Term Structure of Interest Rates

We may ask why the Fed targets one interest rate when there is a plethora of interest rates. Why shouldn't it have a policy regarding all or at least many interest rates? The answer is that interest rates are connected to each other and affecting one will affect all albeit in different degrees. Interest rates can be distinguished by two main features: risk and time to maturity.

It is clear that the riskier a bond the higher would be its rate of interest. A bond issued by the US government is considered risk free. An AAA-bond would also

---

[9]Finn Kydland and Edward Prescott (1977), pp. 473–491. See also Allan Drazen (2000), Part II for a more extensive discussion of the subject.

command lower interest than a lower rated bond. This risk is due to issuer's credit-worthiness but it is not the only source of fixed income asset risk. Consider a 7-year US government bond with the face value of $10,000 and interest rate of 5%. Assuming interest is accrued and paid annually, the bond brings its bearer $500 a year. Now suppose that a few days later interest rates increase and a new series of 7-year bonds are auctioned which pay 5.25% interest or $600 per year. How much money do you need to put into the new bonds to get the same $500? The answer is $9523.81. In other words, if you could buy a share of the new bond, 95.2381% of it would be equivalent to the old bond. So the price of your old bond in the market would be $9523.81. Of course, one can keep the old bond to maturity and sell it for the face value, but every year the bearer incurs a loss of $100. Given that this could happen anytime during the life of the bond, the owner faces an interest rate risk.

A second characteristic of interest rates is their term or time to maturity. A 30-year bond is different from a one-year or 3-month bond and they have different rates. Figure 9.5 shows the interest rates of government bonds with different maturity for the day July 5, 2007.

The graph looks odd because interest rates seem to rise, fall, rise again, and fall again with the length of time to maturity. The reason is that the rates are not exactly comparable. We should either compare the yield to maturity of these bonds or the zero coupon interest rates. But such an exercise is beyond the scope of our discussion. If we make such a comparison, ordinarily the shape of the curve will be as shown in Fig. 9.6

This is the normal shape of the yield curve. If the rates with longer maturity are lower than those with shorter maturity then it is called the inverted yield curve. A normal shaped yield curve is essential for financial intermediation.

A characteristic of modern economy is the separation between or dichotomy of savers and investors (here we mean physical investment, that is, buildings, equipment, machinery, and factories). It is the job of the financial sector to direct savings

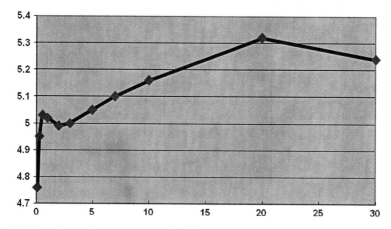

Fig. 9.5 Interest rates of government bonds with constant maturity

Fig. 9.6 Term Structure of
Interest Rates

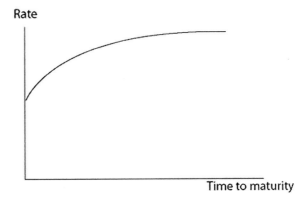

toward investment through financial intermediation. Savers need not commit themselves to long term projects yet they can receive compensation for their abstention
from immediate gratification through consumption. Investors need not worry about
resources as they can borrow in capital markets. But in order for this scheme to
work, the financial sector needs to make money. This requires the long rates to be
higher than short rates. You can collect a certain amount of money with the short
term bonds and lend a portion of it for long term investment, keeping the rest to
repay the savers who may want their money back. If the long rate is less than short
rate the financing firm will go broke. Indeed, this is what happened to Savings and
Loans companies in the 1980s.

While the inverted yield curve has been observed in the US economy, predomi-
nantly the curve has the normal shape. The question is why the long rate is generally
higher than the short. A broader question is: how are the rates connected? In other
words, what determines the term structure of interest rates? Three explanations or
three hypotheses regarding the term structure of interest rates have been offered.

The Market Segmentation Hypothesis

This model contends that the market for bonds is segmented. Some investors prefer
the short term and some the long term fixed income securities. Thus, there need be
no connection between short and long term interest rates. In its extreme form, the
hypothesis reduces to saying that interest rate are different because they are different; hardly an explanation as to why they are different. Furthermore, the existence of
two separate markets opens the door for arbitrage, which would make the rates compatible with each other. One may reformulate the hypothesis by saying that different
investors have different objective functions and needs, and therefore each trades in
the most hospitable segment of the market. At the same time arbitrage by a group of
investors brings the rates in different segments of the market together. Even with a

charitable interpretation, market segmentation is hardly an explanation of the term structure of interest rates.

The Expectations Hypothesis

Consider two alternatives for lending or buying bonds. The buyer could buy a 2-year bond with face value of A dollars and interest rate i_2 which is paid annually. Thus, the total amount at the end of two years will be

$$S = A(1 + i_2)^2$$

Alternatively she can buy an A dollars bond of one year maturity with the interest rate of i_1 for the first year, redeem the bond and buy another one year bond with the *expected* interest rate of i_1^e for the next year. Thus, at the end of the two year period she will have

$$S' = A(1 + i_1)(1 + i_1^e)$$

If we assume rational expectations on the part of market participant, the expected rate for the next year should be such that $S = S'$, that is,

$$i_1^e = \frac{(1 + i_2)^2}{1 + i_1} - 1$$

The same argument implies that in the futures bond market the rate for a one year bond that matures two years from now should be the same as i_1^e.

Note that the 2-year rate is the geometric average of the 1-year rate and the expected rate. In order for the 2-year rate to be higher than 1-year rate, the market should expect the interest rate to rise, that is, we should have $i_1^e > i_1$. While this may be true some of the time, there is no reason to believe that it is true all or even most of the time.

Liquidity Preference Hypothesis

We already have noted that by tying up one's assets in a long term bond, the investor forsakes liquidity and, therefore, exposes herself to the risk of changes in interest rate. It seems reasonable for the investor to demand a compensation for taking the risk. Therefore, generally, the long term interest rate could be higher than the short term interest rate.

We can do even better by combining the expectations and the liquidity preference hypotheses. Let us denote the compensation for the illiquidity of the long term bond by δ and write

$$i_2 = \sqrt{(1 + i_1)(1 + i_1^e)} - 1 + \delta$$

Thus, the long term interest rate could be higher than the short term rate even if investors expect the short term rate to stay constant or decline. But if they expect a sharp decline in the short term rate, then $i_2 < i_1$ and we observe an inverted yield curve.

Now it should be clear why the Fed need only target one interest rate and allow the market to differentiate between bond rates based on their risk and time to maturity.

Chapter 10
Government Budget and Fiscal Policy

> *The subjects of every state ought to contribute towards the*
> *support of the government, as nearly as possible, in proportion*
> *to their respective abilities; that is, in proportion to the revenue*
> *which they respectively enjoy under the protection of the state.*
> *The expense of government to individuals of a great nation, is*
> *like the expense of management to the joint tenants of a great*
> *estate, who are all obliged to contribute in proportion to their*
> *respective interests in the estate.*
>   *The tax which each individual is bound to pay ought to be*
> *certain, and not arbitrary. The time of payment, the manner of*
> *payment, the quantity to be paid, ought all to be clear and plain*
> *to the contributor, and to every other person.*
>   Adam Smith, *The Wealth of Nations*
>
> *et seize et seize qu'est-ce qu'il font?*
> *Ils ne font rien seize et seize*
> *et surtout pas trente-deux*
>   from "Page d'écriture," by Jacques Prévert

In textbook-Keynesian theory, four features distinguish fiscal policy. First, government expenditures and revenues are independent of each other, and issues of how expenditures are financed or what happens to excess revenues are not addressed. A consideration of government budget constraint, however, shows that either the government has to tax the public or its expenditures have monetary implications. Second, the Keynesian model assumes that the public is passive regarding government debt. Higher debt, however, puts the burden of paying interest and repaying debt on the shoulders of the public, both present and future generations. What is the role of government debt and how does the public react to budget deficit? The Ricardian equivalence is one theory that takes the reaction of the public to future increases in taxes into account albeit it is based on extremely unlikely assumptions. Third, the Keynesian model concentrates on the effect of taxes on demand. However, high rates of taxation are disincentives to work and investment, and thus the supply effects of government budgets need to be considered. Finally, the Keynesian model considers government expenditures and taxes as neutral variables that can be manipulated at will. Budget and fiscal policy, however, are political processes and

K. Dadkhah, *The Evolution of Macroeconomic Theory and Policy*,
DOI 10.1007/978-3-540-77008-4_10, © Springer-Verlag Berlin Heidelberg 2009

need to be studied as such. The modern field of political economy has a lot to offer to macroeconomic debates.

Before discussing these issues in this chapter, we shall have an overview of the government budget in the United States.

An Overview of Revenues and Expenditures of the US Government

The total receipts of the United States Federal Government for the fiscal year 2008 is $2521 billion or 17.6% of the GDP. The expenditures add up to $2931 billion or 20.5% of the GDP. Figures 10.1 and 10.2 show the evolution of the US budget since 1925 in absolute values and as percentages of the GDP. As can be seen, with the exception of a few years, the Federal Government has run a deficit. Two points regarding the budget need to be mentioned. First, the fiscal year runs from October first to the end of September of the next year. Thus, the fiscal year 2008 is from October 1st 2007 to September 30th 2008. Second, the budget is divided between "on-budget" and "off-budget" items. In particular, receipt and expenditures of the Social Security trust funds and the Postal Service are off-budget. Here we shall speak of the total budget, on-budget plus off-budget, as the budget. Third, one has to keep in mind that in addition to the Federal Government, there are state and local governments. Each has revenues, expenditures, and budget deficit or surplus. Of course these governments' revenues and incomes are dwarfed by those of the Federal Government. Moreover, no local government has the power to create money. In economics we usually speak of "the government" as if it is a single entity. That is fine as long as it is understood what we are referring to.

The Federal Government budget deficit over many years has resulted in a huge national debt, which in 2008 was estimated to stand at about 9883 billion dollars.

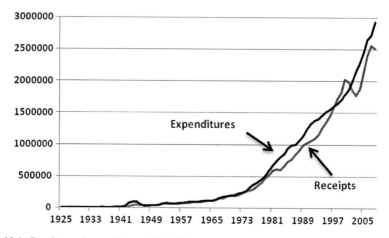

Fig. 10.1 Receipts and expenditures of the US government

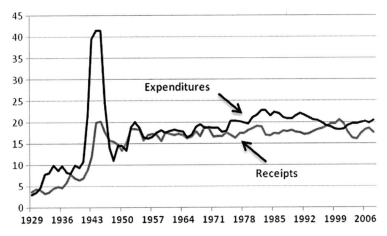

Fig. 10.2 Receipts and expenditures of the US government as percentages of the GDP

The debt is held by the public, the Federal Reserve System, government entities, and foreigners. Of the total debt $5428 billion is held by the public and the rest by Federal Government accounts. In other words, the Federal Government debt to the public was about 38% of the GDP. Of the 5.4 trillion debt held by the public about 14% is held by the Federal Reserve System and more than 40% by foreigners. In 2009 foreign countries with the largest holding of the US Treasury securities were China, Japan, and the United Kingdom.

The interest paid on the debt held by the public amounted to 8.9% of the total Federal Government outlays and 1.8% of the GDP.

Government Budget Constraint

Governments have to finance their expenditures and they have a number of sources: taxes, borrowing from the public, and borrowing from the central bank. The latter would be equivalent to increasing money supply or in everyday parlance, printing money. We can write the government budget constraint as

$$G = T + \frac{\Delta B}{iP} + \frac{\Delta M}{P}$$

where G and T are, respectively, government expenditures and taxes in real terms. B is the number of outstanding bonds; therefore, $\Delta B/i$ is the value of additional government bonds issued. It is divided by the price index to turn it into constant dollars and compatible with G and T, which are in real terms. Finally, $\Delta M/P$ is the additional currency put into circulation in real terms.

In addition, some countries may earn income from government enterprises. Usually such an income is negligible compared to the total expenditures of a government. But in some cases such as oil producing countries in the Middle East, Norway, and Russia oil revenues are quite considerable. Such sources of income could be a blessing but they could also be a source of maintaining autocratic governments in power. A government needs the approval of the citizenry in order to collect taxes; hence it would be responsive to their demands and expectations. A government whose coffers are amply filled with oil revenues need not seek the approval of its people at least not in the short run.

Several features of financing government expenditures by taxation are noteworthy. First, the nation should be convinced that the public good and benefits to the society thus provided are worth the price and could not be attained through the normal operation of the market. This makes taxation the most reasonable and equitable way of financing government expenditures. If a nation believes that everyone should have health care insurance at a certain level, then that nation has to dip into its pocket and pay for it.

Second, the macroeconomic effect on aggregate demand of expenditures financed by taxation is not large. Recall that the multiplier for the balanced budget increase in government expenditures is one. But since an increase in government expenditure raises income, given the money supply, it also raises interest rate. The higher interest rate cuts into investment and therefore reduces to some extent the increase in income. Thus, the multiplier effect is less than one.

Third, if the increase in government expenditures is financed by borrowing from the central bank then it would increase the money supply. An increase in money supply would in the short run reduce the nominal interest rate. But in the long run, particularly if the economy does not have much excess capacity, would raise the inflation rate and the nominal rate of interest. Thus, fiscal policy becomes indistinguishable from monetary policy and will fuel inflation. This is what happens in many developing countries. Unable to collect sufficient taxes and unable to borrow from the public—because of lack of functioning financial markets and people's unwillingness to buy government bonds—many developing countries resort to printing money in order to finance their expenditures. The result is skyrocketing inflation.

Fourth, borrowing from the public has its own consequences, namely, the crowding out of private borrowers from financial markets.

The Ricardian Equivalence

The essence of the Ricardian equivalence is that the way government finances its expenditures would have no effect on the economy. Specifically the effect on the economy would be the same whether the government increases taxes or borrows from the public to pay for its additional expenses. The reason forwarded for this proposition is as follows. When government borrows to pay for its expenditures the taxpayers consider the amount owed as their own debt, which has to be paid sometime in the future. Similarly they do not consider the government bonds as an addition to their assets. Since the debt has to be paid back, the taxpayers start savings for the day when the bill comes due. Thus, government expenditures financed by borrowing would not affect consumption because the additional income is cancelled by saving to pay back the debt.

As far as we can judge the behavior of people, the story is far-fetched. A look around shows that people do not save because they feel one day government would raise taxes to pay back its debt. Robert Barro has suggested that we can think of consumers as consisting of identical families who live forever or families who have children and grandchildren and so on and care deeply about the welfare of the future generations.

This of course is a fiction. Those who benefit from government expenditures are not necessarily the same people who have to pay taxes to repay the debt. Thus, one cannot substantiate the theory by resorting to fiction. We need to say that people behave as if they are infinitely lived families. But then we should show that one or more conclusions of the theory matches known facts.

Note that if the Ricardian equivalence proposition is correct then budget deficit and consumption should be inversely connected. Figure 10.3 shows the government budget deficit and consumption in the United States as percentages of the GDP from 1929 to 2006. As can be seen, except during World War II, the two series are not inversely related. The correlation coefficient between the two series for the entire period is −0.40, but if we consider the post WWII period then the coefficient is 0.10.

Empirical evidence is strongly against the Ricardian equivalence hypothesis. Using meta-analysis, Stanley[1] concludes that

In summary, there already exists quite strong evidence against Ricardian equivalence in the empirical economic literature. The literature, as a whole, reflects a large and significant non-Ricardian effect. This effect is amplified when results are weighted by quality measures,

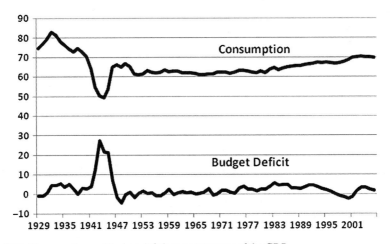

Fig. 10.3 Consumption and budget deficit as percentages of the GDP

[1] T. D. Stanley (1998), pp. 713–727.

degrees of freedom, or the number of separate specification tests passed. Given the inherent bias in favor of RET [Ricardian equivalence theorem], the non-Ricardian effects are quite ubiquitous. Even the simplest and most biased summary procedure, vote-counting, rejects Ricardian equivalence.

The Crowding Out Effect

What are the effects of a budget deficit financed by borrowing from the public on the economy? To answer this question, let us recall two identities from the national income accounts:

$$Y = C + I + G + X - m$$
$$Y - T = C + S$$

The first equation is the definition of the gross domestic product Y, which consists of consumption C, investment I, government expenditures G, exports X, less imports m. The second equation states that the disposable income, that is, GDP less taxes T is either consumed or saved S. Subtracting the second equation from the first and rearranging terms, we get

$$G - T = (m - X) + (S - I)$$

In other words, government budget deficit has to be financed either by trade deficit or by the excess of saving over investment. And this is a matter of accounting not theory.

For the time being let us consider a country other than the United States and other than countries which have been running a trade surplus over time, for instance, Germany in the 1960s and 1970s, and Japan, and China at present. Let us consider a country that cannot run a chronic trade deficit nor is able to have trade surplus year after year. For such a country, we have

$$G - T = S - I$$

In other words, the budget deficit has to be financed by the private sector increasing its savings or reducing its investment. The process is as follows. In order to pay for its expenditures, the government auctions off bonds. An increase in the supply of bonds drives their price down. Since the price of bonds is the inverse of the interest rate, the latter will rise. The increase in the interest rate would encourage more savings and less investment. In other words, the government "crowds out" the private sector in the credit and loan market.

Now consider the case of the United States, which can run a trade deficit for a long stretch of time. The budget deficit has to be financed by the trade deficit, the excess of savings over investment, or both.

Given the ability of the US government to borrow internationally the question is: to what extent the budget deficit raises the domestic interest rate and causes

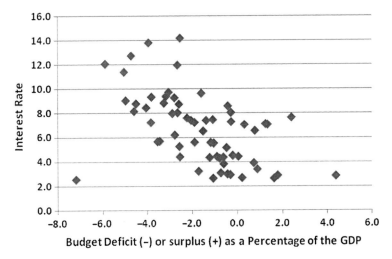

Fig. 10.4 Nominal interest rate vs. Budget deficit

crowding out? A partial answer is Fig. 10.4, which shows that the interest rate rises with the budget deficit. Indeed the correlation coefficient between the corporate AAA rate and the budget deficit is 0.52 for the years 1946–2007. If we look at the period 1972–2007, that is, the post Bretton Woods era, the correlation coefficient is 0.44.

Taxes and Incentives to Work and Save

The main source of revenues for the United States Federal Government is income tax. Moreover, the tax system is progressive in that individuals with higher income are taxed at higher rates than those in lower brackets. It is argued that taxing income reduces incentive to work and to save. From those who put more effort into work or are more skilled and earn more, the government extracts a bigger chunk of their income. The amount of work is determined by a comparison between the utility of leisure and the income from work. Taxing income lowers the wage rate and, therefore, provides more incentive for leisure. Increasing taxes would reduce work and impedes production and economic progress. Lowering taxes gives incentive to work harder and more. On the other hand, government provides assistance to those who cannot find work or have low incomes, thus further reducing incentives to work. One way to minimize the effect of taxes on an individual's incentive to work is to institute a flat rate tax with a certain amount of exemption (see below).

From a philosophical point of view, it is observed that taxing income is equivalent to requiring everyone to contribute to government revenues proportional to what they earn, that is, proportional to what they have contributed to the society. On the other hand a welfare state provides for the population based on their needs. The argument is based on the assumption that everyone earns the value of her marginal product. Moreover, that marginal product is assumed to be beneficial to the society; otherwise why would the market put a positive price on it. This argument does not hold much water. Are we to believe that all hedge fund managers are contributing something to the "society"? Are we to believe that bandit executives who get their rewards even when the company is in the red and share values are plummeting are receiving the value of their contributions?

From a practical point of view taxes are detrimental to work and effort. Many have observed that no country has ever taxed itself to prosperity. But to bestow some kind of philosophical or moral rationale on this affair is simply nonsensical.

Income tax has a negative effect on savings too. Those who save out of their current income hope that in the future they will have more income. But once they try to draw on that income they are hit by further taxes on the income in the form of the taxation of interest and dividend income and by the capital gains tax. In other words, they are taxed twice.

To remedy this it is proposed to tax consumption instead of income (see below).

Flat Tax and Negative Income Tax

By flat tax we mean one tax rate, say 20%, which will apply to all levels of income. There will be a cutoff point below which the individual or family would not pay any tax. Income above that threshold will be taxed at a constant rate. Thus, the tax burden of each family or household is determined as follows:

$$T = \begin{cases} 0 & \text{if} \quad Y \le Y_0 \\ \theta(Y - Y_0) & \text{if} \quad Y > Y_0 \end{cases}$$

where T, Y, Y_0, and θ are, respectively, taxes, income, threshold income, and the tax rate.

Negative income tax, suggested by Milton Friedman, is the idea of paying those with low income proportional to the amount that their income falls below a threshold. Such a payment could replace all other subsidies paid to low income families such as welfare payments, food stamps, and even unemployment benefits. In this case the tax burden of each family or household would be

$$T = \theta(Y - Y_0)$$

with the understanding that a negative T represents the amount that the government will pay the family or household in the form of subsidy.

If a flat tax is instituted, in order for the Federal Government to collect revenues equal to its present intake, the flat rate should be approximately 28.5%. This is a back of the envelope calculation with a threshold of $24,000 for a family of four and based on the 2007 distribution of income. If the threshold is increased or a negative tax is also instituted, then the rate must be higher.

Consumption Tax

It is argued that the tax system discourages savings. In addition, Americans are given incentives to consume. As a result the saving rate in the United States is lower than in some other countries, for example, Japan. To rectify the situation, some have proposed to abolish the income tax and institute a consumption tax. The latter comes in three different forms: a simple sales tax, consumption tax, and value added tax (VAT). Although all three have the same purpose, each comes with its own features.

Sales tax. This is similar to sales taxes levied by many states in the United States. Sellers of final goods and services are given the task of collecting sales tax. The customer buys a pair of shoes for $99.95. The seller adds a 5% tax charging the customer $104.95 and sends the additional five dollars to the tax office. States that have levied a sales tax have certain exemptions such as clothing up to a certain value. In order for the US government to collect the same amount of taxes it received in 2007, the sales tax rate has to be 20.5%. Critics have argued that a sales tax is regressive. Lower income people spend more of their income and therefore will be disproportionately burdened with paying taxes and supporting the government.

Consumption tax. To envisage this type of tax, consider the current IRA's (individual retirement arrangement also referred to as individual retirement accounts) which allow individuals to set aside a part of their income in a retirement savings account and subtract the amount from their taxable income reported to the Internal Revenue Service. There is a limit on such accounts. Suppose that the limits are lifted and the taxpayers can save as much as they want and subtract it from their incomes. Thus, what is taxed is the difference between income and savings, that is, consumption. Such a system would be a strong incentive to save. Consider a country with 25% income tax rate and interest rate of 5%. Suppose a worker, who earns $100,000 a year wants to save 10% of her income this year for her retirement 20 years hence. Further, assume that taxes are paid at the time income is earned. At the end of the 20 years her saving would be

$$\$10,000 \times (1 - 0.25) \times (1 + 0.05 \times (1 - 0.25))^{20} = \$15,661.14$$

If the tax is deferred and paid only at the time of withdrawing from the retirement account, the saving available for consumption would reach

$$\$10,000 \times (1 - 0.25) \times (1 + 0.05)^{20} = \$19,899.73$$

Needless to say the income earner has a greater incentive to save if her income is not taxed. Similarly, we can think of an income earner that every year for 20 years sets aside $100. With a tax rate of 25% and interest rate of 5% the total savings would reach $2332.92 which she can spend on consumption. Without an income tax the savings would reach $3571.93. If all of it is withdrawn for consumption and we tax the consumption at 25% the amount available would be $2678.94, which again provides more incentive to save.

In order for the government to collect consumption tax equivalent to its present income tax revenue, the tax rate should be set at about 26.5%. If some exemptions are included then the rate has to be increased accordingly.

Value added tax (VAT). This kind of tax started in France and now is a main source of income for European governments. The idea is that at each stage of production the value added at that stage is taxed. Consider a company that buys certain amount of inputs say X, turns them into an output worth Y. The value added at this stage of production is $Y - X$, which is taxed at the rate α, that is, $T = \alpha(Y - X)$. Alternatively, we may think of VAT as the company paying the sales tax αY and being reimbursed for what it already paid in VAT to obtain its input, that is, αX.

A full discussion of the implications of switching from income to consumption tax is beyond the scope of this book. But we need to be cognizant of several issues here. First, if the Lucas critique had ever had a serious application, it is here. The change is not a marginal one and would change the structure of incentives and expectations. Therefore, it would be difficult to gauge its effects using econometric models whose coefficients have been estimated using past data. In addition, a large number of people work as tax returns preparers. What will happen to their jobs and the rate of employment?

These considerations do not imply that all structural changes in the economy are undesirable and we should confine all reforms to marginal changes. Rather any structural change requires a comprehensive analysis where information from diverse sources is brought in to shed light on the question at hand. In the case of a consumption tax a comparison of states with sales tax with those with income tax or a combination of both as well as an evaluation of the experience of European countries with VAT could be instructive.

Political Economy of Budgets and Reforms

Economic theory usually assumes a representative economic agent with known preferences, who will live forever. Similarly, the policy maker is assumed to be a benevolent entity, which maximizes the welfare of the society over the long horizon. The real world consists of heterogeneous individuals and groups with conflicting interests. The policy maker has to balance these conflicting interests and try to keep his job. Thus, while the economic theory may suggest a certain policy to be optimal, in reality, some may consider it optimal and others may find it detrimental to their interests. When the dust settles, the compromise may not be optimal in the sense of a constrained maximum for a known objective function. Indeed, such an optimal point may be quite irrelevant.

The new political economy is a study of the intersection of politics and economics.[2] It offers insight into the process of formulating economic policy. For instance, we noted that an increase in government spending, which is not financed by taxes or borrowing from the public, will increase money supply and, therefore,

---

[2] A good beginning on the study of political economy is Allan Drazen (2000).

has inflationary consequences. It may seem obvious that to curb inflation, the government should reduce its budget deficit. But, to reduce the deficit, the government has to cut some of its expenses. Each constituency and lobbying group, while agreeing that the cut is needed, would oppose a cut in its own projects. Similarly, any tax increase would be opposed by those who feel that they have to shoulder the extra burden.

To cut carbon emission and save the environment, we need to use clean energy, for instance by having wind farms. They are great, but not in my backyard.

These considerations also point to the fact that, to carry out a policy, one needs to build a political consensus around it. Moreover, even if at the outset the majority agrees with a policy, as the cost of the policy becomes apparent and some feel the pinch, the support starts to wane. The political consensus has to be strong enough to see the policy through. Examples of such policies and the political determination to see them through are the fight against inflation during Volcker's chairmanship of the Fed, and the balancing of the budget during President Clinton's administration, which was supported by Speaker of the House, Newt Gingrich.

Another area where we need to be mindful of politics is economic reform. Any reform will upset the status quo and would be detrimental to some while benefiting others. Thus, one should expect a tug of war whenever economic reforms are proposed and implemented. The new laws and institutions need to be designed and implemented in such a way as to navigate through conflicting interests with minimum damage. The damage could come from those who would lose under the new arrangements and from those who would want to rig the rules of the game in their own favor. The story of economic reforms in the former socialist economies in Eastern Europe and Russia are quite instructive. The same is true about attempts at reforms in many developing countries.

The Illusion of Populist Economic Programs

We cannot end this chapter without mentioning populist economic programs which have ruined many developing economies and once in a while are praised by politicians and activists in advanced economies.

Populist economic programs have a long history and still are being imposed on some developing countries with calamitous effects. A fertile ground for populist economic policies is a country with skewed distribution of income and where a large segment of the population, rightly or wrongly, believes that they are disenfranchised. Examples of such countries are Venezuela, Bolivia, Nicaragua, and Zimbabwe. But some oil exporting countries, such as Iran, have also been victims of such policies.

The idea is simple. Poverty and want are not caused by a lack of production. The country has everything; only some are taking more than their share. Worse, there are foreign companies and powers that are holding down the country and its people.

Here comes a "knight in shining armor." He will nationalize foreign companies, take over all aspects of economic life, redistribute income, expand social and welfare expenditures, and bring happiness to all.

The nationalization drives entrepreneurs, foreign and domestic capital, as well as many professionals out of the country. Welfare programs, a large bureaucracy, corruption, and an attitude of entitlement and dependency on handouts ensue.

Even if at the beginning the government largesse succeeds in making some happy, soon the government runs out of money. Worse, social spending, financed by printing money, results in inflation. At the end, even those who were going to be helped suffer more. Examples abound; Zimbabwe and Cuba are extreme cases. Iran and Venezuela would have had the same fate were it not for oil revenues.

Chapter 11
The Reagan-Thatcher Revolution: The Age of Hayek and Schumpeter

Representative political institutions cannot alone guarantee liberties. It is economic liberty that nourishes the enterprise of those whose hard work and imagination ultimately determine the conditions in which we live. It is economic liberty that makes possible a free press. It is economic liberty that has enabled the modern democratic state to provide a minimum of welfare for the citizen, while leaving him free to choose when, where, and how he will make his own contribution to the economic life of the country. If the economic life of the country is dominated by the state, few of these things are true.

Margaret Thatcher, the Winston Churchill Memorial Lecture,
October 1979

When tax assessments and imposts upon the subjects are low, the latter have the energy and desire to do things. Cultural enterprises grow and increase, because the low taxes bring satisfaction. When cultural enterprises grow, the number of individual imposts and assessments mounts. In consequence, the tax revenue, which is the sum total of (the individual assessments), increases.

Ibn Khaldun (1332–1406), *The Muqaddimah,* translated by
Franz Rosenthal, Vol. 2, pp. 89–90

The Great Depression changed the economic discourse around the world. The working assumption was that market economies could not function on their own. Government had to intervene through regulations, intervention, and if needed by planning for the economy. In other words, the rule was that government intervention was needed and the exception was to leave the market to itself. The Reagan-Thatcher revolution strived for making free market the rule and government intervention the exception.[1]

Many factors combined to bring about the change. The first was the dismal economic performance around the world. During the decade of 1970s many economies were beset by low growth rate, unemployment, inflation, and high energy prices.

---

[1] A highly readable book describing the transition of these years is *The Commanding Heights* by Daniel Yergin and Joseph Stanislaw, 2002 (revised edition).

K. Dadkhah, *The Evolution of Macroeconomic Theory and Policy,*
DOI 10.1007/978-3-540-77008-4_11, © Springer-Verlag Berlin Heidelberg 2009

Second, it seemed that the traditional remedies did not work. The problem was not confined to market economies; the former Soviet Union and its satellites were affected, particularly because of high energy prices.

But if Keynes did not have the answer, could we turn to his intellectual rivals. In particular one could think of Friedrich Hayek and Joseph Schumpeter. Hayek was a champion of market economy and freedom of choice. Schumpeter, who died in 1950, had made his reputation as a theoretician of economic growth, innovation, and entrepreneurship.

With the Reagan-Thatcher revolution also came a change of emphasis in economic research. Economists shifted their attention from market failures and how to regulate it to ways of unleashing market power and to deregulation, from managing the aggregate demand to enhancing aggregate supply, and from stabilization theories and policies to theories of growth and policies to achieve it.

Hayek's Vision

Hayek's influence has been more through his philosophical vision of a market economy rather than his economic theory. Hayek noted that the economic and social rules, institutions, and arrangements add up to a very complicated system. The system is the outcome of many decisions, actions, and most importantly, many years of trial and error. This is in contrast to imagining the system as the result of the intelligent design of one or a few human beings. One person or a group does not have the information or the ability to set up such system. Should they try their hands, as in social engineering, the result would be pain and even disaster.

Examples of such grand designs leading to environmental or social disasters are aplenty. Consider the homestead policy of the US government in the Great Plains and the misguided agricultural practices that together with the drought and the Great Depression created the environmental and human disaster known as the Dust Bowl.[2] Many settlers had to leave their farms. The plight of these migrants is captured in John Steinbeck's *The Grapes of Wrath* .

The Soviet Union irrigation plan led to the shrinkage of 25% of the Aral Sea's surface and the increase of its salinity, killing its flora and destroying the fishing industry around it. Furthermore, industrial waste, weapons testing, and runoff of fertilizers heavily polluted the lake. All of this happened while the Soviet Union advertised its scientific socialism and comprehensive planning.[3] We should also mention Mao Zedong's Great Leap Forward , which created an economic disaster leading to the death of millions.

---

[2] On this issue see *The Worst Hard Time: The Untold Story of Those Who Survived the Great AmericanDust Bowl* by Timothy Egan, 2006.

[3] The good news is that after the demise of the Soviet Union, Kazakhstan has implemented projects to revive the Aral Sea.

Another example is the well intentioned policies of the Great Society to help black Americans. There is no question that for centuries blacks were mistreated in America and the crime of racism is a blemish on American history. The Civil Rights movement of the 1960s tried to bring about equality before the law and in politics. No doubt American blacks needed assistance to overcome years of discrimination. But paying welfare money as an incentive not to work, and to spread the idea of victimhood has done the black community untold harm.[4]

Thus, for Hayek, state planning, macroeconomic policy to promote stability and growth, and tax policy to engender a more equitable distribution of income are out. The system works best when the rules of the game are specified in advance and are not changed in the middle of the game. Individuals follow their own interest and the overall outcome is the best possible result for society.

Schumpeter's Theory of Business Cycles and Growth

Joseph Schumpeter was among the first economists who realized that business cycles are inherent in a decentralized capitalist system and that short term fluctuations and long term growth of the economy were connected. In the Schumpeterian model the engine of growth, which also causes the short run fluctuations, is innovation. Economic agents who take risk and introduce these innovations into the economy are entrepreneurs. In order to finance their ventures entrepreneurs rely on credit. Thus, credit creation plays an important role in both the fluctuations and the growth of the economy.

Schumpeter's model starts with an economy in equilibrium or balance. Such a state, of course, may be a fleeting moment or a convenient theoretical construct. To this state of calm an intrepid entrepreneur (or perhaps several of them) introduces an innovation. One can think of railways, electricity, telephones, cars, airplanes, computers, and the Internet. The entrepreneur may or may not be an inventor or the originator of the idea. Rather he/she sees the profit opportunity and is ready to take risk. But he/she needs financing. The financial sector, that is, the intermediary between those who save and invest, provide the credit so that the entrepreneur can embark on his/her venture.

The introduction of innovation into the market disturbs the equilibrium by introducing new activities, higher profit, and increased production and income. Other entrepreneurs and investors enter this market and increase the production even further. Some innovations are interconnected, and once one is introduced others may more easily find a market. There will be induced investment as the increase in income increases demand for other products. Not all new ventures will succeed;

---

[4] On this issue one should read John McWhorter's *Winning the Race: Beyond the Crisis in Black America*, 2006. See also his piece in *Sunday Times* of September 11, 2005: "Focus: White do-gooders did for black America. Black poverty is the result of 30 years of misguided welfare rather than racism says John McWhorter."

there will be losers and winners. At some point the wave created by the innovation is exhausted. Entrepreneurs repay their loans and the reduction in money in circulation causes auto-deflation. The economy enters the phase of recession and adjustments are made toward a new equilibrium. In the new equilibrium the level of production and its composition are different from those of the old equilibrium.

Since there are different innovations with different impacts, we could expect many cycles superimposed on each other. We can think of an innovation such as cars that created a long wave and induced other innovations connected with it such as highway systems, and fast food restaurants along the highways. Or we can think of different waves created by unrelated innovations, for example, automobiles and telephones.

If innovations are the engine of growth, then it follows that a free enterprise economy is more viable and thriving. The less restrictions the system puts on entrepreneurs and in general on economic agents, the better off is the society. This should be a noncontroversial conclusion. In an economy with too many restrictions there will be no innovation, no risk taking and no progress. Compare economies of countries like the former East Germany, North Korea, and Cuba with former West Germany, South Korea, and Chile. Similarly, one can compare China's economy prior to Deng Xiaoping's economic reforms that started in 1978 to economies of Taiwan, Hong Kong, and China after reforms.

Schumpeter assigns a great role to credit creation in the process of economic growth. The implication is that the financial sector too should be freed from too many rules and regulations to be able to innovate and play its role. Here perhaps a note of caution is in order. While the idea of freedom for the financial sector is correct, we should note that finance and money are ultimately based on confidence and trust. Therefore, total freedom or a frontier attitude toward this sector may be detrimental to the health of the economy. Nowhere is this illustrated better than in the Great Depression and in the financial crisis of 2007–2009 (Chap. 13).

Supply Side Economics

Supply side economics was the name given to a set of principles that informed economic policies of the Reagan revolution and administration. In some quarters it is derided, caricaturized, and dubbed "voodoo economics." No doubt some supply side proponents have gone too far and have expressed an almost religious belief and zeal for market. They have also espoused extremist policies or mottos, such as "the best government is no government" and "greed is good." But supply side economics comprises principles that could be defended on logical and empirical grounds and are followed around the world.

The first principle is the importance of economic freedom, which could be realized only within a market economy. Indeed, economic freedom is perhaps the most important facet of freedom in general. The market allows each individual to express his/her preferences in the same manner that democracy allows citizens to vote for candidates and policies. In the same manner that democracy provides an arena in which different ideas compete and citizens choose the most desirable, the market is the arena where innovators, entrepreneurs, producers, and suppliers compete and consumers vote with their wallets.

In recent years many who are by no means associated with supply side economics have reached the conclusion that capitalism and a market economy are necessary conditions for democracy. One can imagine a country where all economic activities are controlled by the government and everyone works for the state. In such a society how can an individual or group of individuals stand up to authorities or express their views?

But if a free market is a precondition of freedom, the less restraints are put on it the better it shall function. Hence, supply-siders were against regulations and government meddling in the market. Deregulation became a by-word and many industries and activities such as airlines, banks, gas companies, telephone companies, and others were deregulated or witnessed a substantial reduction in the volume of regulations imposed on them. Here we should note that the idea is not whether to regulate or not regulate, but how much to regulate. In general the question is not whether government should or should not intervene in the market. Rather the question is how far government should intervene. Left to itself the market could spin out of control and not only bring misery to many but also threaten the existence of the market itself. We have seen this problem in Chap. 1 and will encounter it in a modern reincarnation in Chap. 13.

The next issue is the incentive effect of taxes. Supply-siders argued that taxes, particularly the income tax, takes away the incentive to work and invest. Note that in the Keynesian model an increase in taxes reduces aggregate demand but leaves aggregate supply unaffected. Supply-siders argued that taxes reduce the supply in the economy. The argument is compelling. If a worker's income is taxed at 15%, for every hour he/she works the compensation is 15% less. To the extent that the supply of labor depends on the wage rate, a reduction in wages will lower the supply of labor and production. Similarly, a higher tax rate on capital gain or dividends would reduce incentives to invest, hence reducing production.

Thus, supply-siders shifted the emphasis from aggregate demand to aggregate supply. Let us recall that during the Great Depression Keynes argued that the problem was a lack of effective demand. Hence policies espoused by governments around the world concentrated on managing aggregate demand. All the way to the 1970s these policies were effective. But, as we saw in Chap. 6, they ran into the double trouble of stagflation. There developed a mentality that the limit of growth has probably been reached. In other words, the standard of living of those days was all that this planet could support. The supply side economics was a reaction to this pessimistic view. Why not expand the supply? The way was to release the productive forces from the shackles that government regulations and excessive taxation had put on them. Hence, the Reagan-Thatcher movement to deregulate, reduce taxes, and oppose the power of labor unions.

Regarding taxes two points need to be mentioned. First, some have argued that people may have an incentive to pay taxes because they value services provided by the government. This may be true although people usually want services paid by other people's taxes. But the issue is excessive taxation. Like any other organism, governments like to get bigger. It is hard to find a government that easily accedes to getting smaller. The second issue is the *Laffer curve,* which we shall discuss in the next section.

The Laffer Curve

The idea behind the Laffer curve is that a decrease in tax rates would encourage more production and income to the point that the total amount of taxes collected would increase. The original Laffer curve is depicted in Fig. 11.1.

A better representation would be Fig. 11.2. It is clear that as the tax rate increases it entails two effects. On the one hand, a higher tax rate brings more revenue on existing income; on the other hand, a higher tax rate would reduce people's incentive to work and invest, thus reducing the revenue. Similarly, a tax cut would reduce tax revenues on the one hand and on the other give more incentive to people to increase output, income, and consequently total tax revenues.

To make these points more precise, let θ be the tax rate, Y aggregate income, and T the total taxes collected. The total tax revenues would be $T = \theta Y$ and the effect of a reduction in the tax rate can be calculated as

$$\frac{\partial T}{\partial \theta} = Y + \theta \frac{\partial Y}{\partial \theta}$$

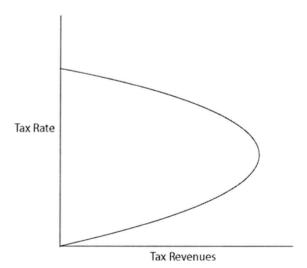

Fig. 11.1 The Laffer curve

Fig. 11.2 A more logical representation of the Laffer curve

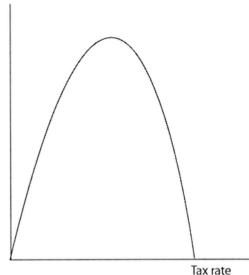

Tax Revenues

Tax rate

Note that $\partial Y/\partial \theta < 0$. Now if

$$Y < \theta \frac{\partial Y}{\partial \theta}$$

then an increase in the tax rate would reduce the total revenues and, conversely, a tax cut would increase tax revenues. If we take the shape of the Laffer curve in Fig. 11.2 to be literally correct, then we could represent it as

$$T = \theta Y = \theta(1 - \theta)A$$

where $\theta = 0$ means no taxes and $\theta = 1$ means a 100% tax rate. In both cases the total tax revenue would be zero.

In terms of Fig. 11.2, we need to be on the descending part of the curve to observe the positive effects of tax cuts on total revenues. Whether the above holds, or in what range of values of Y it holds, are matters for empirical investigation. But if indeed any country was on that part of the curve, then a tax cut should immediately, i.e., in the same fiscal year, effect an increase in total tax revenues. It is difficult to document such an instant in any country.

Yet as we have seen President Kennedy   forwarded this argument when proposing his tax cut, and as the quotation at the beginning of this chapter shows, the idea dates back to the 14th century. Thus, it seems that proponents of the Laffer curve have something else in mind. Perhaps they mean that the tax cut would affect the rate of growth of income and, over time, there would be an increase in total revenues. Suppose that the tax rate is θ_1 and the economy is growing at an average rate of ρ_1. Now the tax rate is lowered to θ_2 and the growth rate is increased to ρ_2. We can calculate the ratio of tax revenues under the two alternatives and after the passage of s years.

$$\frac{T_2}{T_1} = \frac{\theta_2}{\theta_1} \left(\frac{1 + \rho_2}{1 + \rho_1} \right)^s$$

If indeed the new growth rate is higher than the old, sooner or later this ratio would be greater than one. In other words, the main proposition is that no country has taxed itself to prosperity, and higher taxes would bring nothing but economic stagnation.

A Change of Emphasis from Stabilization to Growth

Immediately after WWII the emphasis of economic policy was on stabilization, neutralizing short run fluctuations, and above all, avoiding another depression or prolonged recession. The same concern was evident in macroeconomics textbooks where the discussion began with the IS-LM model of short run behavior. This is not to say that the issue of long run growth was neglected. We already have seen that several models of growth were proposed. But the emphasis was on short run stabilization.

In the 1970s with the memory of depression subsiding, the issue of growth attracted more attention. The first macroeconomics book to reflect the change of emphasis was *Macroeconomics: A Neoclassical Introduction* by Merton Miller and Charles Upton. With the advent of the 1980s and the Reagan -Thatcher revolution more attention was turned to long run issues.

To model the behavior of the economy over time, that is, the dynamics of aggregate variables, a few devices had been proposed and now gained a central role in macroeconomic modeling. These include the Ramsey problem and the overlapping generation model. Below we discuss them in turn. The reason for discussing them in one place is that they have so many features in common and the reader can see the common thread between them.

The Ramsey Problem

Ramsey posed the problem of optimizing consumption over time. In other words, how much should a nation consume now and how much should it save in order to consume in the future? Letting u to denote utility, c_t the per capita consumption at time t, and ρ the rate of time preference, the objective function to be maximized would be[5]

---

[5] Note that all variables are continuous and the subscript t signifies their time dependence.

$$U = \int_0^\infty u(c_t)e^{-\rho t}dt$$

The constraint is the amount of income available, which is the result of production

$$Y_t = F(K_t, L_t)$$

where K denotes capital and L labor, which is assumed to be equal to the population. The production function has constant returns to scale, that is, F is homogenous of degree one. Thus, letting $k=K/L$ we can write the per capital output (=income) as

$$\frac{1}{L_t}F(K_t, L_t) = F\left(\frac{K_t}{L_t}, 1\right) = f(k_t)$$

The output is divided between consumption C and investment I. Investment, in turn, is equal to addition to capital stock less depreciation.

$$Y_t = C_t + I_t = C_t + \frac{dK_t}{dt} - \delta K_t$$

Recalling that

$$\frac{dk}{dt} = \frac{d\left(\frac{K_t}{L_t}\right)}{dt} = \frac{L_t\frac{dK_t}{dt} - K\frac{dL_t}{dt}}{L_t^2} = \frac{1}{L_t}\frac{dK_t}{dt} - k_t\frac{1}{L_t}\frac{dL_t}{dt}$$

we can write the output per capita as

$$f(k_t) = c_t + \frac{dk_t}{dt} + (n - \delta)k_t$$

where n is the rate of growth of the labor force (=population).

Maximizing the objective function subject to the above constraint is a dynamic optimization problem that could be solved using the maximum principle (see Dadkhah 2007, Chap. 12). The solution is

$$\frac{1}{c_t}\frac{dc_t}{dt} = -\frac{u'(c_t)}{c_t u''(c_t)}[f'(k_t) - \rho - n + \delta]$$

which shows the rate of growth of per capita consumption as a function of elasticity of substitution of consumption over time, marginal product of per capita capital, rate of time preference, rate of growth of population, and the rate of depreciation.

The Overlapping Generations Model

In Ramsey's problem we assumed the population and the labor force to be the same. In the overlapping generations model we relax this assumption by dividing the population N_t into the young which is the labor force L_t and the old $N_t - L_t$.

since the old of this period were the young of the last period. Both the population and labor force grow at the same rate of n per year. We can write

$$N_t = L_t + L_{t-1} = \left(1 + \frac{1}{1+n}\right) L_t$$

Since the population and labor force are proportional, we shall define all variables as per laborer. The reader should keep this point in mind. Of course, it would be easy to convert all per laborer variables to per capita by dividing them by

$$\left(1 + \frac{1}{1+n}\right)$$

Each generation lives for two periods: the young work, save and consume, while the old consume what they saved in the previous period plus the interest accrued to their savings.

$$\begin{aligned} C_t &= C_{1t} + C_{2t} \\ &= c_{1t}L_t + c_{2t}(N_t - L_t) \\ &= \left(c_{1t} + \frac{1}{1+n}c_{2t}\right) L_t \end{aligned}$$

The production function remains as in the Ramsey problem. The output per laborer is divided between wages w_t and the remuneration of capital r_t.

$$w_t = \frac{\partial L_t f(k_t)}{\partial L_t} = f(k_t) - L_t \frac{\partial k_t}{\partial L_t} f'(k_t) = f(k_t) - k_t f'(k_t)$$
$$r_t = f'(k_t) - \delta$$

where, as before, δ denotes the depreciation rate.

The youth receive the wage and either consume or save it. Their saving is equal to the amount of existing capital.[6]

$$w_t = c_{1t} + s_t$$

With the saving the youth buy the entire stock of capital which provides them with the income to be consumed in their old age in the amount of

$$c_{2t} = (1 + r_{t+1})(w_t - c_{1t})$$

Again note that all variables are per laborer. We can pose the Ramsey problem and ask what would be the optimal allocation of consumption between the two periods in order to maximize the utility of each generation.

---

[6] This is a shortcoming of the model as the only way to end up with a stable model is to assume that in each period the entire capital stock has to be renewed.

$$U = U(c_{1t}) + \frac{1}{1+\rho} U(c_{2t+1})$$

subject to the constraint

$$c_{1t} = w_t - s_t, \quad c_{2t+1} = (1 + r_{t+1})s_t$$

or combined together

$$c_{2t+1} = (1 + r_{t+1})(w_t - c_{1t})$$

Solving the optimization problem, we arrive at the Euler equation

$$\frac{\partial U(c_{2t+1})/\partial c_{2t+1}}{\partial U(c_{1t})/\partial c_{1t}} = \frac{1+\rho}{1+r_{t+1}}$$

For example if $U = ln(c)$ then

$$c_{2t+1} = \frac{1 + r_{t+1}}{1+\rho} c_{1t}$$

Also we should note that since

$$K_{t+1} = s_t L_t$$

we have

$$k_{t+1} = \frac{s_t}{1+n}$$

Endogenous Growth Theory

Endogenous growth means that the sources of growth of an economy emanate from within the system and are not superimposed from outside. This concept is particularly relevant regarding technological progress and within the neoclassical model. Recall that in Solow's model after accounting for labor and capital still one third of the US economy's growth rate is left unexplained. Usually this is attributed to technological progress. But the concept is left up in the air. It is not clear from where and how technological progress emanates. Neither is it clear why the American economy experiences such high rates of technological progress while many countries cannot master simple technologies. We also saw in Chap. 8 that the real business cycles theory represents technological progress as random shocks without specifying or speculating on their origin or why they show up at all.

In 1990 in a truly path breaking article Paul Romer introduced an endogenous growth model in which technological progress played a starring role.[7] His model was based on three premises. (1) Technological change defined as "improvement in the instructions for mixing together raw materials" is the main reason for growth. (2) Technological progress is the result of conscious efforts of people who are motivated by profit incentives. This is not to say that all research is undertaken by the private sector and for profit. It is true that academic research sponsored by the government results in discoveries. Yet it is the private sector that turns this invention into a marketable product. The distinction is between invention and innovation which was noted by Schumpeter. (3) Technologies, instructions for mixing inputs, are different from other economic goods. There is a fixed cost involved in producing a new technology which is incurred by the inventing and innovating company. Yet when the technology becomes available there is no cost associated with its use. It can be used by anyone again and again with no cost. In general the cost of replicating the instruction or using it is trivial compared to the fixed cost of producing it.

There are two features of knowledge. One is that it is not tied to any physical object or person so it can be used simultaneously in many places. This is termed the *nonrival* property of technology. Second, a firm cannot easily exclude others from using the technology it has developed without protection from the legal system. Since the knowledge developed through research supported by government is publicly available, technology is only *partially excludable* .

These properties imply that, (1) Technology per capita as a nonrival good could be accumulated indefinitely, whereas human capital, for example, cannot. (2) There could be spillover because technology is neither a rival good nor completely excludable. (3) The production function cannot have constant returns to scale with respect to all inputs. This is because by doubling investment in R&D a company could increase the output of a production unit by a factor of λ while holding capital and labor constant. On the other hand, the same technology could be used in many factories, say, three. Then the total output is increased by 3λ. Romer gives the example of spending 10,000 hours of engineering work to design a computer disk with 20-megabyte (forgive the example, it was the 1990s and the days of megabytes). Then a factory with $10 million capital and 100 workers could produce 100,000 units equivalent to 2 trillion megabytes. Now suppose the firm spends 20,000 hours of engineering and designs a 30-megabyte disk and produces its output in two factories each with $10 million capital and 100 workers. In other words, each and every input is doubled. Yet the output is now 6 trillion megabytes or three times that prior to the increase in output. The example illustrates the nonrival and non-excludible nature of technology.

The formal model includes a knowledge production sector with production function

$$\dot{A} = \delta H_A A$$

[7] Paul Romer (1990), pp. S71–S102.

A denotes the existing store of knowledge which is accessible by everyone and used in the production of further knowledge $\dot{A}$ with the help of human capital H_A employed in the knowledge industry. Production function for consumer goods is specified as[8]

$$Y = (H_Y A)^\alpha (LA)^\beta K^{1-\alpha-\beta}$$

where Y, K, and L are, respectively, output, capital, and labor, and H_Y is the human capital used in the production of final goods. Finally, the addition to capital stock is the result of saving.

$$\dot{K}(t) = Y(t) - C(t)$$

Romer derives the path of balanced growth equilibrium and discusses its welfare implications.

In Search of the Elements of Growth

Inspired by new theories of growth and the availability of panel data for a large set of countries, economists looked for the causes of growth and discrepancies in the growth rates of different countries. In the 1950s and 1960s the emphasis was on the accumulation of capital. After the 1980s the focus shifted toward prerequisites of growth and environments that engender growth.

Since then researchers have compiled a wealth of data on factors such as corruption, ease of doing business, democracy, the rule of law and others. At the same time panel data econometrics has been used to find which of these factors contribute to growth and to what extent.[9]

This is an exciting subject and a field with promise.

The Reagan Years

President Reagan was elected on a platform of conservative economics, strong defense, pride in American values, and optimism about the future. As to his economic program, he noted that "If we look to the answer as to why for so many years we achieved so much, prospered as no other people on earth, it was because here in

---

[8] Romer derives this production function by first assuming that capital stock K is the sum of a number of durable goods x_i 's. However, his derivation involves an algebraic error. Therefore, we simply deal with the final version of the function. Also, he posits that there is a third sector producing durable goods to be used in the production of consumer goods. He does not formalize this sector and we skip it here.

[9] For a recent survey of these issues see *The Economics of Growth* by Philippe Aghion and Peter Howitt, 2009; and *Introduction to Modern Economic Growth* by Daron Acemoglu, 2008.

this land we unleashed the energy and individual genius of man to a greater extent than has ever been done before." He added that "it is time to reawaken this industrial giant, to get government back within its means and to lighten our punitive tax burden." Thus, "in the days ahead I will propose removing roadblocks that have slowed our economy and reduced productivity." [10]

> So, with all the creative energy at our command let us begin an era of national renewal. Let us renew our determination, our courage and our strength. And let us renew our faith and our hope. We have every right to dream heroic dreams.
> Those who say that we're in a time when there are no heroes—they just don't know where to look. You can see heroes every day going in and out of factory gates. Others, a handful in number, produce enough food to feed all of us and then the world beyond.
> You meet heroes across a counter—and they're on both sides of that counter. There are entrepreneurs with faith in themselves and faith in an idea who create new jobs, new wealth and opportunity. [11]

We already have noted that during the 1980s Volcker's Federal Reserve embarked on a policy to root out inflation (see Chap. 9). The contractionary monetary policy resulted in the unemployment rate rising above 10%. But once the inflation was under control, gradually policies to stimulate both supply and demand worked to reduce the unemployment rate such that when President Reagan left office in January 1989, the unemployment rate was 5.4%. Reagan era economic policies had five components to it.

The first component was deregulation of many industries and activities. This process was already underway. The law to deregulate airlines had been signed in 1978 by President Carter. The Depository Institutions Deregulation and Monetary Control Act was passed in 1980. The law removed some of the restrictions on the banking system including Regulation Q , which restricted the rate of interest banks could pay on saving deposits. The breakup of AT&T was initiated by the Justice Department in 1974, which resulted in a settlement in 1982. This effectively created the modern communication industry we are enjoying today. Yet it is true that the Reagan administration was less interested in regulating the economy and espoused an environment of reliance on free enterprise and the operation of market forces. Moreover, the administration pushed for deregulation of other industries including natural gas.

The second component was privatization. It is difficult to find a major public enterprise that was privatized during the Reagan era. This may reflect the structure of the American economy. After WWII, England had nationalized many industries and Margaret Thatcher reversed that trend. On the other hand, there had been no waves of nationalization in the US. Instead the Reagan revolution created an atmosphere where letting the private sector do any job was praised and accepted. As a result some of the government functions even in law enforcement and defense were outsourced to the private sector.

---

[10] The inaugural speech of President Ronald Reagan, January 20, 1981.
[11] Ibid.

Privatization was more important in countries other than the United States. Deng Xiaoping's reforms in China; privatization of North Sea oil and gas, ports and airports, Telephone Company and others in England; and economic reforms in India were of far greater magnitude. We should also mention privatization of many companies in Russia after the collapse of the former Soviet Union.

The third was adopting a tough stance against labor unions. This is exemplified by firing of striking members of the Professional Air Traffic Controllers Organization (PATCO) in 1981.

Tax cuts were the fourth and definitely the most important part of the revolution. The Economic Recovery Tax Act of 1981 sponsored by representative Jack Kemp and Senator William Roth was passed. The bill aimed at reducing tax rates to encourage economic growth. It also provided incentives to small business and incentives to save. In fact this is the major tax cut enacted during the Reagan era.

In 1986 the Congress passed the Tax Reform Act sponsored by Representative Richard Gephardt and Senator Bill Bradley. This bill aimed at simplifying the tax code and eliminating some tax shelters but did not have much an impact on reducing taxes. As Fig. 11.3 shows, the total federal government tax collection fell from more than 19% of the GDP to 17%, although later on it increased to 18%.

The fifth component was to reduce government expenditures and shrink the size of government. As Fig. 11.3 shows, this project never got off the ground. When President Reagan took office, government expenditures were somewhat above 21% of the GDP and when he left office they were slightly less than 21%.

It is true that Reagan cut taxes and emphasized free market and private initiatives. But he did not reduce government spending by a significant measure (Fig. 11.3). During his administration and indeed during the next Republican administration the government incurred budget deficits as high as 5.88% and never less than 2.52% of the GDP. True, the economy experienced one of the longest periods of expansion in the post WWII era, and unemployment rate after an initial surge decreased

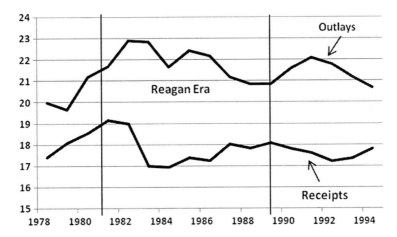

Fig. 11.3 Government receipts and outlays as a percent of the GDP

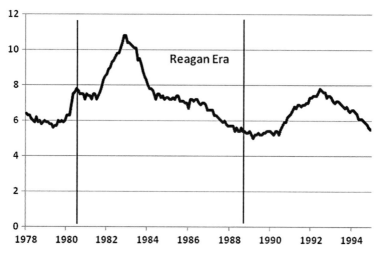

Fig. 11.4 Unemployment rate

throughout 1980s (Fig. 11.4), but it is hard to credit these accomplishments to supply side economics. It is possible to argue that Reagan implemented a conventional Keynesian policy of deficit spending. The issue is open to discussion and perhaps the credit for economic progress should be shared by supply side and Keynesian economics.

The essence of the Reagan -Thatcher revolution was an emphasis on free enterprise and a market economy. This revolution was not confined to the United States and the United Kingdom; it was a worldwide movement. With the exception of a few, all countries around the world enacted reforms to encourage entrepreneurship, competition, and risk taking. The reforms have borne fruits as we can see in the economic emergence of countries such as India, China, Turkey, Columbia, and Brazil.

The Great Moderation

After 1984 the volatility of the world economies, particularly the United States, as measured by the variance of major macroeconomic variables (see Table 11.1 and Figs. 11.5, 11.6 and 11.7) decreased. This was termed *the great moderation*. This moderation is different from the observation that after WWII, economies around the world were more stable due to Keynesian policies. That assertion has been disputed based on the incomparability of aggregate data before and after the War.[12] The data between pre and post the great moderation are reasonably compatible and the same conclusions could be reached if instead of comparing 1984–2008 period to

---

[12]Christina Romer (1986).

Table 11.1 Variance of macro variables before and after the great moderation

	Growth rate of the GDP	Inflation rate (CPI)	Unemployment rate
1948–1983	24.31	13.82	3.03
1954–1983	21.13	13.34	2.75
1984–2008	4.44	1.20	1.07

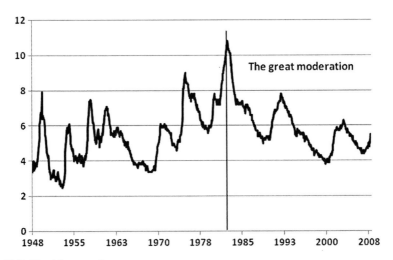

Fig 11.5 Monthly unemployment rate

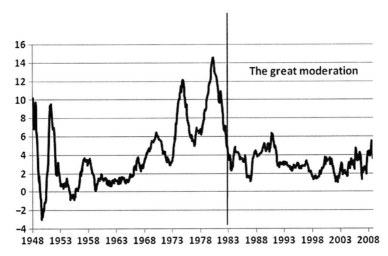

Fig 11.6 Monthly inflation rate (the rate of growth of the CPI over the same month of the last year)

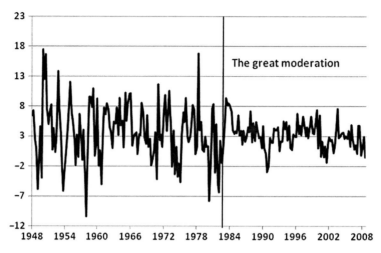

Fig 11.7 Quarterly growth rate of GDP

1948–1983 we compare it to 1954–1983, thus excluding the volatile years of the Korean War.

Economists have attributed this development to several factors.[13] These include: (1) the improvement in monetary policy which reduced volatility in the inflation rate and economic activity; (2) financial innovation and globalization; (3) improved methods of inventory control as evidenced by the fall in output volatility more than sales volatility; and (4) smaller exogenous shocks aka "good luck."[14] Finally, it is argued that the moderation did not happen abruptly in the mid 1980s. Rather this has been a process in the making since the end of World War II.

---

[13] See Steven Davis and James Kahn (2008), pp. 155–180.

[14] For example, Alejandro Justiniano and Giorgio Primiceri (2008), pp. 604–641.

Chapter 12
Macroeconomics of Globalized Economies

> The commerce of one country with another, is in fact merely an
> extension of that division of labour by which so many benefits
> are conferred upon the human race. As the same country is
> rendered the richer by the trade of one province with another.
> James Mill, *Commerce Defended*, 1808 (reprinted 1965), p. 38

> No man is an island, entire of itself; every man is a piece of the
> continent, a part of the main; if a clod be washed away by the
> sea, Europe is the less, as well as if a promontory were, as well
> as if a manor of thy friend's or of thine own were; any man's
> death diminishes me, because I am involved in mankind, and
> therefore never send to know for whom the bell tolls; it tolls for
> thee.
> John Donne, "Devotions Upon Emergent Occasions,
> Meditation XVII"

> Something there is that doesn't love a wall,
> That sends the frozen-ground-swell under it,
> And spills, the upper boulders in the sun;
> And make gaps even two can pass abreast.
> Robert Frost, "Mending Wall"

> Mr. Gorbachev, tear down this wall!
> President Ronald Reagan Remarks at the Brandenburg Gate,
> West Berlin, Germany June 12, 1987

Globalization is a natural process that has been going on for millennia. The alternative to globalization is the isolation of each country from all others, each state from
others, and even isolation of a village from the next. All the way to the twentieth
century you could find areas of the world where the inhabitant of one village could
not understand the language of people in a nearby village. But there has always been
a natural process of interaction and even integration among people and nations.

We need not dwell on the advantages of international trade and integration. The
advantages of free trade are amply discussed in many books.[1] The same can be said
about economic integration. Just imagine if the 50 states in the United States had
declared their independence and each were a separate country. Would any of them

---

[1] A good start in reading about free trade is *Against the Tide, An Intellectual History of Free Trade*
by Douglas Irwin, 1996.

K. Dadkhah, *The Evolution of Macroeconomic Theory and Policy*,
DOI 10.1007/978-3-540-77008-4_12, © Springer-Verlag Berlin Heidelberg 2009

be the economic and political superpower that the United States is today? Would the inhabitants have the level of well being they are enjoying today? Alternatively, suppose that all Latin American countries had formed a federal government similar to that of the United States. Mightn't it have become the great economic and political power in the world?

Figures 12.1 and 12.2 show the exponential rise in aggregate trade in the world both in nominal and real terms. Humankind is one species and indeed there is a tendency for walls to come down. Those who erect walls, oppose trade, oppose exchange of ideas, and isolate their nations are often also those who set up dictatorships.

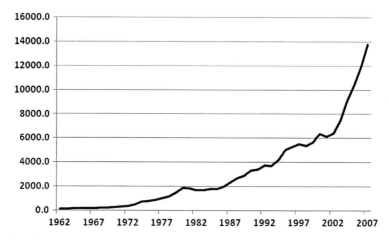

Fig. 12.1 Total world exports (billion dollars in Current Prices)

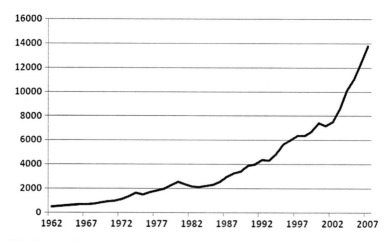

Fig. 12.2 Total world exports (billion dollars in Constant 2007 Prices)

In recent years, the pace of globalization has accelerated, and so has opposition to it. The problem is that the opponents of globalization have masked their basic intentions behind high sounding and ostensibly sensible concerns over fair treatment of workers and children or the protection of the environment. But the fact remains that often they want only to preserve certain perceived privileges for themselves. Sometimes, also, they are idealistic youth who are conned into supporting isolationist ideas.

But no matter how severe the opposition, the trend toward globalization and integration of the world toward one unified economy will continue. Globalization is not a process that certain countries such as the United States, China, India, and Japan have started and, therefore, when faced with strong opposition, they could call off. Rather globalization is a natural process and will continue whether certain groups like it or not. Indeed, as Robert Frost described, "there is something that doesn't love a wall" between individuals and nations.

The movement toward globalization has progressed through several channels. One route has been to remove all obstacles to free trade. That means lowering tariffs and removing quotas and other quantitative restrictions as well as reducing the red tape. First GATT and now the World Trade Organization (WTO) have been the forums to pursue this road to a world of free trade.

In addition, groups of countries have banded together to form free trade areas. These include the European Union and the North American Free Trade Area that encompasses the United States, Canada, and Mexico. In one sense such agreements run counter to the idea of multilateral free trade. Such free trade areas treat their members and outsiders differentially. Nevertheless, to the extent that they remove barriers to trade they are welcome developments.

The opponents of free trade have argued that globalization sends local jobs abroad, lower wages, and circumvents labor standards; that it damages the environment because emerging countries do not have the same standards for the protection of the environment as developed countries; that it encourages child labor because labor laws are lax in countries such as India; that it is harmful to women; that it makes poor countries poorer through deterioration of terms of trade; and finally that it destroys national and cultural identities. Proponents of free trade and globalization argue that even if in some instances such assertions could be supported by facts, overall globalization has a positive effect in all of these areas. They point out that goals of increasing wages and improving labor standards, protecting environment, eliminating child labor, protecting women and improving their lot, alleviating poverty, and safeguarding cultures are better served by promoting globalization. Furthermore, by working together and in line with globalization we can rectify any shortcoming in these areas. Therefore, the battle should not be against globalization but for making it to work even better.[2]

---

[2]For a detailed discussion of these issues see Jagdish Bhagwati (2004).

World Trade Organization (WTO)

The World Trade Organization is an offshoot of GATT (Chap. 2), which was established during the Uruguay Round (1986–1994).[3] It started operation in 1995. While GATT was concerned with trade in goods, the new agreement extended the principle of free trade to services and intellectual property (inventions and creations). At present WTO has 153 members, and other countries would like to join it.

WTO is based on certain principles:

1. Subject to some exceptions, WTO requires its members to treat all members equally. In other words all members are most favored nations. This principle does not preclude countries from forming a trading area where they could treat goods and services from inside the area more favorably than those from outside. Examples of such areas are the European Union and NAFTA.

2. Local and imported goods, including intellectual property (copyright) should be treated equally. This does not mean that the importing country is prevented from imposing import tariffs. Rather, after goods are entered into the country, they are treated in the same way as domestically produced goods. Similarly, intellectual property after reaching the country is afforded the same protection as domestic inventions and creations.

3. WTO continues the tradition of GATT to advance the goal of free trade through negotiation. At present members are engaged in the Doha round of negotiations. Ultimately, it is up to members to make concessions that will move the world toward a free trade zone. On the other hand, each country has to deal with its own interests and lobbying groups. Japan has to satisfy its farmers even if its consumers have to pay a hefty price for meat. French farmers don't like competition and American farmers like their subsidies. It is the same as in other areas of international concern, such as the environment. The United States asks the emerging economies of China and India to curb their gas emissions. But that does not seem right to these countries. The United States and Europe attained their present economic stature by literally messing up the earth, and the US is still a major polluter. In these international negotiations a formula has to be found to make everyone happy and that is not easy. Hence, the Doha round has stalled over conflicting demands from advanced and developing countries.

4. WTO tries to engender stability in international trade by requiring its members to bind themselves to tariff rates and other policies. The idea is that when exporters and importers are sure that no unexpected changes may be sprung upon them, they can more confidently plan their business.

5. Other principles of the WTO include promoting competition and encouraging its members to carry out economic reforms.

---

[3] More information on WTO can be found on the organization's website: http://www.wto.org/ and in *An Introduction to the WTO Agreements* by Bhagirath Lal Das, 1998.

The North American Free Trade Agreement (NAFTA)

In 1992 President George H. W. Bush signed the North American Free Trade Agreement (NAFTA). A year later it was ratified by the United States Congress at the urging of President Bill Clinton and its implementation began on January 1, 1994.

The agreement between the United States, Canada, and Mexico aims at removing barriers to trade and investment between the three countries. Article 101 of the Agreement establishes a free trade zone consistent with the provisions of GATT. Article 102 enumerates the objectives of the Agreement:

a) Eliminate barriers to trade in, and facilitate the cross-border movement of, goods and services between the territories of the Parties;
b) Promote conditions of fair competition in the free trade area;
c) Increase substantially investment opportunities in the territories of the Parties;
d) Provide adequate and effective protection and enforcement of intellectual property rights in each Party's territory;
e) Create effective procedures for the implementation and application of this Agreement, for its joint administration and for the resolution of disputes; and
f) Establish a framework for further trilateral, regional and multilateral cooperation to expand and enhance the benefits of this Agreement.

The NAFTA has two supplements: the North American Agreement on Environmental Cooperation and the North American Agreement on Labor Cooperation.

From the start the Agreement has been the subject of many criticisms. During the presidential campaign of 1992, one of the candidates kept harping at the idea that should the Agreement be ratified jobs will be sucked away from the United States into Mexico. After the ratification of the Agreement (from December 1993 to December 2007), employment in the United States grew from 121.5 to 146.2 million or by more than 24.7 million jobs. Indeed, we have witnessed Mexicans crossing the border, legally and illegally, to work in the US and not the other way around. Some have emphasized the loss of manufacturing jobs. Indeed manufacturing jobs declined from 16.8 million in December 1993 to 13.8 million in December 2007. But the loss of manufacturing jobs has nothing to do with the NAFTA. The growth of manufacturing employment in the United States came to a halt in 1969 and the decline started in 1979. The main cause of the loss of manufacturing jobs is technological progress. Note that while 3 million manufacturing jobs have been lost since 1993, the real value added of manufacturing has increased by 61.4%.

The fact of the matter is that all three countries have benefitted from the Agreement. It is time to concentrate on expanding and improving the Agreement rather than rethinking or renegotiating it. One idea would be to form a monetary union between the three countries. In theory all three will lose their monetary independence. But practically, the United States would dominate the central bank set up to manage the monetary policy of the union. The benefits to Canada and Mexico would be lower transaction costs and the elimination of currency risk. But the deal could be sweetened for Canada and Mexico by allocating them a somewhat bigger share in seignorage.

The European Union

The European Union is the culmination of a half century of effort to forge a unified Europe with enough economic power to stand shoulder to shoulder with the United States and, more recently, with emerging giants such as China and India.

It started in 1951 with Belgium, France, Italy, Luxembourg, the Netherlands, and West Germany forming the European Coal and Steel Community . It was a common market for coal and steel. In 1957 the European Economic Community , a customs union, was formed. Later, the European Community (EC) was formed by merging the European Coal and Steel Community, the European Economic Community, and the European Atomic Energy Community.

The turning point was the Maastricht Treaty that established the European Union (EU) in 1993. Furthermore, it stipulated the formation of a monetary union. This was particularly important as the previous arrangement of the European Monetary System (EMS) with its exchange rate mechanism (ERM) was abandoned.

The monetary union established a single currency, the euro, and a European Central Bank (ECB). By joining the monetary union each government gave up its independent monetary policy. The benefits are lower transactions costs in trade between the member countries and the elimination of exchange rate risk in such transactions.

Over time the membership in the European Union has grown to 27 countries with some standing in line to join. Not all members of the EU are members of the European Monetary Union. Notable exceptions are Denmark, Sweden, and the United Kingdom.

Other Aspects of Globalization

Expansion of trade is only one aspect of globalization. Freedom of capital movement has turned the world into one financial system. Every day a few trillion dollars move across the borders. In comparison the total GDP of the United States is less than 15 trillion dollars per year. At the same time, international direct investment and international borrowing have been increased tremendously. Thus, the international monetary system, financial entities such as sovereign funds, and issues such as sovereign debt attain added importance.

The International Monetary System

The last time we visited the international monetary system was in Chap. 6 at the time of the collapse of the Bretton Woods Agreement . In the intervening four decades, the international monetary system underwent changes and faced several severe crises. A review of these developments is beyond the scope of this book. Nevertheless, certain characteristics of the international monetary system and their bearing on macroeconomic policy need discussion.

The Bretton Woods Agreement set up an international monetary system with known rules that obligated the signatories to keep their exchange rates fixed. Moreover, there was a central authority to oversee the adherence to these rules. In earlier chapters we noted that any international monetary system has four ingredients: the manner in which exchange rates are determined, the international money, a central authority, and the way the system corrects imbalances. After Bretton Woods, countries around the world have groped toward a new system.

It is usually said that the new system is one of flexible exchange rates. Yet, as of 2006, by one accounting, only 50 out of 182 countries, or 27.47%, have floating rates. The largest group (45.60%) adheres to soft pegs, and the rest (26.92%) have hard pegs.[4]

Thus, the determination of exchange rates for many advanced and emerging economies is left to the market. But this is not universal; the majority of these countries as well as developing countries have yet to make their exchange rates fully flexible.

The international currency for the most part is the dollar. Figure 12.3 shows the share of the dollar and euro in international reserves. Although since its introduction the euro has increased its share, it accounts only for a quarter of reserves. The dollar accounts for slightly less than two thirds of reserves, and the rest is in other currencies.

The system does not have a central authority. But the hub of the system is the US economy.

The normal mechanism for correction of imbalances for economies with a floating exchange rate has been the market mechanism. Countries whose currencies have been in demand, for trade or investment, have appreciated. On the other hand

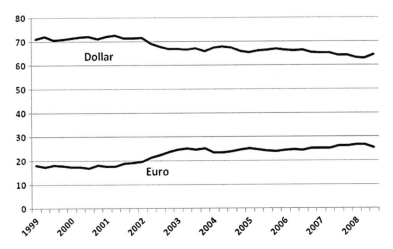

Fig. 12.3 Composition of international currency reserves

---

[4] Barry Eichengreen (2008), p. 188.

economies experiencing a net outflow due to trade deficits and investment abroad, have experienced depreciation of their currencies.

The financial and economic crisis of 2007–2009 (see the next chapter) has underlined the shortcomings of the present international monetary and financial arrangements. There is a definite need to revamp the system.

Sovereign Debt

One government borrowing from another or from the people of another country is not a new practice. But, since the end of the Bretton Woods, the scale of sovereign debt has increased dramatically. Indeed, borrowing from abroad is not an exception but a normal occurrence. To get an order of magnitude of the US foreign borrowing, according to the Department of Treasury as of December 2008, the amount of Treasury securities held by major foreign holders was $3.1 trillion.

Some countries, particularly in Latin America, have frequently defaulted on their sovereign debt. This brings up a host of legal and economic issues. But more important, from a macroeconomic point of view, is that sovereign debt increases the interdependence of economies. When China is holding close to three quarters of a trillion dollars in US debt, the health of the US economy becomes even more important to China. On the other hand, China's decisions regarding the US debt could potentially have dramatic effects on the US economy. Hence the necessity of working together.

Sovereign Funds

In recent years some countries with huge surplus in their international trade have set aside part of their surplus in entities known as sovereign funds. The distinctive features of these funds are their ownership by governments (hence the designation sovereign) and their extraordinarily large amount of assets. Consider, for example, Saudi Arabia, China, and the United Arab Emirates. Saudi Arabia earns billions of dollars every year from its oil exports. The same is true for the UAE. Similarly, China has amassed more than a trillion dollars in assets around the world from its trade surplus. Now what are these countries supposed to do with this money? They cannot simply deposit it in checking accounts in the hope of using it. But should these countries buy government bonds of the United States and other countries and settle for a low return? Note that even a 5% interest on a trillion dollars brings $50 billion in revenues. Why shouldn't they do what all other investors are doing? They can form a fund and appoint a manager, directing him/her to optimize their profit. This is indeed what they have done. The countries mentioned as well as a number of others have funds worth hundreds of billions of dollars, which engage in investment around the world.

There are certain worries associated with the operation of these sovereign funds. The most important issue is that the owners of these funds are not individuals and private companies solely concerned with profit. What if the funds use their money and influence to political ends? Worse, what if they pose some kind of security threat to the host country where they have invested? So far there is no evidence of such behavior. Yet the concern is legitimate.

As we shall discuss in the next chapter there is a need for a new international monetary and financial system. Perhaps the issue of sovereign funds as one among many other concerns could be addressed in such a system.

International Economic Policy Coordination

Openness and freedom of capital movement means that economic policy in one country would have repercussions in others. In Chap. 5 we discussed the effect of monetary policy in an open economy with a flexible exchange rate. An increase in money supply, we argued, will lead to a lowering of the interest rate which, in turn, would cause a net outflow of capital. As a result, a country's currency depreciates, thus its exports increase and its imports decrease. The upshot is higher income, but the interest rate would revert to the international level.

It is clear that the higher income of the country has been achieved at the expense of other countries. By reducing its imports from other countries, it has reduced their exports and income. As long as we are talking about a small country, perhaps these secondary effects are negligible. Certainly the same thing cannot be said if the country in question is the United States or advanced countries such as Germany and Japan.

On the other hand, if simultaneously all countries increase their money supplies, it is hard to imagine that any of them will experience the anticipated effect. These considerations have necessitated thinking about policy coordination, at least among economic powerhouses. During the 1970 s in response to an oil crisis, leaders of six democracies, the United States, the United Kingdom, France, West Germany, Japan, and Italy, agreed to meet annually to discuss economic issues. Later, Canada joined the group to make it the group G7. After the collapse of the former Soviet Union, Russia first informally attended the meetings of the G7 and in 1997 became the eighth member to make it G8.

While the group is an excellent forum for economic coordination, most of their meetings are taken up with immediate political issues. As a result, economic issues, let alone economic policy coordination, have been neglected. A permanent vehicle for international policy coordination is sorely missed in the present global economy. Such a forum should also include emerging economic powers such as China, India, Brazil, South Korea, and perhaps Saudi Arabia.

Chapter 13
The Financial and Economic Crisis of 2007–2009

The record is unmistakable: If you seek economic growth, if you seek opportunity, if you seek social justice and human dignity, the free market system is the way to go. And it would be a terrible mistake to allow a few months of crisis to undermine 60 years of success.
> President George W. Bush, speech in Federal Hall National Memorial, New York City, hosted by Manhattan Institute, November 13, 2008

Capitalism is that form of private property economy in which innovations are carried out by means of borrowed money, which in general, though not by logical necessity, implies credit creation.
> Joseph Schumpeter, *Business Cycles*, 1939, p. 223.

The salary of the chief executive of the large corporation is not a market award for achievement. It is frequently in the nature of a warm personal gesture by the individual to himself.
> John Kenneth Galbraith, *Annals of an Abiding Liberal*

Enough Blame to Go Around

The financial and economic crisis of 2007 started without warning and before long it had spread to many countries around the globe. Many have tried to blame one or another factor for the crisis. The fact of the matter is that such a crisis could not possibly have had a single cause. A combination of elements conspired to create it. It was first felt in the housing market. From there it spread to the credit market and ultimately affected the real part of the economy. In order to understand it we need to start from the beginning and we need to understand a few concepts in finance.

The American Dream of Homeownership

To own a house is an integral part of the American dream. In the United States both the government and the private sector have done their utmost to make this dream come true. Figure 13.1 shows the number of homes in the country as well as those occupied by their owners.

K. Dadkhah, *The Evolution of Macroeconomic Theory and Policy*,
DOI 10.1007/978-3-540-77008-4_13, © Springer-Verlag Berlin Heidelberg 2009

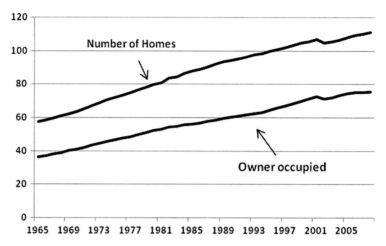

Fig. 13.1 Home ownership in the United States (million)

This is an achievement of the free market in operation aided by government. Builders motivated by profit have built the houses, banks have provided the necessary finance for the buyers, and the government has ensured liquidity in this market. Indeed, the idea of more and more families owning their homes has been a goal of public policy.

A mortgage is a loan made to a person(s) to buy a house. The borrower needs to meet certain criteria to be eligible for the loan. This is not unusual as any lender wants to make sure that it is taking a reasonable risk and would receive the interest and principal. Thus, the potential borrower is asked about his/her ability to repay the loan (creditworthiness), the value of collateral (in this case the house), and the amount of the down payment.

Fig. 13.2 Monthly 30-Year Fixed Mortgage Rate

Figure 13.2 shows monthly data for the 30-year fixed mortgage rate from 1971 to 2008. In recent years the rate has been around 6%, which in many countries around the world causes envy. It should be noted that the rates for 15-year mortgages were lower and for adjustable loans are even lower.

The US government has facilitated homeownership by providing liquidity to the market and by guaranteeing certain loans. In particular, two government sponsored corporations, Fannie Mae and Freddie Mac, have created a secondary mortgage market whereby banks can sell mortgages they have generated and obtain money for further loans.

Fannie Mae and Freddie Mac

The Federal National Mortgage Association (FNMA) or Fannie Mae was established by the government in 1938. As a government agency its mission was to guarantee loans and provide resources to the housing market. In 1968 it became a private corporation but it retained the backing of the government. In 1970, the Congress created the Federal Home Loan Mortgage Corporation (FHLMC) or Freddie Mac for the same purpose. The two companies have been successful in carrying out their mission. They own or guarantee half the amount of mortgages outstanding in the country, which amounts to a staggering $12 trillion.

Over time both companies, being private and at the same time government sponsored, grew too big. As a result neither could they be managed effectively nor could the government afford to let them go bankrupt. At the same time both organizations used their vast resources to lobby the Congress for their own benefit.

Toward the end of the 1990s both the Administration and the Congress demanded that the two companies buy loans extended to low income families. The fact is that the mortgage market worked well for anyone who had a decent income, did not have credit problem, and was not a member of certain minorities. The idea was now to extend the facilities to buy mortgages to individuals with a problematic credit history or minorities who may have been deprived of homeownership due to their alleged credit problem. In other words Fannie and Freddie were entering the *sub-prime mortgage* market (see the next section).

To help low income families gain homeownership is one thing but to lend to people who cannot afford the loan or are high risk is an entirely different matter. In 2003 the Bush Administration proposed to tighten Fannie Mae and Freddie Mac regulations. The two corporations brought immense lobbying pressure to bear on the members of Congress, and Democrats led by Representative Barney Frank of Massachusetts opposed the legislation. Another bill introduced in 2006 by Senator Chuck Hagel had no better fate.

During the financial crisis that started in 2007 the two corporations experienced severe financial troubles and the value of their shares plummeted. In September 2008 both corporations were placed under the conservatorship of the Federal Housing Finance Agency.

The experience documents the sub-optimality of such hybrid arrangements and points to the necessity of breaking up the two corporations into smaller companies once the crisis is over.

Subprime Mortgage

Subprime mortgage refers to housing loans extended to individuals with credit problems, those who cannot document their income, or those whose ability to service the loan is questionable. In order to extend credit facilities to these people, some financial regulations were relaxed. By offering teasers some lenders enticed the borrowers, who might have known better, into borrowing. The interest rate for the first two years of the loan would be low, say 4.5%. After that the interest rate would go up to 6.5–7.5%. Others used what is known as predatory lending, taking advantage of the lack of information on the part of borrowers.

While the housing market was experiencing a boom, there was little to worry about. The idea was that you borrow $300,000 and buy a house. Let us assume that you could afford to service the loan for the time being, but the future is uncertain. In a year the price of your house increases by 15%. You already have gained $45,000. You could get a line of credit based on the equity in your house and keep paying your monthly payments. If the interest rate goes up then you refinance your loan. Suppose none of this works, then you simply sell the house. You have lived in it for a year or two and have made a handy profit.

When the housing bubble burst, this fairy tale came to an end. House prices started to decline and borrowers found themselves holding mortgages that they could not afford. Worse, the amount of the mortgage was more than the market price of the house. They could not borrow more, because they did not have any equity in their home. They could not refinance, because the new loan, even if they secured one, would be less than the amount of the old one. They could not sell their house because there were few buyers, but even if they did, they would not be able to pay back the loan. Some abandoned their houses and some faced foreclosure.

The Housing Crisis

After the recession of the 2001, the Federal Reserve, under the chairmanship of Alan Greenspan, kept the interest rate low for too long. This provided a lot of liquidity to the market and prompted financial institutions to scramble to lend. Housing was a ready outlet.

In Chap. 11 we discussed the Schumpeterean theory of growth and fluctuations and noted that the engine for both was innovation financed by credit expansion. In the 1980s it was personal computers and in the 1990s the Internet. After 2001 no such innovation was forthcoming. The combination of abundant liquidity and the lack of investment outlets turned the investors and banks toward buying mortgages and assets backed by such mortgages.

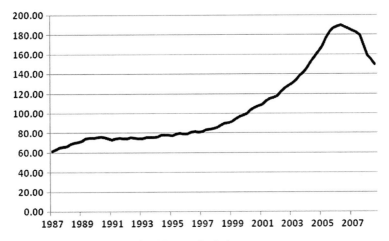

Fig. 13.3 S&P Case-Shiller US national home price index

When in late 2006 house prices started to decline (Fig. 13.3), mortgages and assets based on them lost their value. Perhaps if the originating bank was holding the mortgage, the problem could be contained. The bank could write it off or negotiate with the customer to find a mutually agreeable compromise. But the bank had sold the mortgage together with many others to an investment bank. The latter had made it into an asset backed security (see below) and sold it in pieces to other institutions and investors. Moreover, derivatives and insurances were issued based on these assets. Again each piece was owned by God knows who. When the underlying asset lost its value a pyramid of assets lost their values. Worse, no one knew which one and by how much. This precipitated the financial crisis. But before getting to that, we need to familiarize ourselves with a few concepts in finance.

The Function of Finance and Financial Institutions

An understanding of finance is essential to macroeconomic analysis. There are many excellent books on finance. The present section is not intended as a substitute for reading them nor is there any pretension here of serving as an introduction to the subject. Rather, the present section is intended to whet the appetite of readers and perhaps jog the memory of those who already know the material.

Finance and the financial system are essential to the workings of modern economies. The financial system connects savers and investors and is a bridge between the present and future. A group of young entrepreneurs have an idea about setting up a high tech company but they are just out of school and have no money to realize their dream. There are a large number of individuals with small and large savings but they have no idea what to do with it. Just putting it under the mattress doesn't sound like a great idea. Yet they don't want to take the risk of lending their money out or investing it outright. A financial institution takes their money with the promise of paying them back with interest. The money is lent to entrepreneurs who invest it and should they be successful they will pay back their loan with interest. Of course not all projects are successful and some investments do not pan out. Thus, the interest rate paid to depositors is lower than that charged to investors. The difference is the cost of risk (default by some borrowers), the cost of running the institution (say the bank), and profit for the institution.

Similarly, workers would like to provide for their retirement. So they set some of their money aside and deposit it with a financial institution. At the same time, young couples just starting their lives together who want to buy a house borrow from the financial institution. The bank charges them interest and adds part of it to the account of workers who are saving for the future. The young borrowers enjoy their homes long before they can afford them outright and the savers have more resources for their retirement.

This is the essence of finance. But of course, the world is not quite this simple. To begin with, the savers hand their money to the financial institution on trust. What prevents those running the institution taking the money and running away or investing it in dubious, high risk ventures? Here we need rules and regulations and regulatory bodies. Hence the central bank, FDIC and other regulatory agencies. Ultimately money and finance are based on trust and confidence. It is the role and duty of the regulatory framework to engender an environment of confidence and trust within which all actors, that is, investors, savers, lenders, and borrowers, can make decisions. We shall return to this theme below.

But even if everyone plays by the rules and everyone is honest, there is the element of risk. No one can forecast the future perfectly. Our lives and definitely any investment involve risk. We need to measure risk and find a way to deal with it.

Assets, Risk, and Diversification

We are familiar with physical assets. Financial assets are in the form of a piece of paper or a record that certifies the ownership of a physical asset or command over some amount of resources that could be used to obtain physical assets. For instance, a stock of a particular company (say Verizon, Honda, or Google) shows that the owner is entitled to a share of all the assets of that company. A government bond signifies that the bearer would receive $10,000 at maturity.

These are financial assets and each can be characterized by two parameters: return and risk. For a stock, the return consists of dividends plus any increase or decrease in the value of stock. The risk measures the volatility of the return. For a government bond the return is the interest paid and if the bond holder keeps it till maturity the asset is risk free. However, if the bond holder sells it prior to maturity he/she will realize a loss (gain) in price if there has been an increase (decrease) in interest rate. To realize a higher return the investor has to accept a higher risk.

Each investor chooses a number of assets to invest in. The bundle is referred to as a portfolio. The question is how to choose a portfolio to maximize the return for a level of risk that the investor can accept. This necessitates a way to measure risk. In a seminal paper Harry Markowitz, Nobel laureate 1990, suggested the use of standard deviation as a measure of risk.[1]

Markowitz showed that a portfolio of equally risky assets would have less risk compared to each of those assets. This is the idea of diversification, which simply put, means not putting all your eggs in one basket. An investor is better off, in terms of risk, if she divides her wealth among a number of stocks. To see this, consider an investor who invests in two assets with returns equal to r_1 and r_2 and risks (measured by the standard deviation of returns) of s_1 and s_2. If the investor divides her wealth in the proportion a in the first asset and $1-a$ in the second, then her return and risk will be[2]:

$$R = ar_1 + (1-a)r_2$$
$$S = \sqrt{a^2 s_1^2 + (1-a)^2 s_2^2}$$

Suppose the investor chooses two assets with the same risk and return:

$$r_1 = r_2 = r, \quad \text{and} \quad s_1 = s_2 = s$$

and invests half her wealth in each asset. Then $R = r$ and

$$S = \sqrt{\frac{1}{4}s^2 + \frac{1}{4}s^2} = \frac{\sqrt{2}}{2}s \approx 0.707s$$

In other words, with diversification it is possible to realize the same return with less risk.

Markowitz provided a formal exposition for an idea that investors knew long before. Mutual funds had been created and operated on the principle of diversification.[3] A mutual fund is a portfolio of a set of stocks managed by a money manager. Shares at this portfolio are sold to investors. For instance, suppose the portfolio consists of 120 shares of company A, 400 shares of company B, and 250 shares of stock C. Further assume that the fund is made into 200 shares that are sold to investors. Then each share of the mutual fund would represent 0.6 share of company A, 2 shares of company B, and 1.25 shares of company C. In addition to diversifying risk, a mutual fund allows for pooling of resources and realizing benefits of scale.

---

[1] Harry Markowitz (1952), pp. 77–91.

[2] We have assumed that the two assets are completely independent of each other and, therefore, their returns are not correlated. If the returns of the assets are correlated with correlation coefficient ρ, then we will have $S = \sqrt{a^2 s_1^2 + (1-a)^2 s_2^2 + 2a(1-a)s_1 s_2 \rho}$

[3] The mutual fund was invented by Massachusetts Financial Services Company (now MFS Investment Management) in 1924.

Long, Short, and Neutral

Regarding any asset the investor can take one of three positions. If you own the asset, your position is *long*. If you owe an asset then you have a *short* position regarding that asset. This requires a bit of explanation. Suppose you think that in the next two months the stock of General Motors or the price of a barrel of oil will decline. Of course if you already have that asset you may want to sell it before its price goes down. But suppose you do not have the asset and you want to speculate on your forecast or hunch. You borrow that asset from someone for a fee and you sell it. If your forecast is correct, soon you can buy that asset at a lower price than you sold it. Your profit would be equal to the price difference less the fee and transactions cost. Of course, if you were wrong then you lose money. When you sell a borrowed asset you are shorting it.

In some markets you are allowed to sell an asset even without borrowing it. That is called *naked short selling*. During the financial crisis of 2008, some blamed this practice for part of the troubles in the market and the SEC banned it for a time.

If one neither owns nor owes an asset then she has a *neutral* position.

Hedging, Arbitrage, and Speculation

Many business activities involve risk not necessarily associated with the operation of that business or risks that the management could not or is unwilling to assume. An exporter is in the business of exporting certain products, not speculating on exchange rates. A company exports 100 million euros worth of computers to Europe but would receive payment in six months. The company has to pay for labor and material in the dollar now. A euro is worth $1.28 now, but in six months it could be $1.18. The difference would be $10 million. The company cannot afford to take such a risk. The option is to *hedge* against such an eventuality. Hedging means that the company sells its euros now but delivers it 6 months from now, thus buying insurance against fluctuations in the value of the euro. Of course the company has to pay a premium for such a transaction.

The same is true for an airline that is worried about an increase in the price of fuel, an electricity generating company regarding the price of natural gas, and a food processing factory regarding its raw material. As we shall see these businesses can engage in buying and selling of futures contracts or options to hedge against changes in prices and protect themselves.

Arbitrage involves two simultaneous transactions in two markets to make a profit from the difference in the price of an asset in those markets. Perhaps the idea of arbitrage can best be illustrated with an example from the foreign exchange market although, given the means of communications today, it is difficult to find arbitrage opportunities in foreign exchange markets. Let us consider the exchange rates between the dollar, euro, and yen in three different markets. In New York a euro is worth $1.32, in Frankfurt a euro buys 147 yen, and in Tokyo 106 yens buys a dollar. An arbitrageur buys a euro in New York for $1.32, and with the euro buys 147 yens in Frankfurt and sells his yens for $1.3868 = 147/106$ in Tokyo, thus profiting 6.68 cents for every $1.32 invested less transactions cost. As mentioned before, in today's world there are no such opportunities but it illustrates the idea of arbitrage.

Arbitrage is not confined to the foreign exchange market. For example, there can be arbitrage between short and long term bond markets (see Chap. 9 and the discussion on expectations theory of the term structure of interest rates).

Speculation has gotten a bad rap, but frankly it is not as bad as it sounds. If you think that next week the price of toothpaste will go up, it seems logical to buy a few tubes of toothpaste now. Of course if the price goes down you have paid too much. That is the idea of speculation: acting on your forecast or hunch to make money from ups and downs of the market.

Usually politicians blame speculators any time something goes wrong when in fact a good deal of the time politicians themselves are the culprit. First, note that if a market solely consists of speculators, as a group they cannot make any money. The market would resemble a poker table; if someone wins it must be at the expense of someone else. The market has to have some hedgers who would want to divest themselves of risk and the speculators assume that risk. In fact, speculators make markets more efficient by exploiting available information and moving prices in the right direction.

Financial Innovations

Like any industry, financial institutions have been engaged in innovation. The basic motives have been to tailor the risk of assets to the tastes of their clients. Of course, like any other industry some innovations have been successful and some have produced loss and calamities. We also mentioned the necessity of regulations and, in general, a framework for the operation of financial system. One effect of financial innovation is that the existing framework cannot guarantee the trust and confidence of market participants.

The main purpose of the financial system could be summarized as: (1) to marshal resources from small and large savers and to allocate it to investors and consumers; (2) to separate risk from return to the degree possible and to sell the risk taking to those who could and are willing to assume it; and (3) to allow investors, regardless of the size of their wealth, to realize the highest return possible given the risk they are comfortable with. Financial innovation has aimed at achieving these goals more efficiently and extending it to more people. This is not to say that there haven't been missteps or outright criminal acts by financiers. Perhaps the financial system has more than its share of crooks. Because of the possibilities of wrongdoing, because not everyone is well versed in the intricacies of financial dealings, and because, as was mentioned before, finance and money are based on trust and confidence, the regulatory agencies have an immense role to play.

Derivatives

Derivatives are assets the value of which depends on another underlying asset. For instance a barrel of oil may have a price of $45. But you may want to buy oil not for today but two months hence. You buy a futures contract of 1000 barrels delivery of Cushing, Oklahoma for $46 per barrel. This way you guarantee that no matter what the price of oil is two months from now you will have it for $46 a barrel. Needless to say, if the price is substantially lower than $46 then you have made a bad decision and have to live with it. Futures are available for commodities as well as financials such as stocks and bonds.

Futures and options contracts for commodities and financials are traded in NYSE Euronext, the New York Mercantile Exchange (NYMEX), the Chicago Board of Trade (CBOT), and in other exchanges.

A futures contract obligates the buyer to the full value of the contract. For instance, a futures contract on oil at $46 means the buyer has to pay $46,000 and take possession of the 1000 barrels of oil or somehow sell it in the market. But suppose you just want to hedge against a contingency or speculate on the price change without obligating yourself to the purchase of the whole contract. As an example, suppose that you have sold a shipment of your product to a European company for a sum of €50 million. But the payment will be made by the European buyer in six months. Since each euro today is $1.35, you are counting on $67.5 million. But six months from now the euro may be much less. Could you insure yourself against a depreciation of the euro against the dollar? You could buy an *option* to sell your euros at $1.35 in six months. The price of that option would be, for example, $202,500. By paying this price you guarantee that whatever the price of the euro is six months hence, you will get your $67.5 million. Thus, if for instance the price of the euro is $1.30, you have avoided a loss of $2.5 million. Of course someone has lost that much. This is called a *put option*. An option that allows you to buy at a certain price is called a *call option*.

What would happen if you have a put option and the price of the euro increases to $1.37? You simply throw away the option; it is worthless. You will get $68.5 for your euros and you have paid an insurance premium of $202,500. Thus, an option is a right but not an obligation to sell (put) or buy (call) a commodity or asset.

Options are of two types: American and European. With an American option you can exercise your right from the time of purchase to the expiration date of the option. With a European option you can exercise it only at the expiration date. Most options in the market are of the American type. Yet the computation for the valuation of options is based on the Black-Scholes formula that considers a European option.

It should be noted that the mathematics behind the valuation of options is rather involved. Tables for valuation of options have been compiled based on the Black-Scholes formula. But it is not unfair to say that most of those who use these tables have no clue as to their meanings. The situation gets worse when innovation is piled on top of innovation. Securities are based on assets, and options are created on top of these assets and sold around the world. Men and women in suits may go around and talk the talk and collect salaries without knowing what they are talking about. Many great financial houses have lost tremendous fortunes on such assets. An ordinary investor is best advised to stay away from investing in options or derivatives in general.

Asset-Backed Securities, Collateralized Debt Obligations (CDOs), and Credit Default Swaps (CDSs)

Asset-backed securities. Among the more recent financial innovations were *asset-backed securities*. Consider a bank or a mortgage company that has lent money to a number of customers. Each mortgage generates a given amount of revenue in the form of interest payment. The same is true for car loans, credit card loans, etc. Now suppose that we put a large number of such obligations into a portfolio and sell shares in it to customers who will be entitled to a cash flow from these assets. The advantage of such securitized assets is that the investor could receive the cash flow while assuming less risk than if she had to deal with each of these assets alone. The disadvantage is that it may be difficult for the investor to ascertain what it is that she has invested in.

In addition to mortgages, asset backed securities are formed from car loans, credit card debts, student loans, and other cash flow generating asset. Consider a credit card company that has lent money to its cardholders. Each cardholder is obligated to pay certain amount of money every month, which could be considered revenue if it does not include payment of the principal.

Collateralized debt obligations. Asset-backed securities made of fixed-income securities are called collateralized debt obligations. Where fixed income securities are financial instruments with a definite stream of income over a period of time. Examples are government and corporate bonds. Again cash flows from a number of such assets are sold to investors.

Credit default swaps. Suppose you are a bank manager and you have lent a million dollars to a client. There is a danger of the default on the loan. Wouldn't it be nice if you could insure your bank against such a loss? Suppose someone sells insurance for such contingencies. You buy the insurance and periodically make payments, similar to insurance premium, to the issuer. Should the borrower default on his loan then you collect your loss. Such derivatives are called *credit default swap*. There is, however, one catch. You need not have lent the money to your client to buy the CDS nor need you suffer a loss to collect. Rather the credit default swap is like betting on the happening of an event. The price (or spread) of CDS of a company reflects the perception of the solvency of that entity. A higher price means investors are betting that the company will default. During 2007–2009 CDSs were blamed for exacerbating the crisis.[4]

---

[4] Credit default swaps were invented at JP Morgan Chase in 1997 and found legal status in the Commodity Futures Modernization Act of 2000.

Fraud in Financial Markets

We noted several times that money and finance are ultimately based on trust; hence the necessity for the government to supervise and regulate financial markets. But another aspect is that finance attracts fraudsters. The stakes are high and even those with alleged financial savvy can fall prey to the promise of easy gains. The history of finance is replete with schemes and fraud.

Perhaps nothing exemplifies this better than the case of Bernard Madoff, a former chairman of NASDAQ, who defrauded $50 billion from his quite wealthy and unsuspecting victims. The case is extraordinary because of the amount of money involved, the list of rich and famous victims, and the fact that Madoff was regarded as a quite respectable financier.

Yet the scheme was an old Ponzi[5] game. The idea is that the old investors are paid by the money the new investors bring in. Charles Ponzi offered 50% return on a 45 day investment. The fraudster claims that he has hit upon a scheme to make a lot of money very fast. Of course, he cannot disclose his methods and that is understandable. The early investors are paid on time and the word gets around and everyone wants to believe that indeed there are fairies, a Santa Claus, and that financial schemes can make a lot of money "overnight." Money comes in from the new investors and goes out to the old. Sooner or later the scheme collapses leaving a lot of savvy investors red faced.

There are three lessons to be learned here. First, money and the financial market require more regulations and stricter enforcement than other markets. The idea that the market will take care of itself doesn't work here. It is unfortunate that the SEC as the cop on the beat was found napping or worse. Second, the old adage that "if it is too good to be true, it is" applies like the laws of physics. Why in the world would someone give you 50% or 25% return? The usual answer is that he is reaping an even bigger return, say 200% himself. But then he should be able to borrow at 8% or 10% and make even more for himself. What is his connection to you that he would want to give you a part of the loot? Incidentally, these schemers prey more easily on people with whom they have some affinity such as shared religion, ethnicity, or national origin. The third lesson is that when high rolling financiers, managers of hedge funds, and others with pretensions fall for this, you can conclude that either they are accomplices or have no clue as to what they are doing. Either way, in financial decision making you are on your own.

In his highly readable classic, *A Random Walk Down Wall Street*, Burton Malkiel wrote: "Investors would be far better off buying and holding an index fund than attempting to buy and sell individual securities or actively managed mutual funds." He added that "optimal investment strategies must be age-related. Chapter 14, entitled 'A Life-Cycle Guide to Investing,' should prove very helpful to people of all

---

[5] After Charles Ponzi, an Italian immigrant who at the beginning of the last century set up shop in Boston and defrauded his victims. He spent some years in prison after which he was deported to Italy where he died in poverty.

ages. This chapter alone is worth the cost of a high-priced appointment with a personal financial adviser." The events have proved Malkiel right. One could go a step further and say that his book is worth its weight in gold.

The Financial Crisis

Now that we have a general picture of financial markets, we can go back to the story of the 2007/2009 financial and economic crisis. Banks and mortgage companies had lent to borrowers who did not have the ability to pay the interest and principal on the loans. The loans in turn had been bundled in securities and sold around the world. Then the housing market experienced a downturn. Subprime mortgages stopped performing. In April 2007, New Century Financial, which specialized in subprime mortgages, filed for Chapter 11 bankruptcy. In August Bear Stearns, an investment bank told its investors that the money they had invested in two hedge funds was lost. Soon the crisis became international and banks in France, England, Germany, and Switzerland were in financial trouble. Several banks around the world reported tremendous losses due to their investment in the subprime market. Banks stopped lending to each other and the London Interbank Offered Rate LIBOR (similar to the federal funds rate) shot up.

When subprime mortgages stopped performing, asset backed securities stopped paying the cash flow and lost their value. Recall that the value of an asset equals the discounted value of the income stream it generates. If the income is zero or near zero, the asset's value is zero. This in itself would have created a tremendous problem around the world, but the problem was compounded because no one knew which asset or which part was worthless. Each asset-backed security consisted of portions of many loans. But then there were other securities that were based on these assets and they were losing their value.

By the end of 2007, the extent of losses by major banks became known. The Swiss bank UBS and the American giant Citigroup reported huge losses.

The Stock Market

The reaction of the stock market to the financial crisis is quite fascinating. Figure 13.4 shows the daily movement of the Dow Jones Industrial index from January 2004 to December 2008. In 2006, after the financial crisis had started, the market started an upward movement culminating in a record high for the index in October 2007. After that a downward movement started resulting in a low of less than 8000 in November 2008.

There are several features of the market worth noting. First, there was the excessive daily volatility of the index, at times moving 1000 points in one or the other direction within a day. Second, the market showed great sensitivity to news. Indeed, this sensitivity may have been the cause of the volatility. Finally, the market highlighted the international nature of present day finance. The indexes around the world,

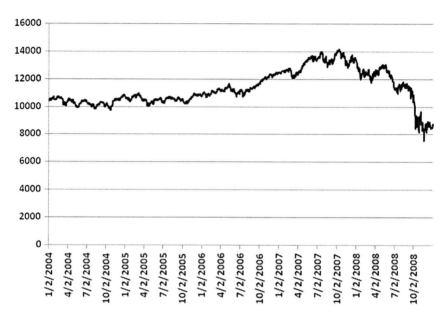

Fig. 13.4 Daily closing of the Dow Jones industrial index

NIKKEI (Japan), KOSPI (South Korea), Hang Seng (Hong Kong), CAC (France), DAX (Germany), FTSE (England), and Dow Jones (USA) reacted to each other and amplified the fluctuations in the market.

The Effects on the Real Economy

The credit crisis affected demand. Consumers relied on credit to purchase goods and services. Firms borrowed to invest in buildings and equipment. When credit tightened, consumers and investors reduced their demand. Nowhere did this hit the economy with a stronger impact than in the auto industry. Car sales fell. Of course, there was the additional impact of high oil prices, which in July 2008 reached $147 per barrel. But since the sharp drop in the price of oil, which happened in the fall of 2008, did not help the situation, we can be confident that the main effect was the unavailability of finance and worries about the future of the economy.

Table 13.1 shows the quarterly growth rates of the GDP and its main components (seasonally adjusted at annual rate). The downturn in the economy started with investment, particularly in residential construction. Consumption which constitutes 70% of the GDP stayed robust and the slack in investment was picked up by exports. The increase in exports and later the reduction in imports were partly due to the depreciation of the dollar. Nevertheless, in the fourth quarter of 2007 the GDP declined by 0.2%. In the next two quarters, due to government action, the GDP rebounded. In particular with the tax rebate of 2008, the GDP showed robust growth of 2.8% in the second quarter. But this was a short lived relief and the GDP fell by 0.5% in the third quarter. That was enough for the NBER to declare that

Table 13.1 Quarterly growth rates of the GDP and its main components[6]

	2005				2006			
	I	II	III	IV	I	II	III	IV
GDP	3.0	2.6	3.8	1.3	4.8	2.7	0.8	1.5
Consumption	1.7	3.6	3.7	1.4	4.3	2.8	2.2	3.7
Durables	0.6	12.1	5.4	−11.7	18.9	1.8	3.5	4.2
Investment	9.1	−5.1	4.0	12.2	6.2	−0.4	−5.3	−15.0
Residential	8.1	9.7	4.0	0.2	−3.6	−16.6	−21.4	−19.5
Exports	8.1	8.8	0.4	10.9	16.7	5.5	3.5	15.6
Imports	3.2	0.6	0.8	15.3	10.3	0.1	3.1	2.0
Government	−0.2	0.9	3.4	−1.7	3.9	1.2	1.7	1.6
Federal	1.1	1.1	9.7	−7.2	10.0	−1.5	1.9	1.8
	2007				2008			
	I	II	III	IV	I	II	III	IV
GDP	0.1	4.8	4.8	−0.2	0.9	2.8	−0.5	−6.2
Consumption	3.9	2.0	2.0	1.0	0.9	1.2	−3.8	−4.3
Durables	9.2	5.0	2.3	0.4	−4.3	−2.8	−14.8	−22.1
Investment	−9.6	6.2	3.5	−11.9	−5.8	−11.5	0.4	−20.8
Residential	−16.2	−11.5	−20.6	−27.0	−25.1	−13.3	−16.0	−22.2
Exports	0.6	8.8	23.0	4.4	5.1	12.3	3.0	−23.6
Imports	7.7	−3.7	3.0	−2.3	−0.8	−7.3	−3.5	−16.0
Government	0.9	3.9	3.8	0.8	1.9	3.9	5.8	1.6
Federal	−3.6	6.7	7.2	−0.5	5.8	6.6	13.8	6.7

the US economy had been in recession since December 2007. The economic conditions became even worse when in the fourth quarter of 2008 the GDP dropped by an annual rate of 6.2%.

The decline in production meant layoffs and the unemployment rate started nudging up (Fig. 13.5). Here the multiplier effect started working in reverse. Less investment meant less output and less employment. But less employment meant less income and less demand for products. Furthermore, the fear of losing one's job darkens the horizon for the consumer. Shouldn't I curtail my expenditures just in case I may lose my job? Indeed, consumption fell by 3.8% in the third quarter of 2008.

Thus, the circle was completed; the housing crisis caused a financial crisis which, in turn, caused an economic downturn.

Government Response to the Crisis

The government response to the crisis was to use monetary and fiscal policies. First, the Federal Reserve lowered the interest rate. Indeed, the Fed kept lowering the federal funds rate getting it to almost zero (Fig. 13.6). In addition, the Fed made available $200 billion liquidity to banks and financial institutions. But this policy,

---

[6]These are annual rates. Thus, −6.2% growth rate for the GDP in 2008-IV means that if the same rate of decline as in the fourth quarter had continued for a whole year, the GDP would have decreased by 6.2%. The decline in fourth quarter compared to the third had been 1.59%.

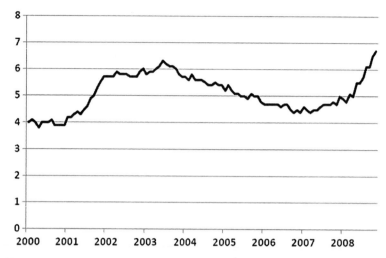

Fig. 13.5   Monthly unemployment rate

Fig. 13.6   Daily federal funds rate: 2006–2008

at least at the beginning, did not seem to have the desired effect. Therefore, a fiscal stimulus was deployed. In spring 2008, taxpayers within a certain income group and depending on whether or not they had qualifying children, received a check amounting to $600–$1800.

Although this stimulus worked for a while, the crisis continued. It became clear that there was a crisis of confidence. Many financial institutions were holding the so called toxic assets. These assets were based on underlying assets, which may have lost their value. As a result there was no market and buyers for them. Hence, if they were going to be priced to the market, their prices would be zero. This meant many financial institutions were insolvent. Furthermore, they did not meet the capital requirements to keep lending. Could they borrow from other solvent institutions? No, because who wants to lend to a bank or company which is on the verge of bankruptcy. Here, the Treasury decided to step in and buy some of these assets and to guarantee some loans. Such a move takes time to work, but as of early 2009, it became much easier to secure a loan. Further, the government engineered or facilitated the acquisition of troubled firms by others. JP Morgan bought Bear Sterns and Bank of America acquired Merrill Lynch. The government went even further and directly rescued some firms by giving them funds in exchange for shares in those companies. In particular, the government prevented the giant insurance company, American International Group (AIG) to go bankrupt. On the other hand it allowed the investment bank Lehman Brothers to go under.

The Treasury proposed the Troubled Assets Relief Program (TARP) with the price tag of $700 billion. Treasury Secretary Paulson had asked for a free hand to spend the money. The Congress approved the program and allotted $350 billion as the first installment. The money was spent, yet the Treasury had difficulty showing where the money went or what the result was. The rescue plan whetted the appetite of other industries. Executives from automakers GM, Ford, and Chrysler, boarded their private jets and went to Capitol to ask for money. They got it.

Nevertheless, the crisis was far from over. It seemed that monetary policy was ineffective because the economy is experiencing a *liquidity trap*. That is, the economy was operating at that portion of the LM curve that is horizontal, which means that the interest rate had reached the lowest possible level, and moving LM to the right would have no effect. Alternatively, one could think that the loss of confidence in financial institutions was such that no amount of money injection would cause them to lend or the public to borrow. Definitely, the fact that the Treasury did not know where the money went, and why banks were not lending, did not help the situation.

The way out was fiscal stimulus and the new administration proposed a massive stimulus plan amounting to $787 billion. The plan included a $212 billion tax cut for individuals and businesses, $267 billion in direct spending, and $308 billion in appropriations for infrastructure, science, and energy.

On the expenditures side, the money was allocated to programs favored by the new administrations supporters. As such it was not clear that they would produce jobs. A more direct approach to creating jobs, for instance more defense expenditures, would have been more successful.

The package also included 'buy American' clauses, although some of these provisions were toned down before the law was passed. The law required the use of American iron and steel in infrastructure projects funded by the package. The protectionist hint of the law alarmed Canadians, Japanese, and Europeans. During his first visit abroad as president, Barak Obama heard the concerns of the Canadian

258   13 The Financial and Economic Crisis of 2007–2009

prime minister and tried to reassure him that he was for the expansion of trade. The protectionist attitude of some members of Congress is a reminder of Smoot-Hawley act that exacerbated the Great Depression.

In addition to the stimulus package, the government received the authorization to spend the second half of the TARP money on helping the financial system. In response to a number of revelations that executives in institutions which had received government money had helped themselves to large bonuses, the second TARP included caps on executive pay. Moreover, the program aimed at enlisting the private sector help in rescuing troubled financial firms. Yet as of the time of writing this book, the Treasury hadn't come up with a definite plan.

There have been talks of nationalizing banks which has both its defenders and critics. The government has rejected such ideas. Yet to help the financial industry back to its feet, the government acquired 40% stake in the Citigroup.

The government announced that $75 billion had been allocated to help home-owners facing foreclosure. The important issue here was to help those who cannot afford their mortgage without encouraging irresponsible behavior. There is a moral hazard involved here. If a homeowner who is delinquent in paying his mortgage, is helped by the government, what is to prevent his neighbors to stop making payments and hoping for government help?

Fed Chairman, Ben Bernanke, however, testified before the House Financial Services Committee that even borrowers who knowingly got into trouble should be helped. He noted that "Some borrowers presumably knew what they were getting into, but from a public policy point of view, the large amount of foreclosures are detrimental not just to the borrower and lender but to the broader system. In many of these situations we have to trade off the moral hazard issue against the greater good."

Needless to say, the government's massive intervention will have repercussions that we need to be cognizant of. First, the amount of the budget deficit and the amount of money infused into the economy will, sometime in the future, cause inflation. The budget for 2010 presented to Congress by President Obama had $1.75 trillion deficit. At present, the argument is that we need to get over this crisis now and deal with the problem of inflation when things are back to normal. The argument is compelling, as no one wants a repeat of the Great Depression. But we still need to prepare for the long run consequences. Second, the massive government intervention in the economy will engender vast bureaucracies, bring efficiencies, and stifle the workings of the market economy. In short, it will go against all that has made the United States an economic powerhouse and brought economic prosperity to its people. Once the crisis is over, a way must be found to smoothly but decisively disentangle government from businesses it has rescued.

Regarding the budget deficit, President Obama pledged to halve the budget deficit by 2013. He said that he intended to achieve this by reducing the Iraq war expenditures, taxing the rich, and streamlining government programs. He also invited 130 members of congress, community leaders, and government officials to discuss the budget deficit issue.

Back to the Future

Sooner or later this crisis will be over. The question on many people's mind is how can we avoid another crisis like this. The answer is that we cannot. Indeed, we can be sure that within 7–12 years from now we will have another crisis, most likely less severe but perhaps as disturbing as the present one. As mentioned in Chap. 8, ups and downs and cyclical behavior is in the nature of a decentralized capitalist system. Indeed, such ups and downs are the engine and the impetus for the progress of the capitalist system. On the other hand, if by "like this" we mean a very similar crisis, history teaches us that hardly any two recessions look alike. There is little resemblance between the recessions of 1982, 1990–1991, the dot.com crisis, and the present one. But what is to be done?

A common attitude is to avoid talking long term at the time of crisis. "Let us get through this then we will have time to implement reforms." But when the crisis is over, a common refrain is "if it is not broken, don't fix it." Then when is the time to reform a system? Indeed, we have an opportunity now to reform the domestic and international financial systems and update them to the requirements of the twenty first century.

To begin with, we have realized the necessity of transparency in financial transactions and the need for a guarantee that what you see is what you get. The financial system is largely based on trust and confidence. Once that trust is broken, it is hard to get back to normal functioning. Furthermore, because trust is a main ingredient, the financial system is more prone to fraud and scams. Recall the story of Bernard Madoff, which was a big scam by no means without precedent; hence, the necessity of regulations and supervision of financial firms and financial markets.

To see the importance of trust and transparency consider the fact that you deposit your money in a bank and in return you get a piece of paper. Without guarantees, you may return and there is no bank, no money, no nothing. This vulnerability of finance over time has brought about the supervision of the central bank over commercial banks, the requirement of keeping reserves with the central bank, and insurance of bank deposits by the FDIC.

The main requirement of new regulations is that they do not interfere with the normal workings of the market. It is private enterprise capitalism that has brought us the current level of well being. The trick is to harness market forces to do the job of policing. The first requirement, therefore, is to make the supervising firms' compensations independent of supervisees. Note that credit agencies make their money from the lenders, that is, the credit card companies, not consumers. Otherwise every consumer would have an incentive to bid for a higher credit rating. In the same way, it is important that auditing firms are paid by the shareholders and credit rating agencies are paid by the buyers of assets.

This leads to the question of corporate governance. Ultimately, the shareholders in a public corporation are the owners. If they want to give their hired hand, the CEO of the company, a billion dollars for her services, that is their prerogative. But the requirement should be that the compensation is approved by shareholders not by a "compensation committee" hired by the CEO or his accomplices on the board of directors, nor by "compensation specialists" hired by the CEO. It does not make sense for an executive to preside over the loss of value of his company's shares, give himself a multimillion dollar bonus, and avoid shareholders meeting. Nor does it make sense for an executive to bankrupt a company, go begging to the government, and still keep his job.

On another front, given present day communication technologies, it would not be too much to ask that any asset traded in the market should list its underlying assets and their shares. For example, a mutual fund consists of certain stocks, some bonds, and cash. These components should be listed on the website with their percentage of the total and updated frequently.

There is a need for a national dialogue on these and many more issues. Without the majority agreeing on these changes, it will be hard to pass legislation or enforce new rules. Of course, no amount of change will preclude another crisis or the fraud of con artists. Bernard Madoff is only one in a long line of crooks. As the *Wall Street Journal* opined: "The real lesson here is about men, not markets. Human nature doesn't change, and crooks will always be with us. . . . Don't assume that passing some new federal law will banish financial fraud . . .. As Shakespeare understood, the fault is not in our stars, but in ourselves."[7]

But one thing can be changed. People can be given the opportunity to be more financially savvy. A hundred years ago learning to drive was not a part of the basic education of every youngster. Today it is. In the same fashion, tomorrow's adults need to know more about finance than their parents and grandparents. Perhaps it is time to make finance a part of high school or even elementary school curriculum.

The international financial system too needs restructuring. In the memorable Frank Capra's "It's a Wonderful Life," George Bailey has lived all his life in Bedford Falls, has done banking there and his customers have been people of the same town. That environment is light years away from our present day world of finance. Even if you live in Bedford Falls, your mortgage may be held partially in Hong Kong, partially in Saudi Arabia, and the rest perhaps somewhere else in the world. We need a new international monetary system and international financial regulations. Perhaps it is time to think of a single currency for the coalition of willing countries and a world central bank to manage the international money.

---

[7] *The Wall Street Journal*, December 15, 2008.

References

Acemoglu, Daron (2008) *Introduction to Modern Economic Growth*, Princeton, Princeton University Press.

Adolfson, Malin, Jesper Lindé, Stefan Laséen, and Mattias Villani (2005) "The Role of Sticky Prices in an Open Economy DSGE Model: A Bayesian Investigation," *Journal of the European Economic Association*, 444–457.

Aftalion, Albert (1927) "The Theory of Economic Cycles Based on the Capitalistic Technique of Production," *The Review of Economics and Statistics*, 165–170.

Aghion, Philippe and Peter Howitt (2009) *The Economics of Growth*, Cambridge, Massachusetts, the MIT Press.

Altig, David, Lawrence Christiano, Martin Eichenbaum, and Jesper Linde (2005) "Firm-Specific Capital, Nominal Rigidities and the Business Cycle," NBER Working Paper.

Arrow, Kenneth (1960) "The Work of Ragnar Frisch, Econometrician," *Econometrica*, 175–192.

Babson, Roger W. (1910) "Barometric Indices of the Condition of Trade," *Annals of the American Academy of Political and Social Science*, 111–134.

Barro, Robert (1977) "Unanticipated Money Growth and Unemployment in the United States," *American Economic Review*, 101–115.

Barro, Robert (1978) "Unanticipated Money, Output, and the Price Level in the United States," *Journal of Political Economy*, 549–580.

Bernanke, Ben and Frederic Mishkin (1997) "Inflation Targeting: A New Framework for Monetary Policy?" *Journal of Economic Perspectives*, 97–116.

Beveridge, Sir William H. (1942) *Social Insurance and Allied Services*, New York, Macmillan.

Beveridge, Sir William H. (1945) *Full Employment in a Free Society*, New York, W. W. Norton.

Bhagwati, Jagdish (2004) *In Defense of Globalization*, New York, Oxford University Press.

Blanchard, Olivier and Stanley Fischer (1989) *Lectures on Macroeconomics*, Cambridge, Massachusetts, the MIT Press.

Brookmire, James H. (1913) "Methods of Business Forecasting Based on Fundamental Statistics," *The American Economic Review*, 43–58.

Chari, Varadarajan V. and Patrick Kehoe (2006) "Modern Macroeconomics in Practice: How Theory is Shaping Policy," *Journal of Economic Perspectives*, 3–28.

Chari, Varadarajan V., Patrick Kehoe, and Ellen McGrattan (2009) "New Keynesian Models: Not Yet Useful for Policy Analysis," *American Economic Journal: Macroeconomics*, 242–266.

Christ, Carl (1994) "The Cowles Commission's Contributions to Econometrics at Chicago, 1939–1955," *Journal of Economic Literature*, 30–59.

Christiano, Lawrence, Martin Eichenbaum, and Charles Evans (2005) "Nominal Rigidities and the Dynamic Effects of a Shock to Monetary Policy," *The Journal of Political Economy*, 1–45.

Clarida, Richard, Jordi Calí, and Mark Gertler (1999) "The Science of Monetary Policy: A New Keynesian Perspective," *Journal of Economic Literature*, 1661–1707.

Cohen, Adam (2009) *Nothing to Fear: FDR's Inner Circle and the Hundred Days that Created Modern America*, New York, Penguin Press.

Crowe, Christopher and Ellen E. Meade (2007) "The Evolution of Central Bank Governance around the World," *Journal of Economic Perspectives*, 69–90.

Dadkhah, Kamran (1992) "Futures Market for Oil," in Katz and Shojai (eds.) *The Oil Market in the 1980s: A Decade of Decline*, New York, Praeger, 207–219.

Dadkhah, Kamran (2007) *Foundations of Mathematical and Computational Economics*, Mason, OH, Thomson/South-Western.

Dadkhah, Kamran and Santiago Valbuena (1985) "Non-Nested Test of New Classical vs. Keynesian Models: Evidence from European Economies," *Applied Economics*, 1083–1098.

Davis, Steven and James Kahn (2008) "Interpreting the Great Moderation: Changes in the Volatility of Economic Activity at the Macro and Micro Levels," *Journal of Economic Perspectives*, 155–180.

De Long, J. Bradford (2000) "The Triumph of Monetarism," *Journal of Economic Perspectives*, 83–94.

Drazen, Allan (2000) *Political Economy in Macroeconomics*, Princeton, Princeton University Press.

Economic Report of the President, Washington, DC, Government Printing Office, different years.

Egan, Timothy (2006) *The Worst Hard Time: The Untold Story of Those Who Survived the Great American Dust Bowl*, Boston, Houghton Mifflin.

Eichengreen, Barry (ed.) (1995) *Europe's Post-War Recovery*, New York, Cambridge University press.

Eichengreen, Barry (2007) *The European Economy Since 1945: Coordinated Capitalism and Beyond*, Princeton, Princeton University Press.

Eichengreen, Barry (2008) *Globalizing Capital, A History of the International Monetary System*, 2nd ed., Princeton, Princeton University Press.

Epstein, Roy (1987) *A History of Econometrics*, New York, North-Holland.

Fisher, Irving (1933) "The Debt-Deflation Theory of Great Depressions," *Econometrica*, 337–357.

Friedman, Milton (1953a) "The Case for Flexible Exchange Rates," in *Essays in Positive Economics*, Chicago, the University of Chicago Press.

Friedman, Milton (1953b) "Lange on Price Flexibility and Employment: A Methodological Criticism," in *Essays in Positive Economics*, Chicago, the University of Chicago Press.

Friedman, Milton (1962) *Capitalism and Freedom*, Chicago, the University of Chicago Press.

Frisch, Ragnar (1933) "Propagation Problems and Impulse Problems in Dynamic Economics" in *Economic Essays in Honour of Gustav Cassel*, reprinted 1967, New York, A. M. Kelley.

Frisch, Ragnar and Harold Holme (1935) "The Characteristic Solutions of a Mixed Difference and Differential Equations Occurring in Economic Dynamics," *Econometrica*, 225–239.

Giancarlo, Gandolfo (2002) *International Finance and Open-Economy Macroeconomics*, New York, Springer.

Gilbert, John Cannon (1982) *Keynes's Impact on Monetary Economics*, London, Butterworths.

Granger, Clive and Paul Newbold (1974) "Spurious Regressions in Econometrics," *Journal of Econometrics*, 111–120.

Granger, Clive and Paul Newbold (1986) *Forecasting Economic Time Series*, 2nd ed., San Diego, Academic Press.

Hayek, Friedrich A. (1983) "The Austrian Critique," *The Economist*, June 11, 39.

Humes, Edward (2006) *Over Here: How the G.I. Bill Transformed the American Dream*, Orlando, Houghton Mifflin Harcourt.

Irwin, Douglas (1996) *Against the Tide, An Intellectual History of Free Trade*, Princeton, Princeton University Press.

Johansen, Leif (1969) "Ragnar Frisch's Contributions to Economics", *The Swedish Journal of Economics*, 302–324.

Jorgenson, Dale W. and Siebert Calvin D. (1968) "A Comparison of Alternative Theories of Corporate Investment Behavior," *American Economic Review*, 681–712.

Justiniano, Alejandro and Giorgio Primiceri (2008) "The Time-Varying Volatility of Macroeconomic Fluctuations," *American Economic Review*, 604–641.

Kapur, Devesh, John Lewis, and Richard Webb (1997) *The World Bank, Its First Half Century*, Washington, DC, Brookings Institution.

Kennedy, David (1999) *Freedom from Fear, the American People in Depression and War, 1929–1945*, New York, Oxford University Press.

Keynes, John Maynard (1936) *The General Theory of Employment, Interest and Money*, New York, Harcourt, Brace.

Keynes, John Maynard (1973) *The General Theory and After, Part I Preparation*, Vol. XIII of the Collected Writings of John Maynard Keynes, Donald Moggridge (ed.), London, Macmillan.

Kydland, Finn and Edward Prescott (1977) "Rules Rather than Discretion: The Inconsistency of Optimal Plans," *Journal of Political Economy*, 473–491.

Kydland, Finn and Edward Prescott (1982) "Time to Build and Aggregate Fluctuations," *Econometrica*, 1345–1370.

Kydland, Finn and Edward Prescott (1996) "The Computational Experiment: An Econometric Tool," *Journal of Economic Perspectives*, 69–85.

Laforte, Jean-philippe (2007) "Pricing Models: A Bayesian DSGE Approach for the U.S. Economy," *Journal of Money, Credit and Banking* (supplement), 127–154.

Laidler, David (1999) *Fabricating the Keynesian Revolution*, New York, Cambridge University Press.

Lal Das, Bhagirath (1998) *An Introduction to the WTO Agreements* New York, Zed Books.

Lindé, Jesper (2001) "Testing for the Lucas Critique: A Quantitative Investigation," *The American Economic Review*, 986–1005.

Lubik, Thomas and Frank Schorfheide (2004) "Testing for Indeterminacy: An Application to U.S. Monetary Policy," *The American Economic Review*, 190–217.

Lucas, Robert (1981) "Econometric Policy Evaluation: A Critique," in *Studies in Business-Cycle Theory*, Cambridge, MA, the MIT Press.

Manchester, William (1974) *The Glory and the Dream, A Narrative History of America 1932–1972*, Boston, Little, Brown.

Mankiw, Gregory (2006) "The Macroeconomist as Scientist and Engineer," *Journal of Economic perspectives*, 29–46.

Mankiw, Gregory and David Romer (1991) *New Keynesian Economics*, 2 vols., Cambridge, MA, the MIT Press.

Markowitz, Harry (1952) "Portfolio Selection," *The Journal of Finance*, 77–91.

McWhorter, John (2005) "Focus: White do-gooders did for black America. Black poverty is the result of 30 years of misguided welfare rather than racism says John McWhorter," *Sunday Times*, September 11.

McWhorter, John (2006) *Winning the Race: Beyond the Crisis in Black America*, New York, Gotham Books.

Moore, Geoffrey H. (1975) "The Analysis of Economic Indicators," *Scientific American*, January, 17–23.

Morgan, Mary (1990) *The History of Econometric Ideas*, New York, Cambridge University Press.

Mundell, Robert (1961) "Flexible Exchange Rates and Employment Policy," *The Canadian Journal of Economics and Political Science*, 509–517.

John (1961) "Rational Expectations and the Theory of Price Movements," *Econometrica*, 315–335.

Nelson, Charles (1972) "The Prediction Performance of the FRB-MIT-PENN Model of the U.S. Economy," *American Economic Review*, 902–917.

Persons, Warren M. (1916) "Construction of a Business Barometer Based upon Annual Data," *The American Economic Review*, 739–769.

Persons, Warren M. (1920) "A Non-Technical Explanation of the Index of General Business Condition," *The Review of Economics and Statistics*, 39–48.

Persons, Warren M. (1927) "An Index of General Business Conditions, 1875–1913," *The Review of Economics and Statistics*, 20–29.

Pesaran, Hashem (1982) "A Critique of Proposed Tests of the Natural Rate-Rational Expecations Hypothesis," *The Economic Journal*, 529–554.

Phillips, Alban William (1958) "The Relation Between Unemployment and the Rate of Change of Money Wage Rates in the United Kingdom, 1861–1957," *Economica*, 283–299.

Reichlin, Lucrezia (1995) "The Marshall Plan Reconsidered," in Barry Eichengreen (ed.) *Europe's Post-War Recovery*, Cambridge, Cambridge University Press.

Romer, Christina (1986) "Is the Stabilization of the Postwar Economy a Figment of the Data?" *American Economic Review*, 314–334.

Romer, David (2006) *Advanced Macroeconomics*, 3rd ed., Boston, McGraw-Hill Irwin.

Romer, Paul (1990) "Endogenous Technological Change," *Journal of Political Economy*, S71–S102.

Samuelson, Paul and Robert Solow (1960) "Analytical Aspects of Anti-Inflation Policy," *The American Economic Review*, 177–194.

Samuelson, Robert J. (2008) *The Great Inflation and Its Aftermath*, New York, Random House.

Santoni, G. J. (1986) "The Employment Act of 1946: Some History Notes," *Federal Reserve Bank of St. Louis Review*, 5–16.

Sargent, Thomas and Neil Wallace (1976) "Rational Expectations and the Theory of Economic Policy", *Journal of Monetary Economics*, reprinted in Robert Lucas and Thomas Sargent (eds.) (1981) *Rational Expectations and Econometric Practice*, vol. 1, Minneapolis, the University of Minnesota Press.

Schlesinger, Arthur, Jr. (1958) *The Coming of the New Deal*, Boston, Houghton Mifflin.

Schuettinger, Robert and Eamonn Butler (1979) *Forty Centuries of Wage and Price Controls*, Washington, DC, the Heritage Foundation.

Smets, Frank and Rafael Wouters (2005) "Bayesian New Neoclassical Synthesis (NNS) Models: Modern Tools for Central Banks", *Journal of the European Economic Association*, 422–433.

Stanley, Tom D. (1998) "New Wine in Old Bottles: A Meta-Analysis of Ricardian Equivalence," *Southern Economic Journal*, 713–727.

Stone, Richard (1984) "The Accounts of Society" printed in *Journal of Applied Econometrics*, 1986, 5–28.

"The battle of Smoot-Hawley," (2008) *The Economist*, December 20, 125–126.

Wallace, Henry (1945) *Sixty Million Jobs,* New York, Simon & Schuster.

Wickens, Michael (2008) *Macroeconomic Theory, A Dynamic General Equilibrium Approach*, Princeton, Princeton University Press.

Woodford, Michael (2009) "Convergence in Macroeconomics: Elements of the New Synthesis," *American Economic Journal: Macroeconomics*, 267–279.

Yergin, Daniel (1991) *The Prize, the Epic Quest for Oil, Money, and Power*, New York, Simon & Schuster.

Yergin, Daniel and Joseph Stanislaw (2002) *The Commanding Heights* (revised edition), New York, Simon & Schuster.

Index

Printed in the United States
153874LV00001B/33/P